Scholastic
VISUAL
Dictionary

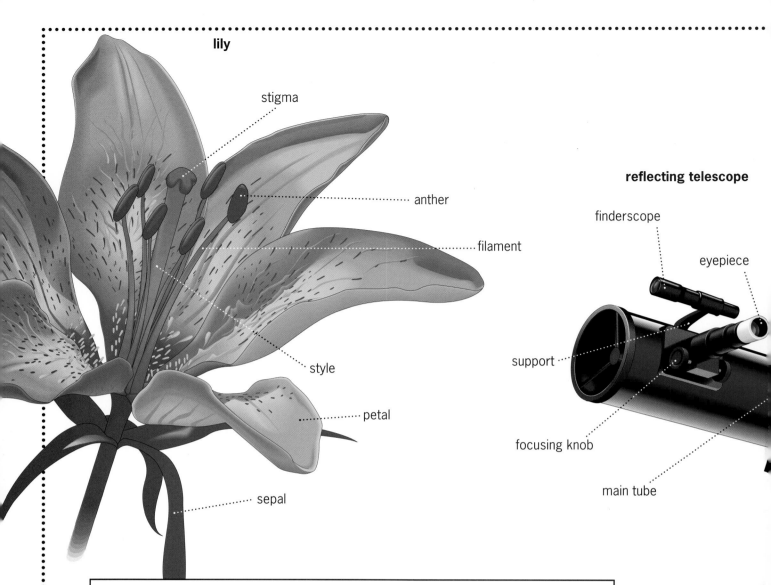

lily

stigma

anther

filament

style

petal

sepal

reflecting telescope

finderscope

eyepiece

support

focusing knob

main tube

counterweight

ISBN 0-439-37649-1

Copyright © 1994 by Éditions Québec/Amérique Inc.
Copyright © 2000 by Les Éditions Québec Amérique Inc. All rights reserved.
First published in the U.S.A. in 2000 by Scholastic Inc. by arrangement with
Les Éditions Québec Amérique, 425 rue St-Jean-Baptiste, Montreal, Quebec, Canada.
Published by Scholastic Inc. SCHOLASTIC and associated logos are trademarks
and/or registered trademarks of Scholastic Inc.

12 11 10 9 8 7 6 5 4 3 2 1   1 2 3 4 5 6/0

Printed in the U.S.A.   24

First Scholastic paperback printing, November 2001

Jean-Claude Corbeil • Ariane Archambault

Scholastic VISUAL Dictionary

Art Directors
Jean-Louis Martin
François Fortin

Graphic Designer
Anne Tremblay

Computer Graphic Designers
Marc Lalumière
Jean-Yves Ahern
Rielle Lévesque
Anne Tremblay

Computer Programming
Yves Ferland

Data Capture
Serge D'Amico

Page Make-up
Lucie Mc Brearty
Pascal Goyette

Production
Tony O'Riley

SCHOLASTIC INC.

New York Toronto London Auckland Sydney
Mexico City New Delhi Hong Kong Buenos Aires

SKY

solar system............................6
Sun..8
Moon......................................9
comet....................................10
solar eclipse..........................10
lunar eclipse..........................10
reflecting telescope 11
refracting telescope 11

EARTH

Earth coordinate system...............12
structure of the Earth 12
earthquake 13
cave 13
coastal features 14
volcano 15
glacier 16
mountain 17
the continents...........................18
seasons of the year 20
structure of the biosphere 20
elevation zones and vegetation ...20
climates of the world.................21
weather 22
meteorological measuring instruments 23
cartography..............................24
compass card 27
ecology....................................28

PLANT KINGDOM

plant and soil...........................34
soil profile 34
germination 34
mushroom.................................35
structure of a plant 36
flowers.....................................38
tree 40
conifer 43

FRUITS AND VEGETABLES

fleshy fruits: berry fruits............44
fleshy stone fruits 45
fleshy pome fruits 46
fleshy fruits: citrus fruits 47
tropical fruits 48
vegetables 49

GARDENING

gardening................................54

ANIMAL KINGDOM

insects and spider....................56
butterfly 57
honeybee 58
amphibians 60
crustaceans 61
fish 62
reptiles....................................64
cat 66
dog..66
horse 67
farm animals.............................68
types of jaws 70
major types of horns 71
major types of tusks 71
types of hoofs 71
wild animals..............................72
bird..74
examples of birds 76

HUMAN BODY

human body, anterior view 78
human body, posterior view 79
skeleton...................................80
human anatomy 81
eye: the organ of sight 82
hand: the organ of touch 82
ear: the organ of hearing 83
nose: the organ of smell............84
mouth: the organ of taste 84
human denture..........................85

ARCHITECTURE

traditional houses.....................86
mosque....................................87
castle.......................................88
gothic cathedral 89
downtown.................................90

HOUSE

house.......................................92
window.....................................94
bed..95
seats 96
table and chairs 97
lights 98
lighting 99
glassware................................100
dinnerware 100
silverware................................101
kitchen utensils 102
cooking utensils 104
kitchen appliances 105
refrigerator..............................106
cooking appliances 107

DO-IT-YOURSELF

carpentry tools 108
electric tools 110
painting upkeep 111

CLOTHING

men's clothing 112
women's clothing 114
sweaters 117
gloves and stockings.................118
shoes......................................119
sportswear 120

PERSONAL ARTICLES

hairdressing 122
dental care 122
glasses 123
leather goods 123
umbrella..................................123

COMMUNICATIONS

communication by telephone.....124
photography 125
television.................................126

video..127
stereo system 128
portable sound systems 129

ROAD TRANSPORTATION

car..130
trucking..134
motorcycle..135
bicycle 136

RAIL TRANSPORTATION

diesel-electric locomotive 138
types of freight cars.............................138
highway crossing 140
high-speed train 140

MARITIME TRANSPORTATION

four-masted bark 141
hovercraft 141
cruise liner 142
harbor 142

AIR TRANSPORTATION

plane 144
helicopter..145
airport...146

SPACE TRANSPORTATION

space shuttle.......................................148
spacesuit 149

SCHOOL

school supplies....................................150
school equipment..................................152
geometry 156
drawing..157

MUSIC

traditional musical instruments 158
keyboard instrument 159
musical notation...................................160
stringed instruments 162
wind instruments 164
percussion instruments 166
symphony orchestra...............................167

TEAM GAMES

baseball 168
football..170
soccer 172
volleyball 174
field hockey 175
ice hockey 176
basketball...178
tennis 180

WATER SPORTS

swimming 182
sailboard 184

WINTER SPORTS

skating 185
skiing 186

GYMNASTICS

gymnastics..188

CAMPING

tents 190
sleeping equipment 191
camping equipment...............................192

INDOOR GAMES

card games...194
dominoes 194
dice 194
chess 195
backgammon...196
checkers 196
video entertainment system 197
game of darts..197

MEASURING DEVICES

measure of time 198
measure of temperature 199
measure of weight 200

ENERGY

oil..202
hydroelectric energy 204
nuclear energy......................................206
solar energy 208
wind energy..209

HEAVY MACHINERY

fire prevention 210
heavy vehicles 212
heavy machinery....................................214

SYMBOLS

common symbols 216
safety symbols 216
protection 216

5

SOLAR SYSTEM

planets and moons

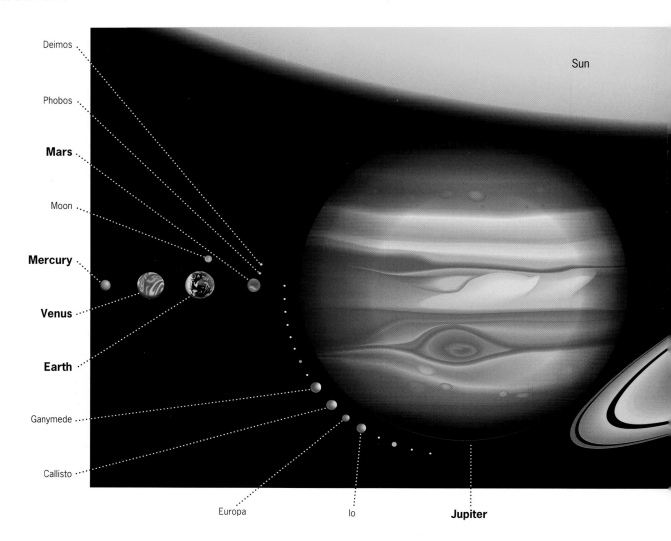

Deimos
Phobos
Mars
Moon
Mercury
Venus
Earth
Ganymede
Callisto
Europa
Io
Jupiter
Sun

orbits of the planets

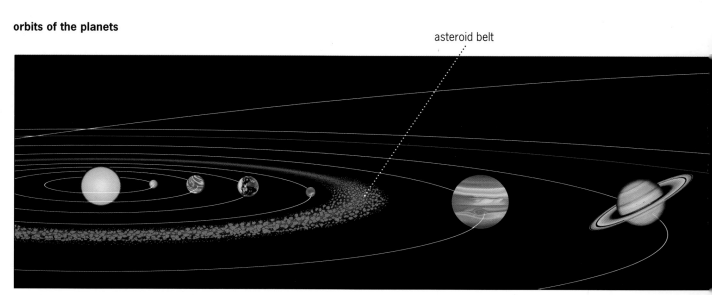

asteroid belt

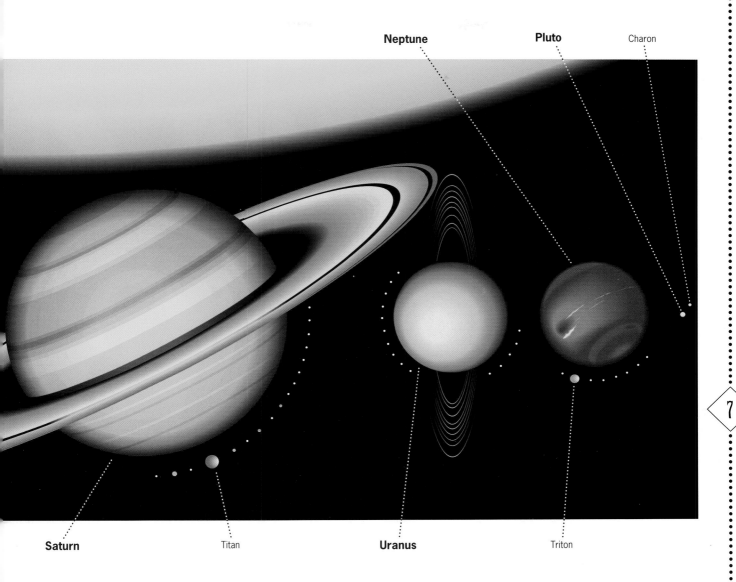

Neptune

Pluto

Charon

Saturn

Titan

Uranus

Triton

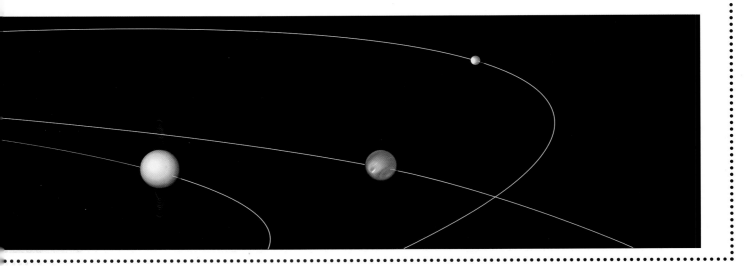

SUN

structure of the Sun

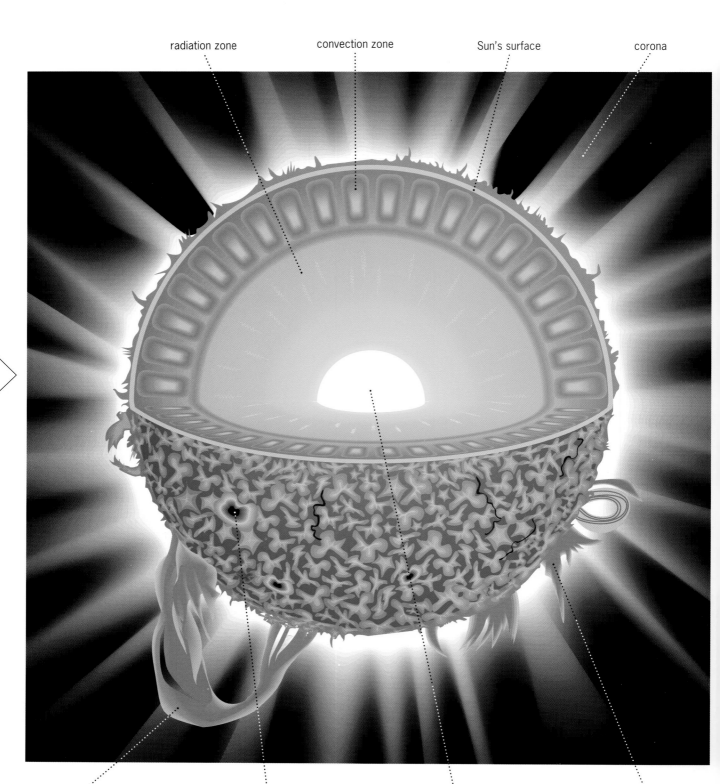

MOON

bay · · · · · · · · ·

cliff · · · · · · · · ·

ocean · · · · · · · · ·

· · · · · lake

· · · · · sea

mountain range

· · · · · crater

· · · · · wall

· · · · · cirque

PHASES OF THE MOON

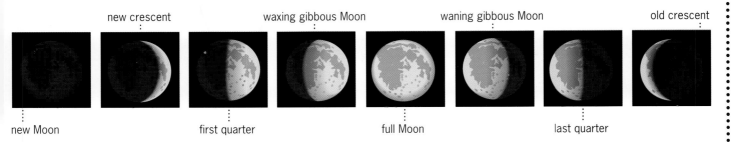

new crescent

waxing gibbous Moon

waning gibbous Moon

old crescent

new Moon

first quarter

full Moon

last quarter

COMET

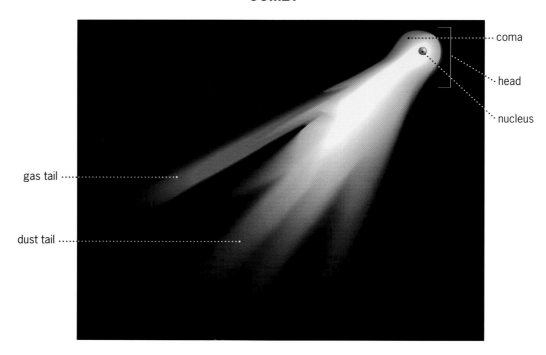

coma

head

nucleus

gas tail

dust tail

SOLAR ECLIPSE

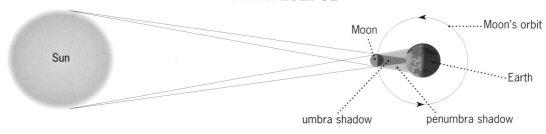

Sun

Moon

Moon's orbit

Earth

umbra shadow

penumbra shadow

TYPES OF SOLAR ECLIPSES

 total eclipse

 annular eclipse

 partial eclipse

LUNAR ECLIPSE

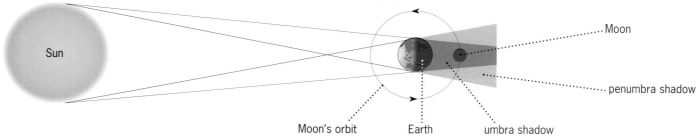

Sun

Moon

penumbra shadow

Moon's orbit

Earth

umbra shadow

TYPES OF LUNAR ECLIPSES

partial eclipse

 total eclipse

REFLECTING TELESCOPE

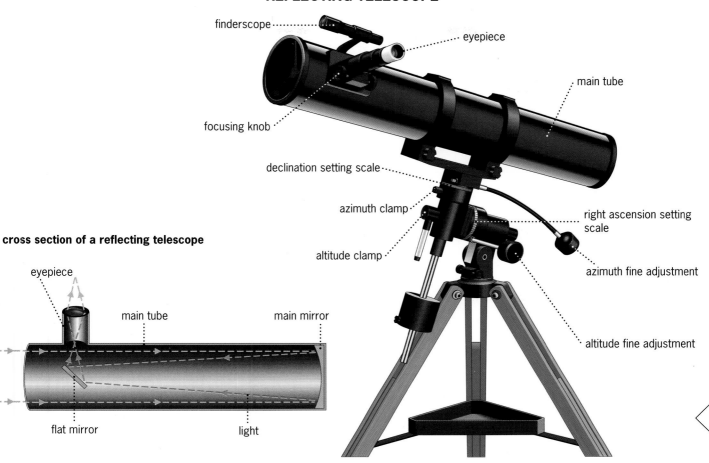

finderscope

eyepiece

main tube

focusing knob

declination setting scale

azimuth clamp

right ascension setting scale

altitude clamp

azimuth fine adjustment

altitude fine adjustment

cross section of a reflecting telescope

eyepiece

main tube

main mirror

flat mirror

light

REFRACTING TELESCOPE

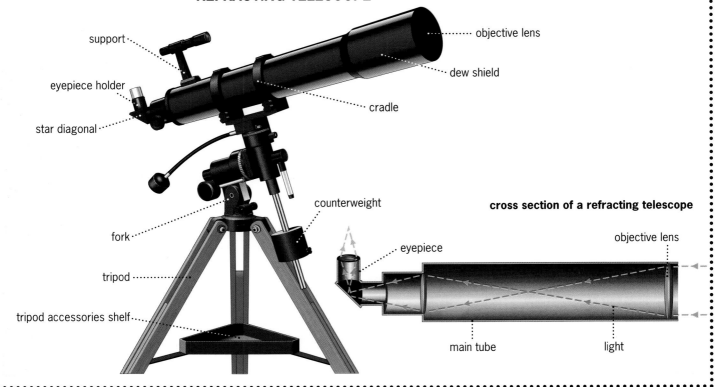

support

objective lens

eyepiece holder

dew shield

star diagonal

cradle

counterweight

fork

cross section of a refracting telescope

objective lens

tripod

eyepiece

tripod accessories shelf

main tube

light

EARTH COORDINATE SYSTEM

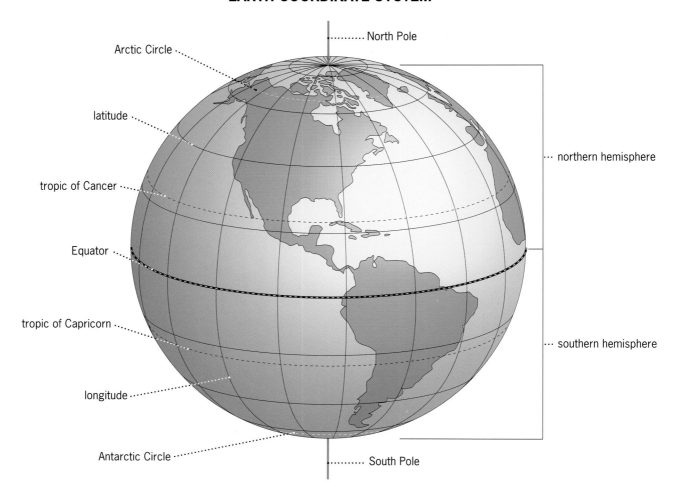

North Pole

Arctic Circle

latitude

tropic of Cancer

Equator

tropic of Capricorn

longitude

Antarctic Circle

South Pole

northern hemisphere

southern hemisphere

STRUCTURE OF THE EARTH

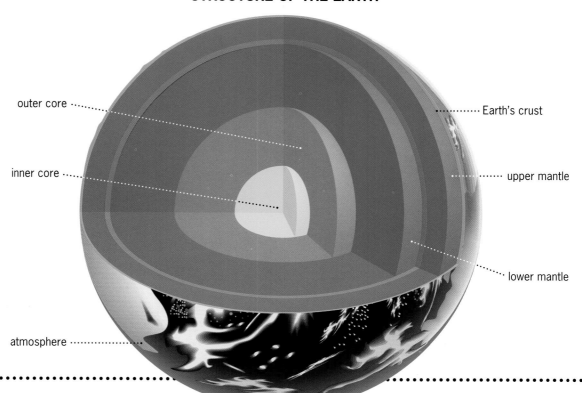

outer core

inner core

atmosphere

Earth's crust

upper mantle

lower mantle

EARTHQUAKE

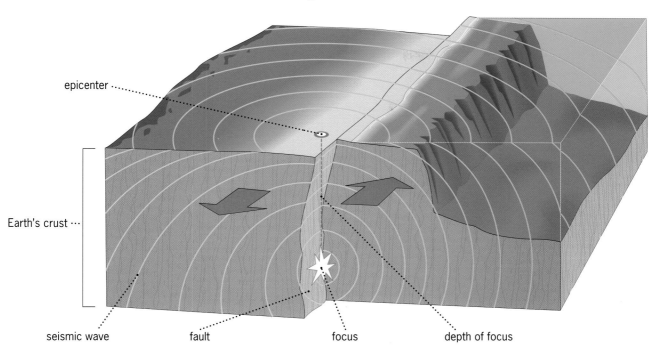

epicenter

Earth's crust

seismic wave · · · · · · · ·   fault   focus   depth of focus

CAVE

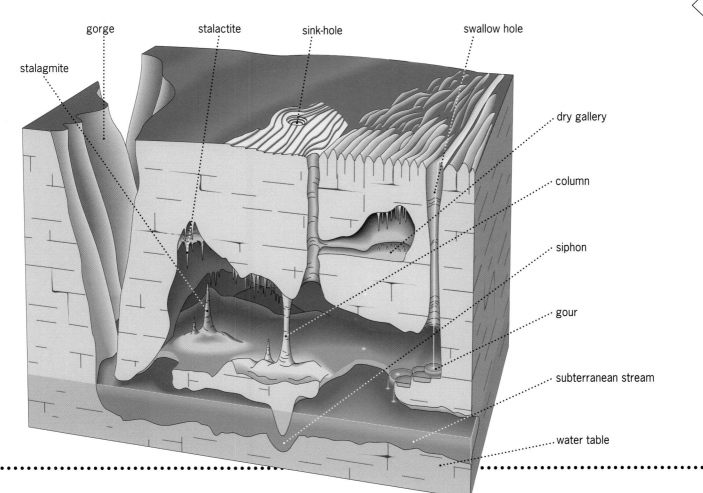

gorge   stalactite   sink-hole   swallow hole

stalagmite

dry gallery

column

siphon

gour

subterranean stream

water table

COASTAL FEATURES

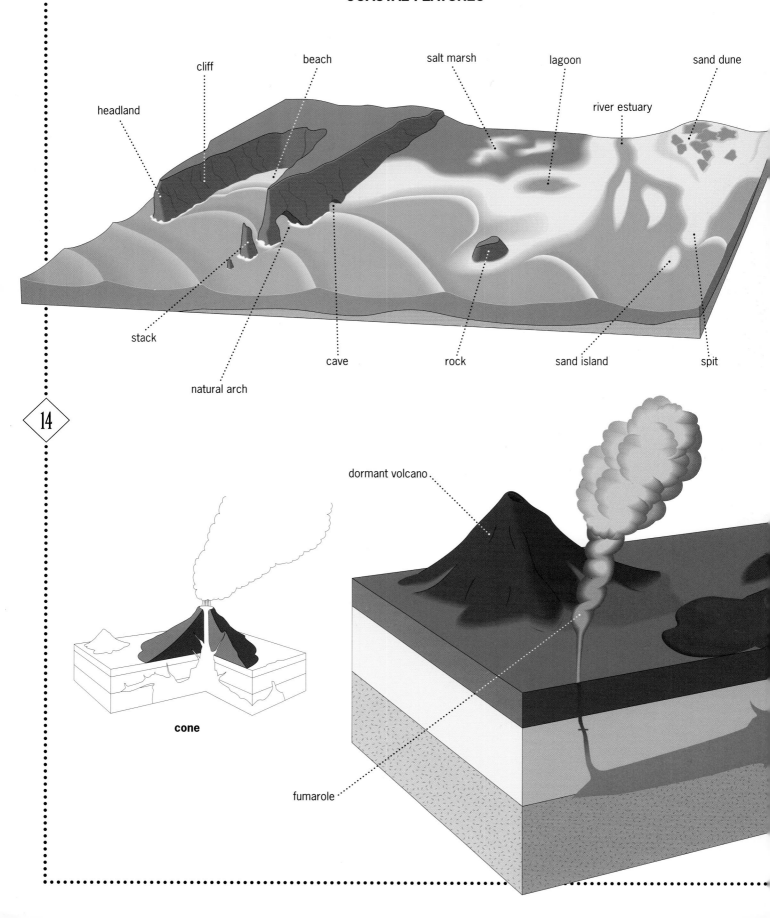

headland

cliff

beach

salt marsh

lagoon

sand dune

river estuary

stack

natural arch

cave

rock

sand island

spit

cone

dormant volcano

fumarole

VOLCANO

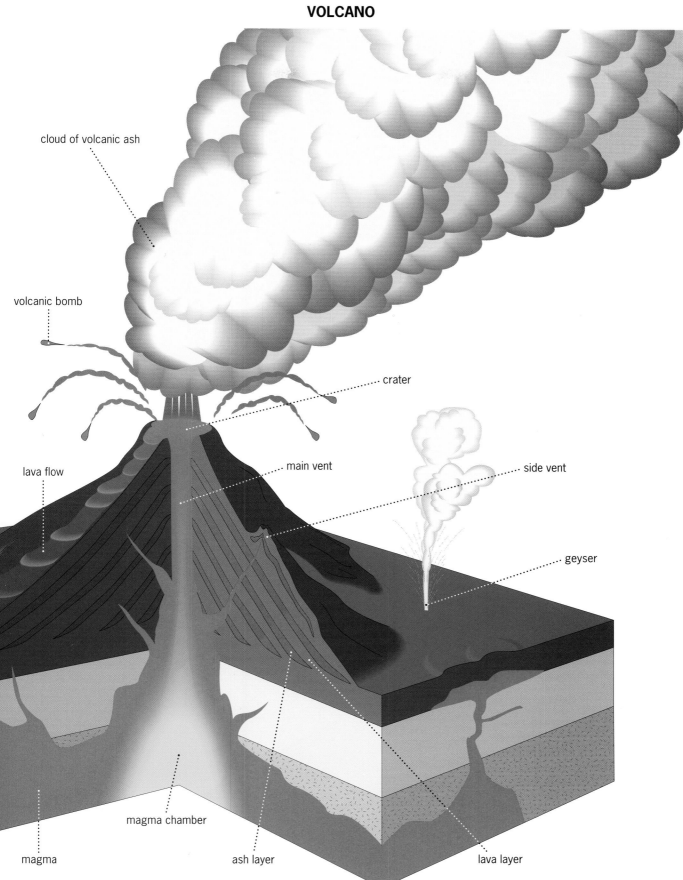

cloud of volcanic ash

volcanic bomb

lava flow

crater

main vent

side vent

geyser

magma chamber

magma

ash layer

lava layer

GLACIER

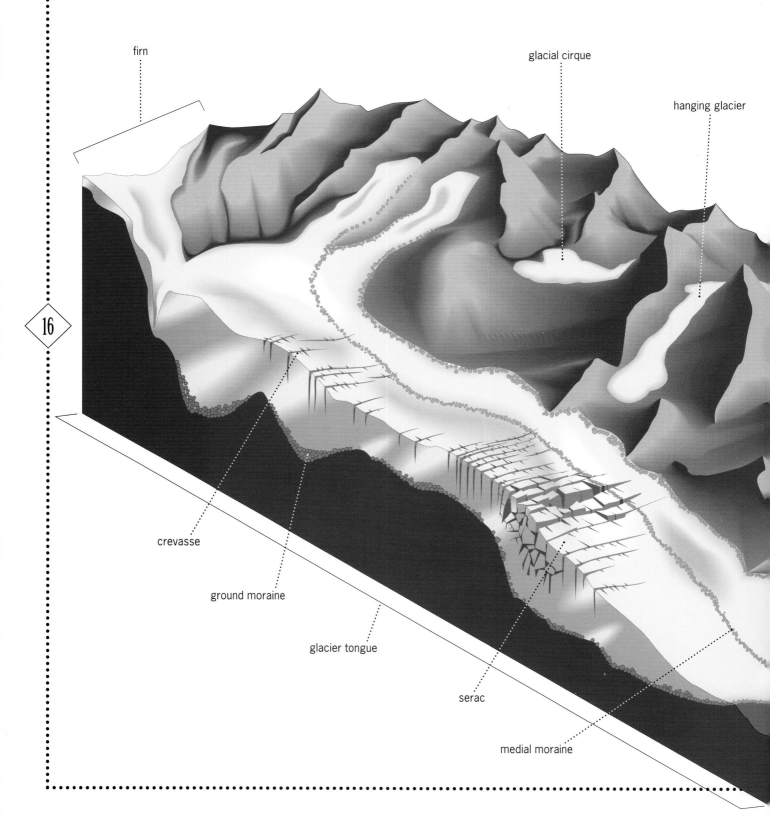

firn

glacial cirque

hanging glacier

16

crevasse

ground moraine

glacier tongue

serac

medial moraine

MOUNTAIN

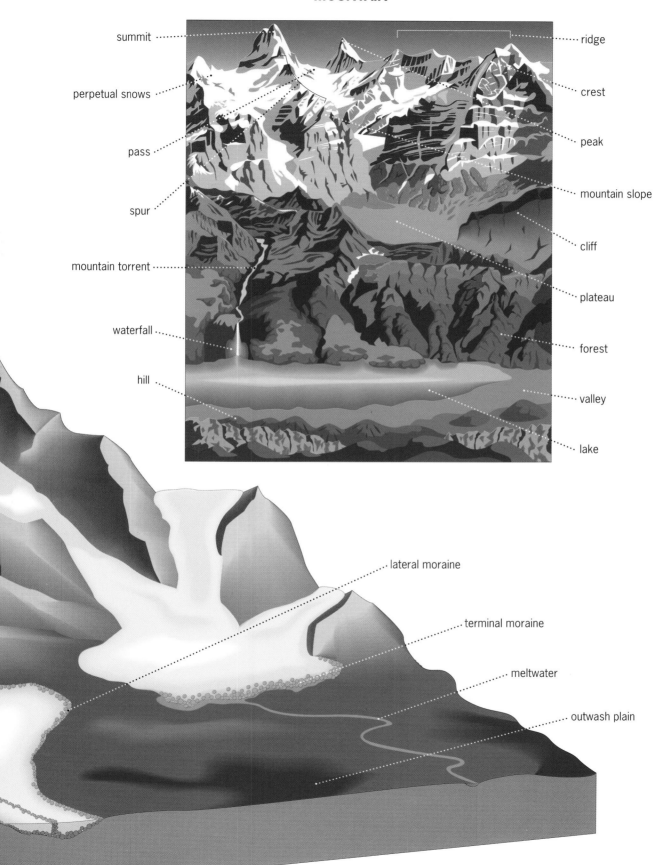

summit

perpetual snows

pass

spur

mountain torrent

waterfall

hill

ridge

crest

peak

mountain slope

cliff

plateau

forest

valley

lake

lateral moraine

terminal moraine

meltwater

outwash plain

THE CONTINENTS

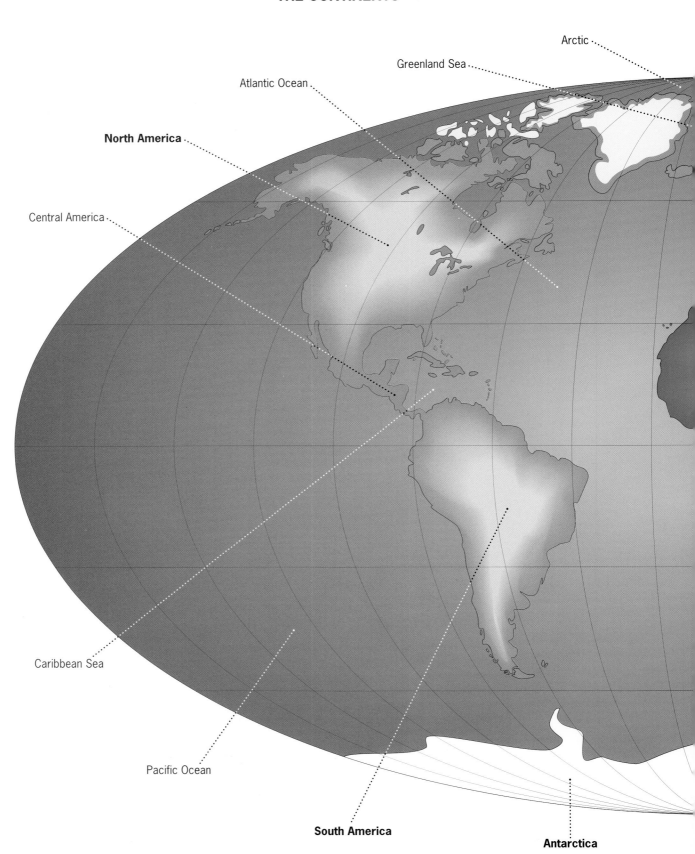

Arctic

Greenland Sea

Atlantic Ocean

North America

Central America

Caribbean Sea

Pacific Ocean

South America

Antarctica

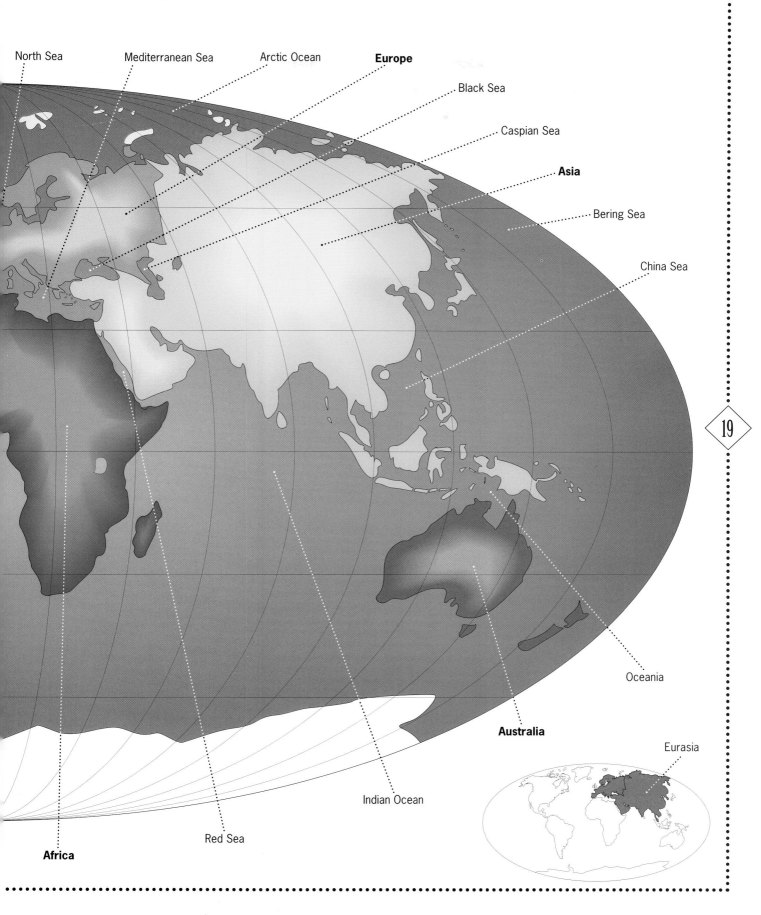

North Sea

Mediterranean Sea

Arctic Ocean

Europe

Black Sea

Caspian Sea

Asia

Bering Sea

China Sea

Oceania

Australia

Eurasia

Indian Ocean

Red Sea

Africa

SEASONS OF THE YEAR

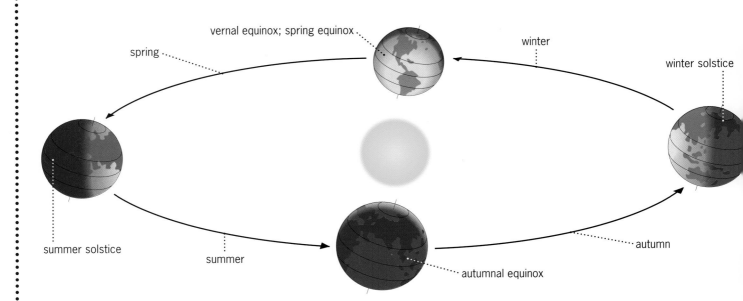

vernal equinox; spring equinox

winter

spring

winter solstice

summer solstice

summer

autumn

autumnal equinox

STRUCTURE OF THE BIOSPHERE

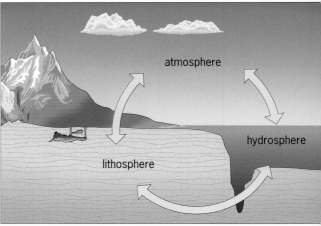

atmosphere

hydrosphere

lithosphere

ELEVATION ZONES AND VEGETATION

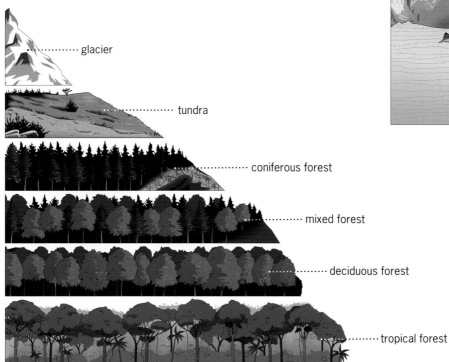

glacier

tundra

coniferous forest

mixed forest

deciduous forest

tropical forest

CLIMATES OF THE WORLD

tropical climates

- tropical rain forest
- tropical savanna
- steppe
- desert

temperate climates

- humid - long summer
- humid - short summer
- marine

polar climates

- polar tundra
- polar ice cap

subtropical climates

- Mediterranean subtropical
- humid subtropical
- dry subtropical

continental climates

- dry continental - arid
- dry continental - semiarid

highland climates

- highland climates

subarctic climates

- subarctic climates

WEATHER

mist

fog

dew

glazed frost

stormy sky

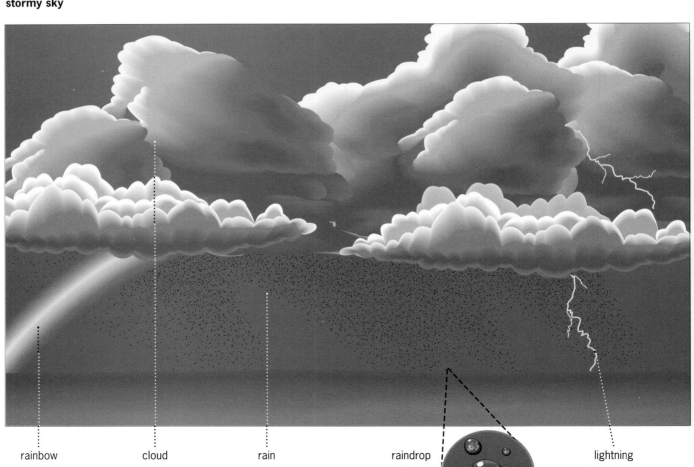

rainbow   cloud   rain   raindrop   lightning

METEOROLOGICAL MEASURING INSTRUMENTS

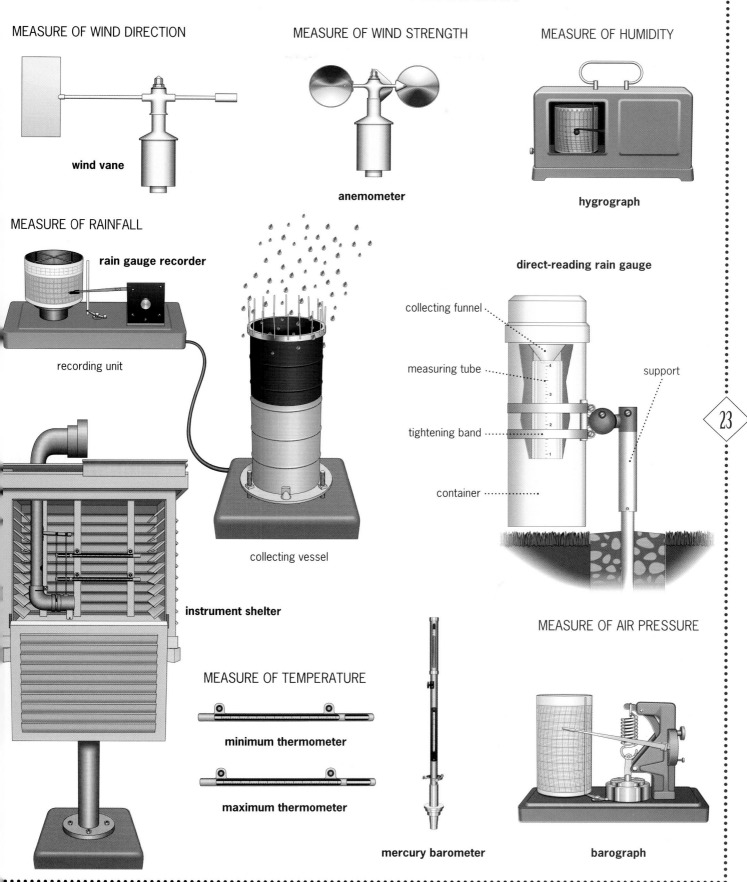

MEASURE OF WIND DIRECTION

wind vane

MEASURE OF WIND STRENGTH

anemometer

MEASURE OF HUMIDITY

hygrograph

MEASURE OF RAINFALL

rain gauge recorder

recording unit

direct-reading rain gauge

collecting funnel

measuring tube

tightening band

support

container

collecting vessel

instrument shelter

MEASURE OF TEMPERATURE

minimum thermometer

maximum thermometer

MEASURE OF AIR PRESSURE

mercury barometer

barograph

23

CARTOGRAPHY

hemispheres

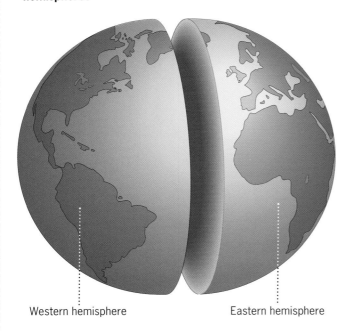

Western hemisphere

Eastern hemisphere

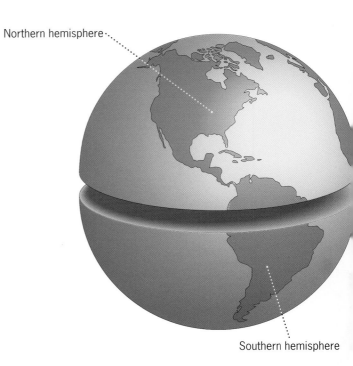

Northern hemisphere

Southern hemisphere

GRID SYSTEM

lines of latitude

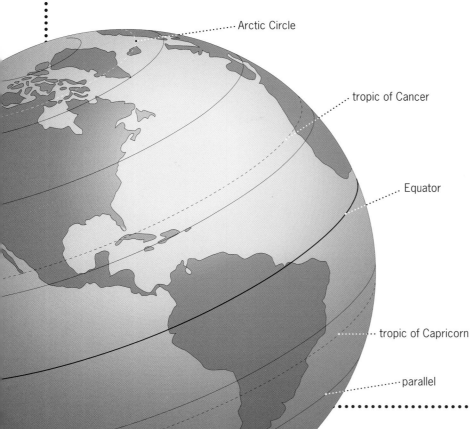

Arctic Circle

tropic of Cancer

Equator

tropic of Capricorn

parallel

lines of longitude

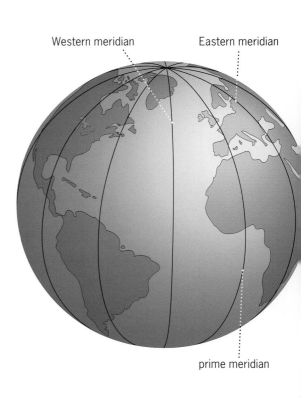

Western meridian

Eastern meridian

prime meridian

MAP PROJECTIONS

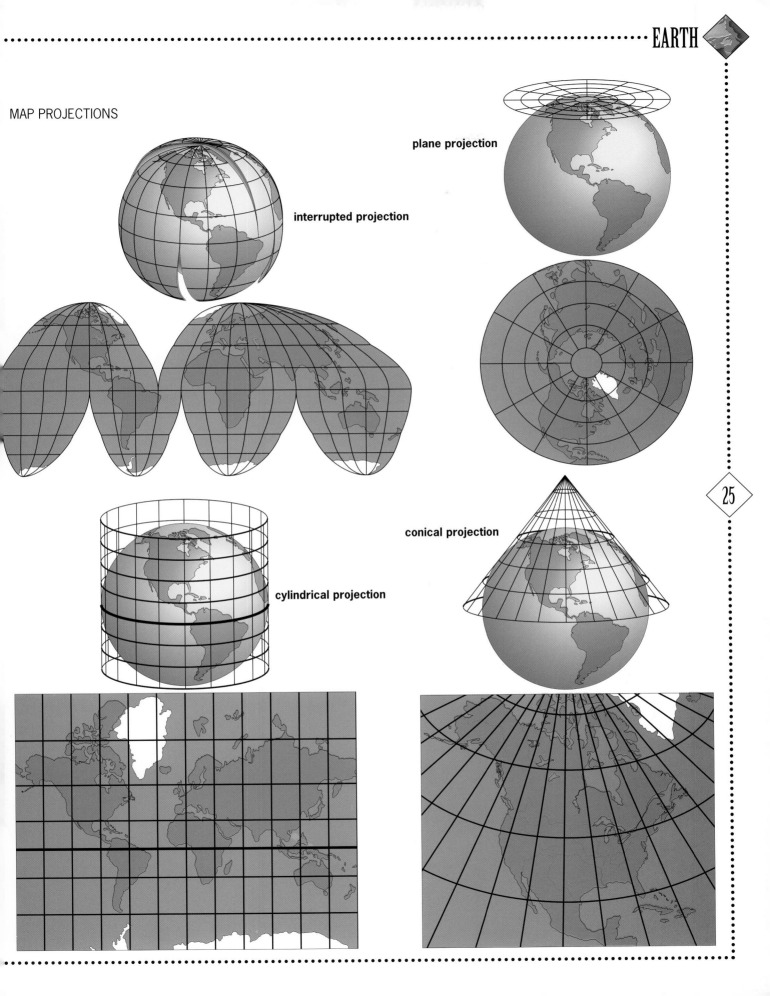

interrupted projection

plane projection

cylindrical projection

conical projection

CARTOGRAPHY

political map

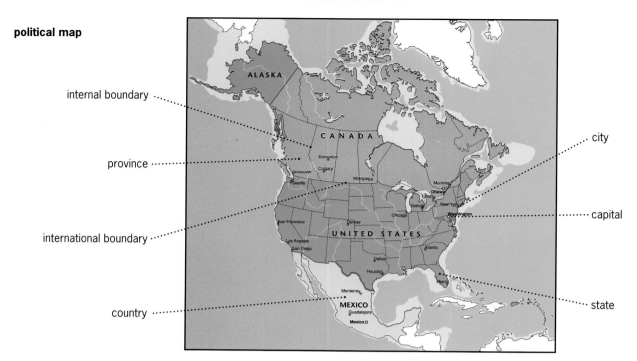

internal boundary

province

international boundary

country

city

capital

state

ALASKA

CANADA

Edmonton
Calgary
Vancouver
Winnipeg
Seattle

Montréal
Ottawa
Toronto
Detroit
New York
San Francisco
Denver
Chicago
Washington
UNITED STATES
Los Angeles
San Diego
Dallas
Atlanta
Houston
Miami

Monterrey
MEXICO
Guadalajara
Mexico

physical map

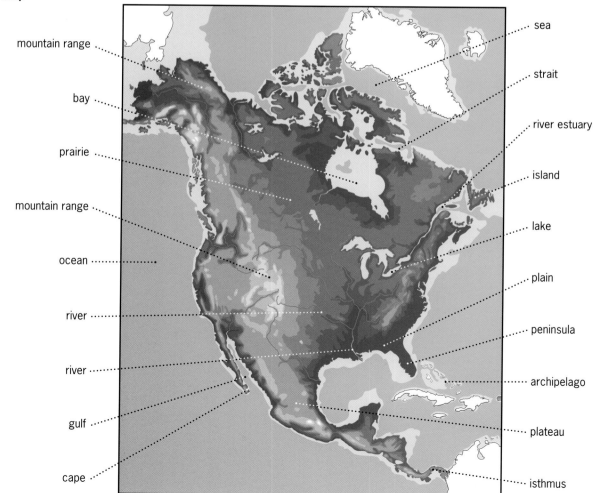

mountain range

bay

prairie

mountain range

ocean

river

river

gulf

cape

sea

strait

river estuary

island

lake

plain

peninsula

archipelago

plateau

isthmus

road map

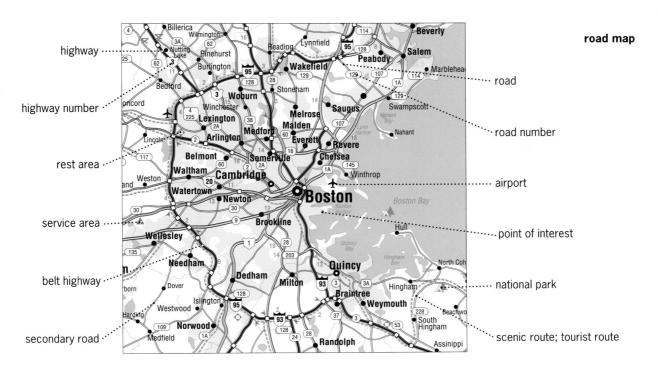

highway ······

highway number ······

rest area ······

service area ······

belt highway ······

secondary road ······

······ road

······ road number

······ airport

······ point of interest

······ national park

······ scenic route; tourist route

27

COMPASS CARD

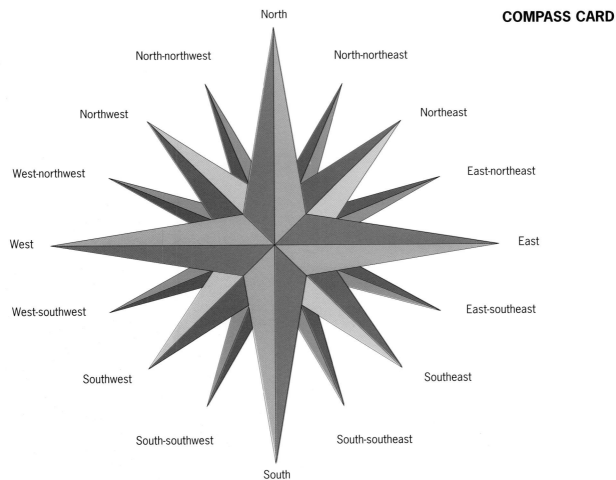

North

North-northwest

North-northeast

Northwest

Northeast

West-northwest

East-northeast

West

East

West-southwest

East-southeast

Southwest

Southeast

South-southwest

South-southeast

South

ECOLOGY

greenhouse effect

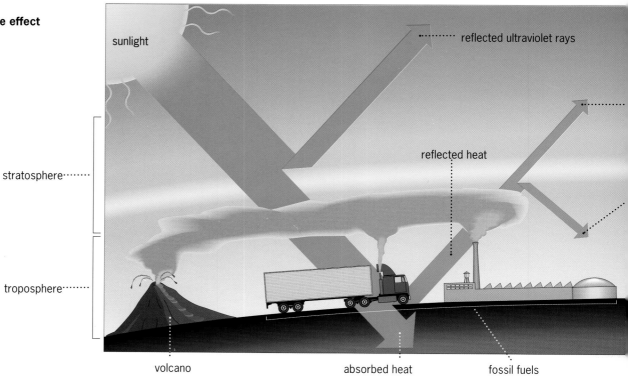

sunlight

reflected ultraviolet rays

stratosphere

reflected heat

troposphere

volcano

absorbed heat

fossil fuels

food chain

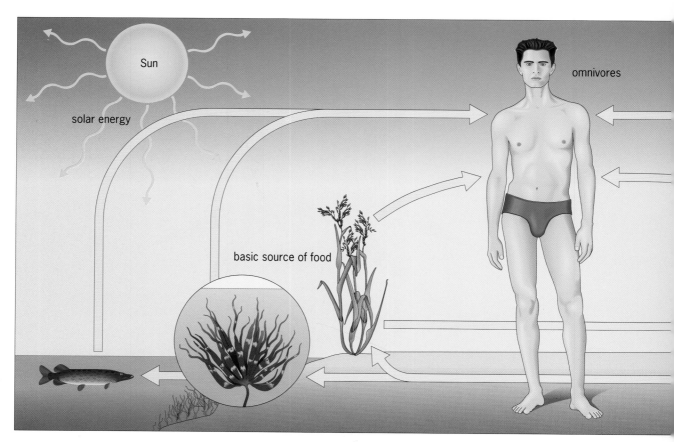

Sun

omnivores

solar energy

basic source of food

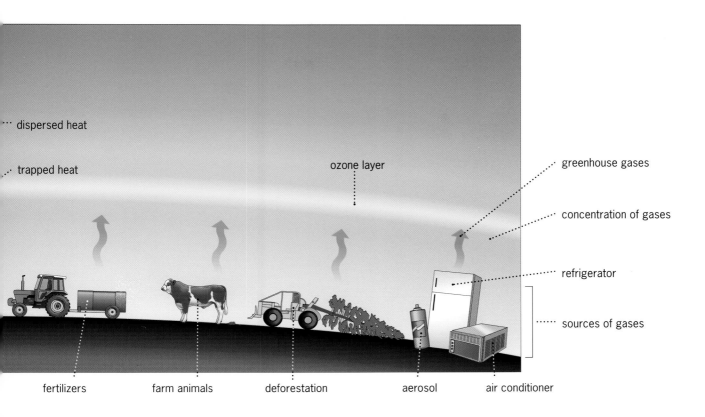

dispersed heat

trapped heat

ozone layer

greenhouse gases

concentration of gases

refrigerator

sources of gases

fertilizers

farm animals

deforestation

aerosol

air conditioner

carnivores

herbivores

insectivores

decomposers

inorganic matter

ECOLOGY

atmospheric pollution

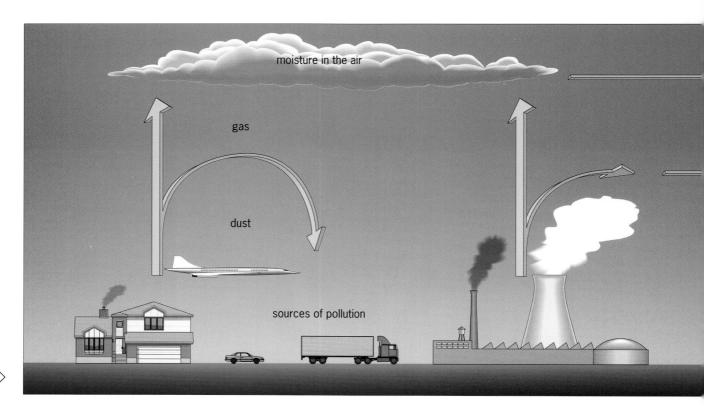

moisture in the air

gas

dust

sources of pollution

water cycle

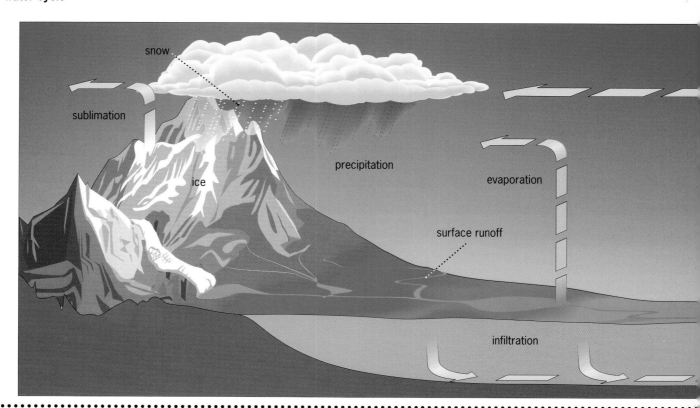

snow

sublimation

ice

precipitation

evaporation

surface runoff

infiltration

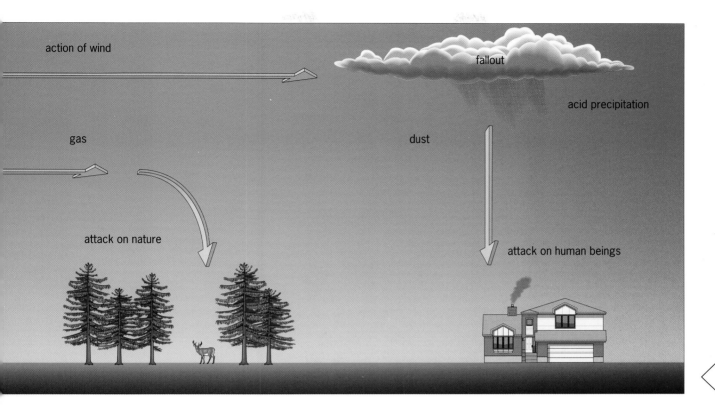

action of wind

gas

fallout

acid precipitation

dust

attack on nature

attack on human beings

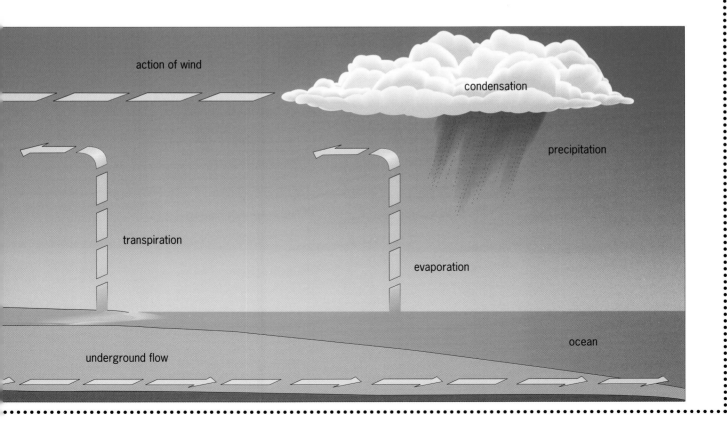

action of wind

condensation

precipitation

transpiration

evaporation

ocean

underground flow

ECOLOGY

food pollution on ground

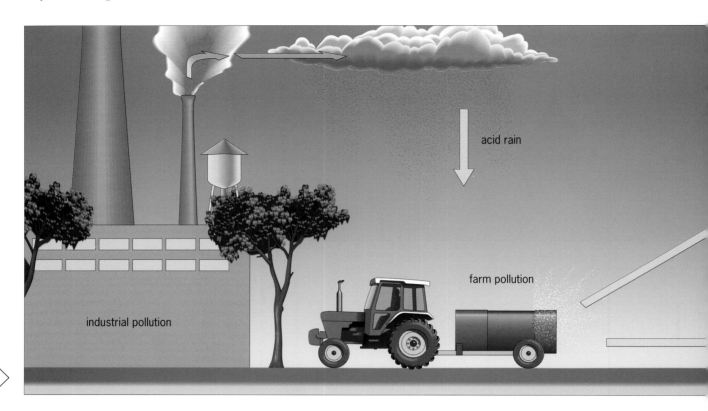

acid rain

farm pollution

industrial pollution

food pollution in water

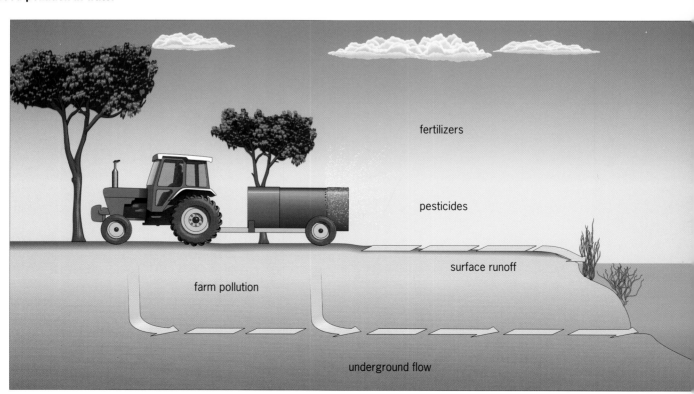

fertilizers

pesticides

surface runoff

farm pollution

underground flow

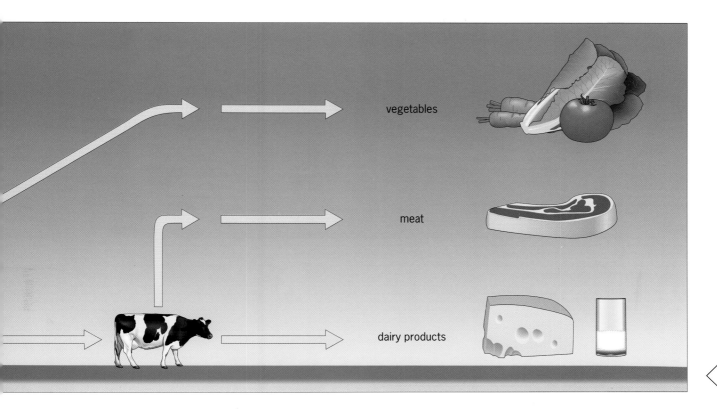

vegetables

meat

dairy products

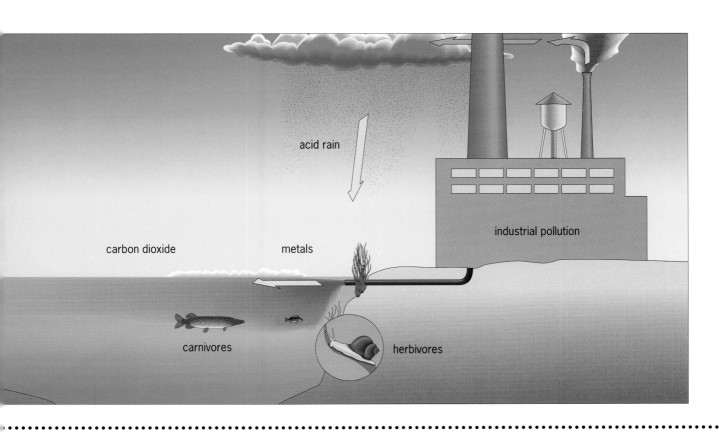

acid rain

carbon dioxide

metals

industrial pollution

carnivores

herbivores

PLANT AND SOIL

SOIL PROFILE

GERMINATION

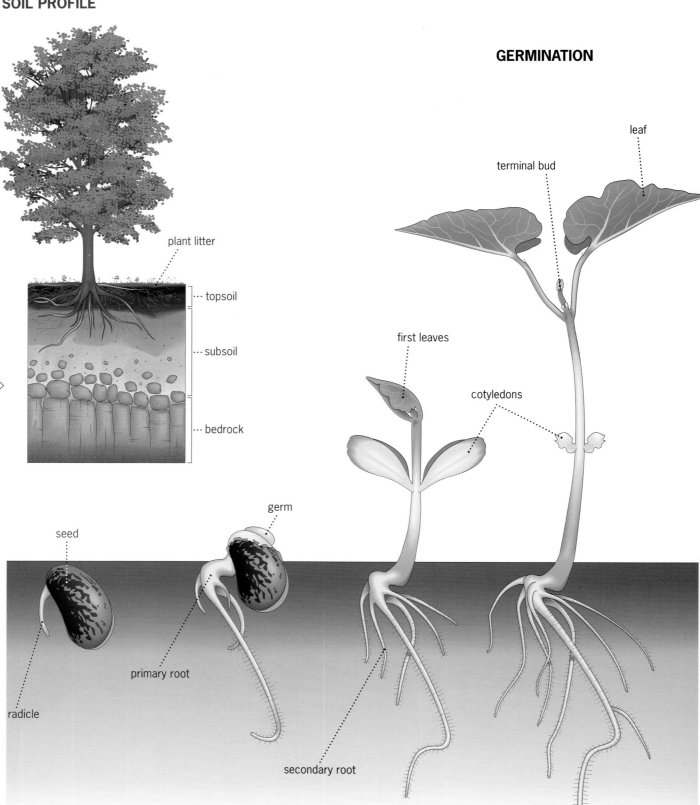

plant litter

topsoil

subsoil

bedrock

leaf

terminal bud

first leaves

cotyledons

germ

seed

primary root

radicle

secondary root

root hairs

34

MUSHROOM

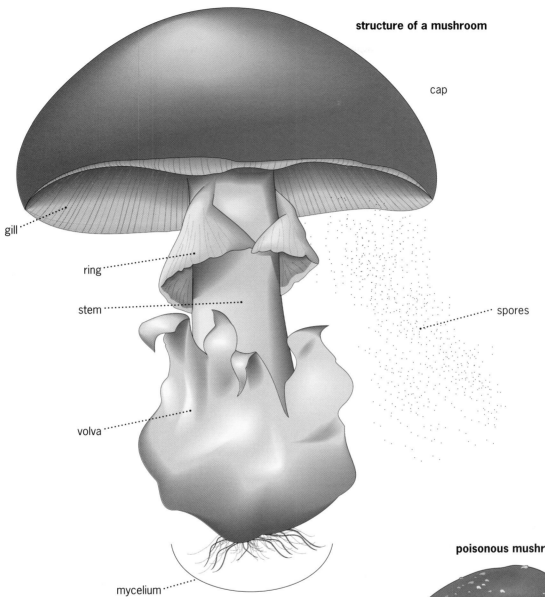

structure of a mushroom

cap

gill

ring

stem

spores

volva

mycelium

edible mushroom

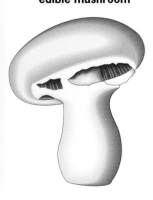

cultivated mushroom

deadly mushroom

destroying angel

poisonous mushroom

fly agaric

STRUCTURE OF A PLANT

COMPOUND LEAVES

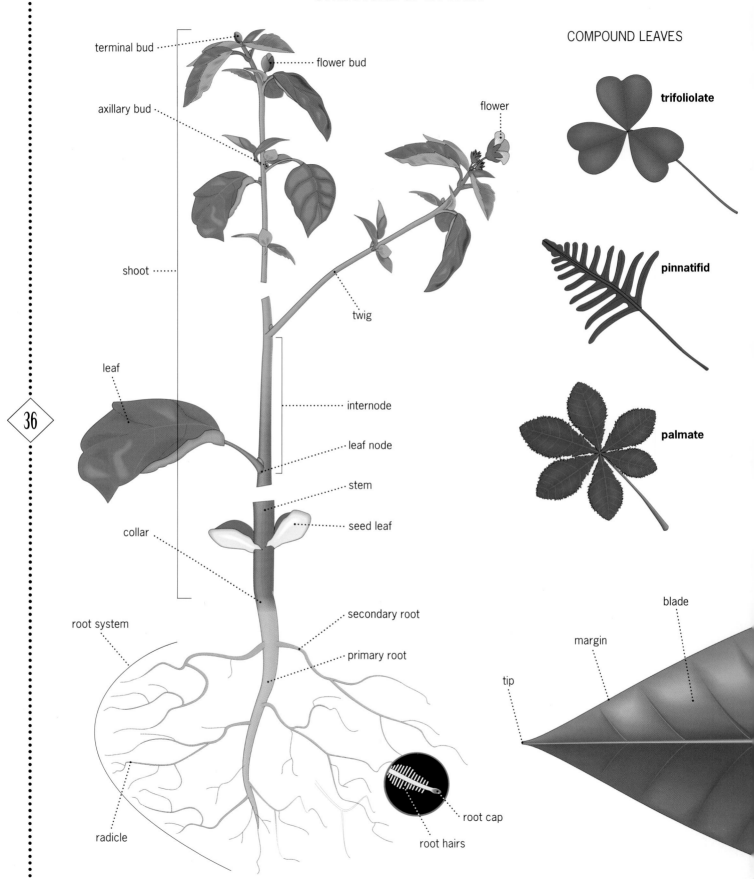

terminal bud

flower bud

axillary bud

flower

trifoliolate

shoot

twig

pinnatifid

leaf

internode

leaf node

palmate

stem

seed leaf

collar

root system

secondary root

primary root

blade

margin

tip

radicle

root cap

root hairs

36

SIMPLE LEAVES

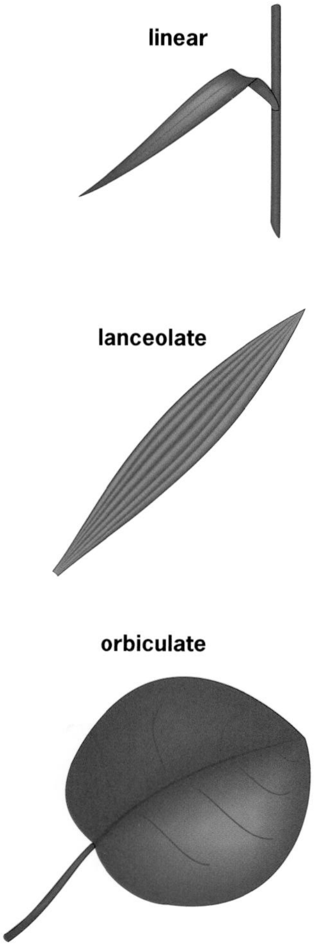

LEAF MARGINS

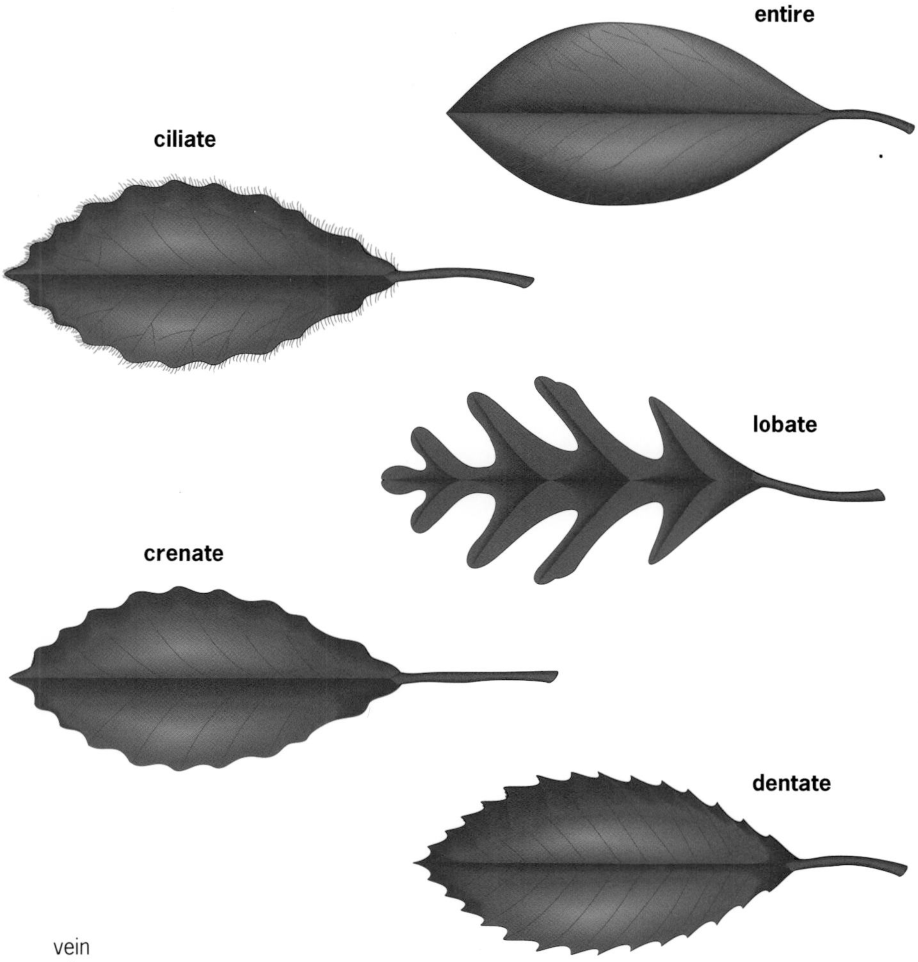

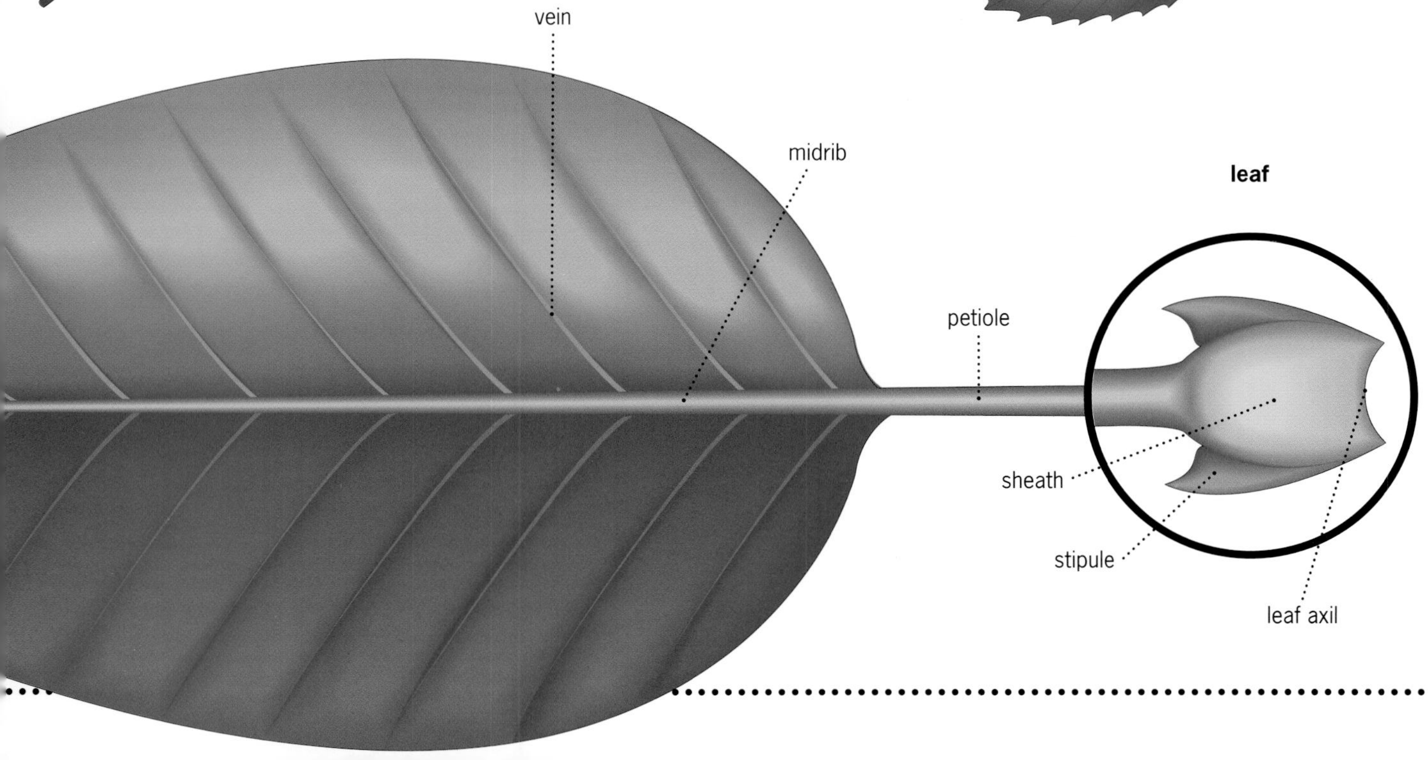

linear

ciliate

entire

lanceolate

lobate

crenate

orbiculate

dentate

vein

midrib

petiole

leaf

sheath

stipule

leaf axil

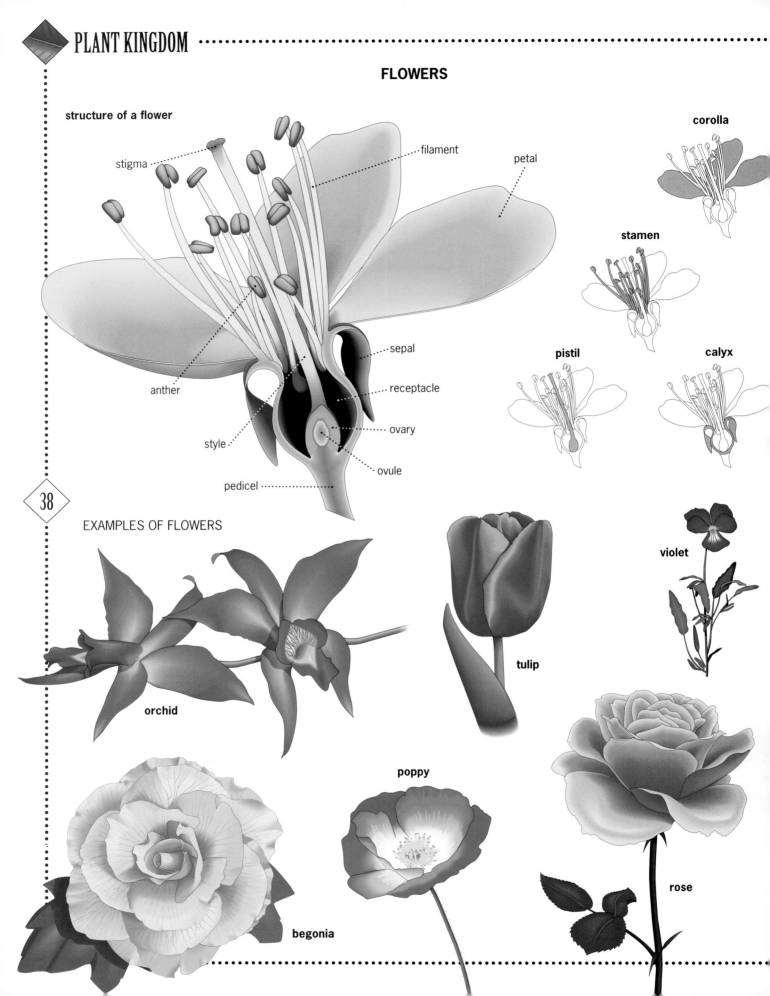

FLOWERS

structure of a flower

stigma
filament
petal
corolla
stamen
anther
sepal
receptacle
style
ovary
pistil
calyx
pedicel
ovule

38

EXAMPLES OF FLOWERS

orchid

tulip

violet

poppy

begonia

rose

lily

sunflower

lily of the valley

39

crocus

carnation

daffodil

TREE

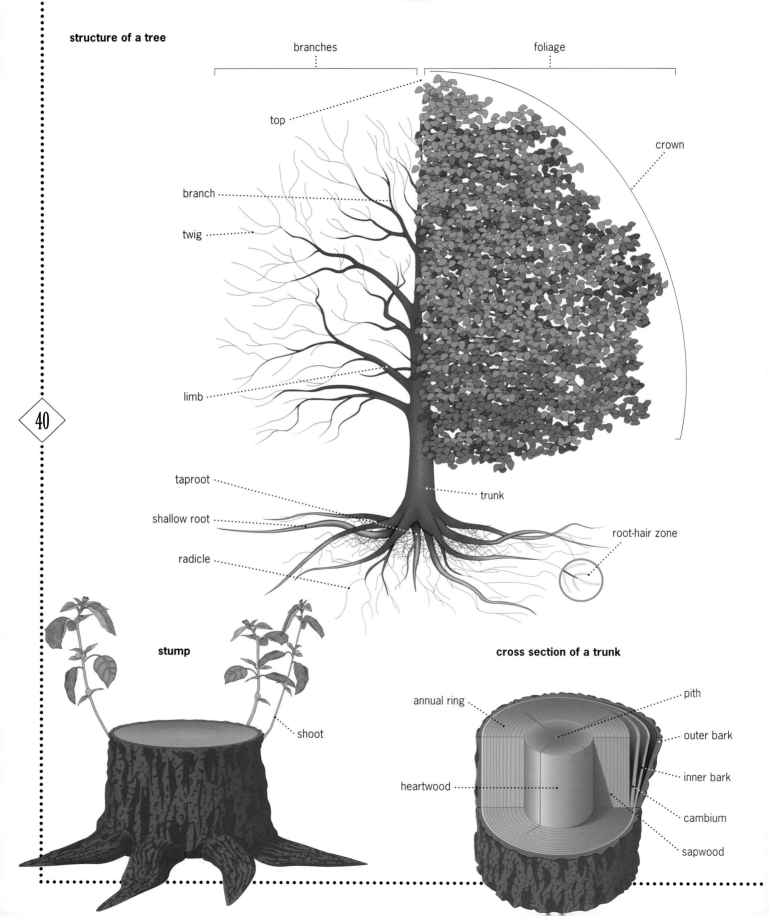

structure of a tree

branches

foliage

top

crown

branch

twig

limb

taproot

trunk

shallow root

root-hair zone

radicle

stump

shoot

cross section of a trunk

annual ring

pith

outer bark

inner bark

heartwood

cambium

sapwood

EXAMPLES OF TREES

poplar

oak

maple

palm tree

weeping willow

birch

42

CONIFER

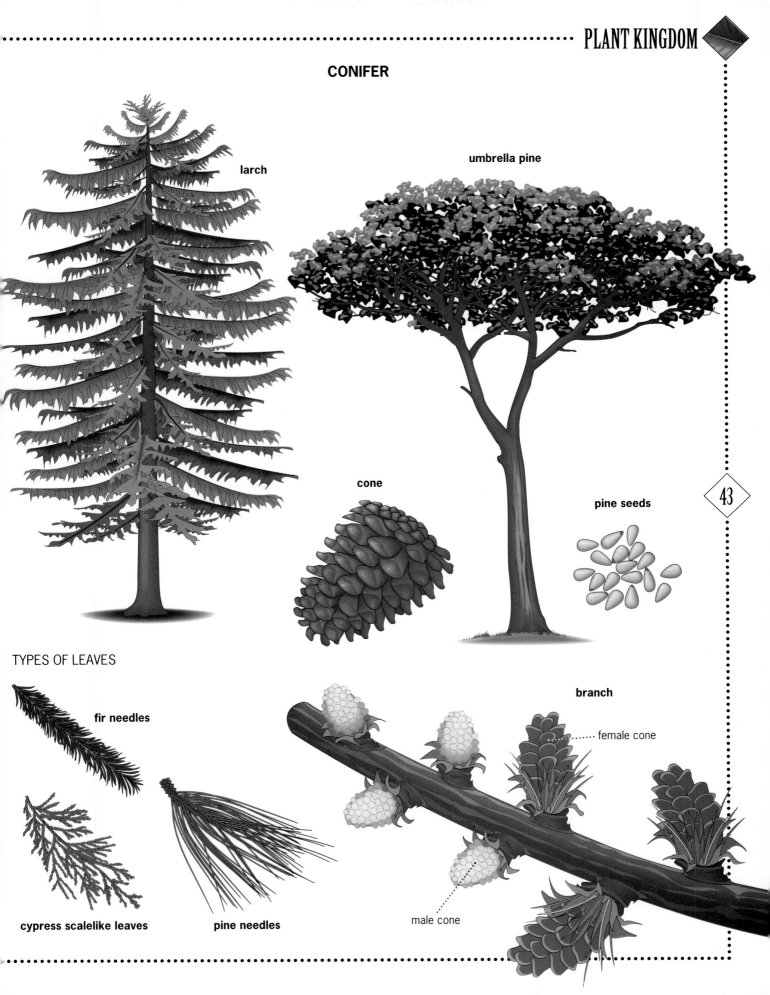

larch

umbrella pine

cone

pine seeds

TYPES OF LEAVES

fir needles

branch

female cone

male cone

cypress scalelike leaves

pine needles

FLESHY FRUITS: BERRY FRUITS

section of a berry

MAJOR TYPES OF BERRIES

grape

usual terms   technical terms

stalk   pedicel

pip   seed

flesh   mesocarp

skin   exocarp

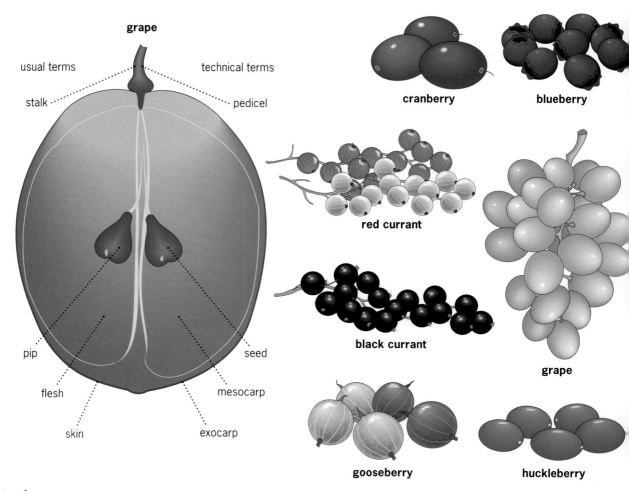

cranberry

blueberry

red currant

black currant

gooseberry

huckleberry

grape

section of a strawberry

flesh

achene

section of a raspberry

receptacle

seed

drupelet

sepal

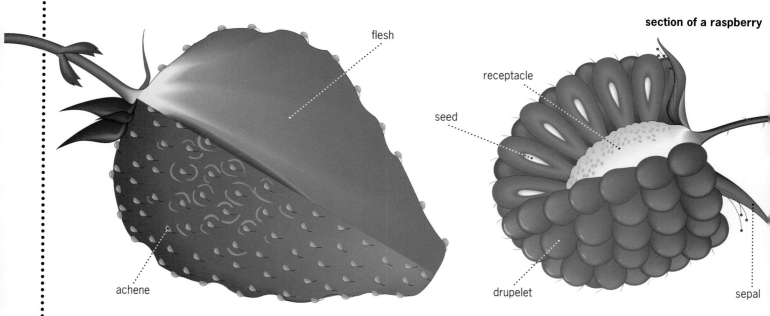

FLESHY STONE FRUITS

section of a stone fruit

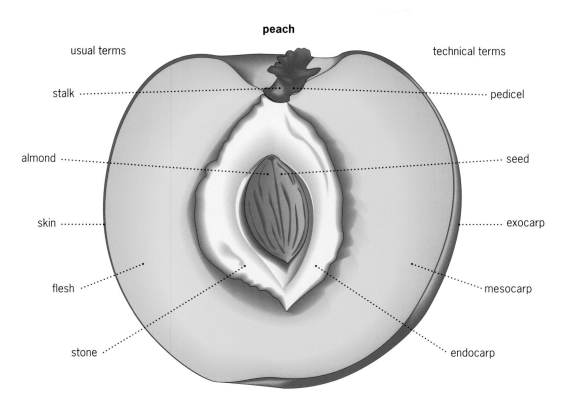

peach

usual terms   technical terms

stalk ·········· pedicel

almond ·········· seed

skin ·········· exocarp

flesh ·········· mesocarp

stone ·········· endocarp

45

MAJOR TYPES OF STONE FRUITS

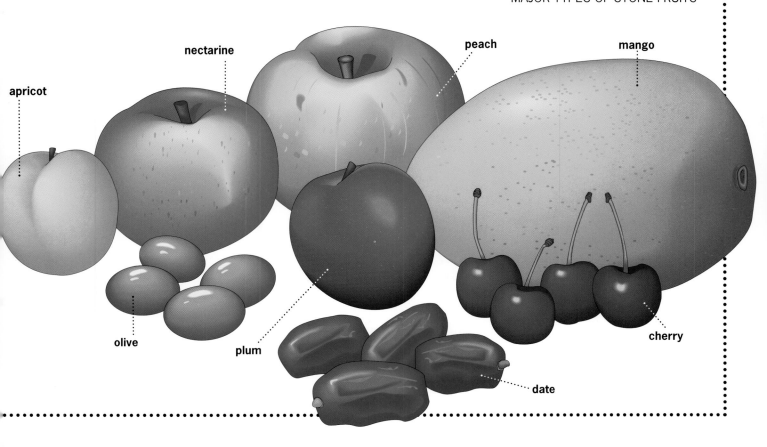

nectarine

peach

mango

apricot

olive

plum

date

cherry

FLESHY POME FRUITS

section of a pome fruit

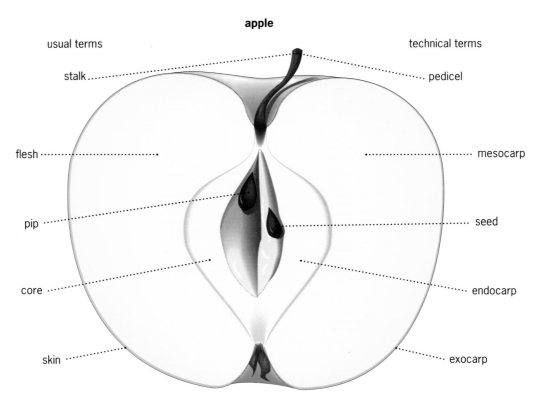

apple

usual terms   technical terms

stalk ·········· pedicel

flesh ········· mesocarp

pip ········· seed

core ········ endocarp

skin ········ exocarp

MAJOR TYPES OF POME FRUITS

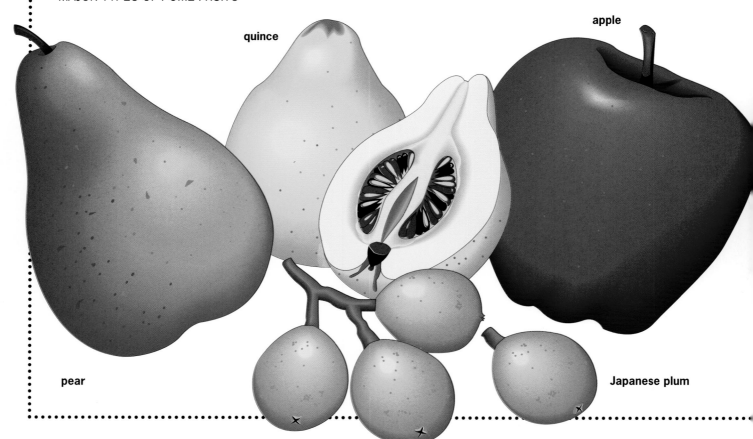

quince

apple

pear

Japanese plum

FLESHY FRUITS: CITRUS FRUITS

section of a citrus fruit

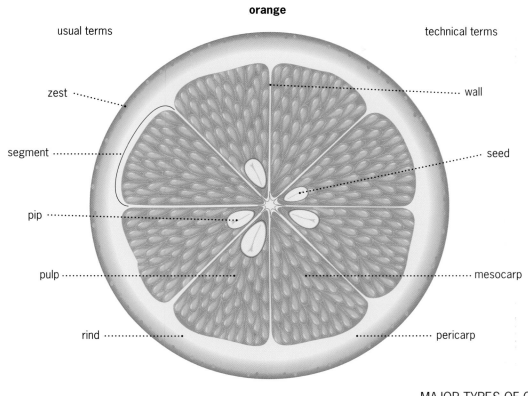

orange

usual terms

technical terms

zest

wall

segment

seed

pip

pulp

mesocarp

rind

pericarp

MAJOR TYPES OF CITRUS FRUITS

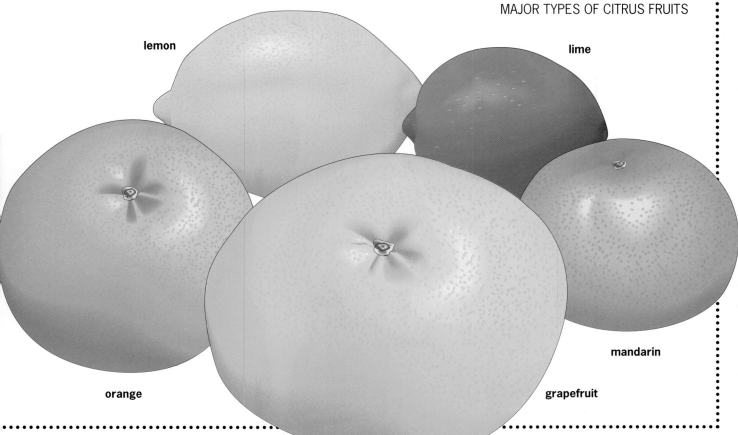

lemon

lime

mandarin

orange

grapefruit

TROPICAL FRUITS

MAJOR TYPES OF TROPICAL FRUITS

litchi

kiwi

guava

Japanese persimmon

Indian fig

cherimoya

fig

48

papaya

pomegranate

banana

avocado

pineapple

VEGETABLES

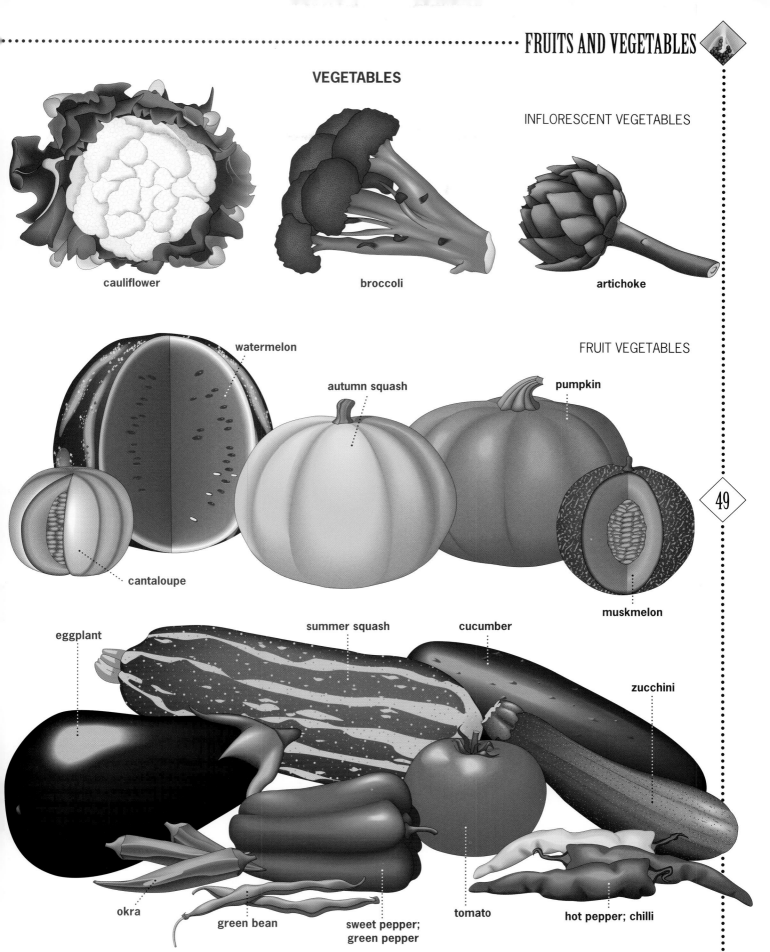

INFLORESCENT VEGETABLES

cauliflower

broccoli

artichoke

watermelon

FRUIT VEGETABLES

autumn squash

pumpkin

cantaloupe

muskmelon

eggplant

summer squash

cucumber

zucchini

okra

green bean

sweet pepper;
green pepper

tomato

hot pepper; chilli

49

VEGETABLES

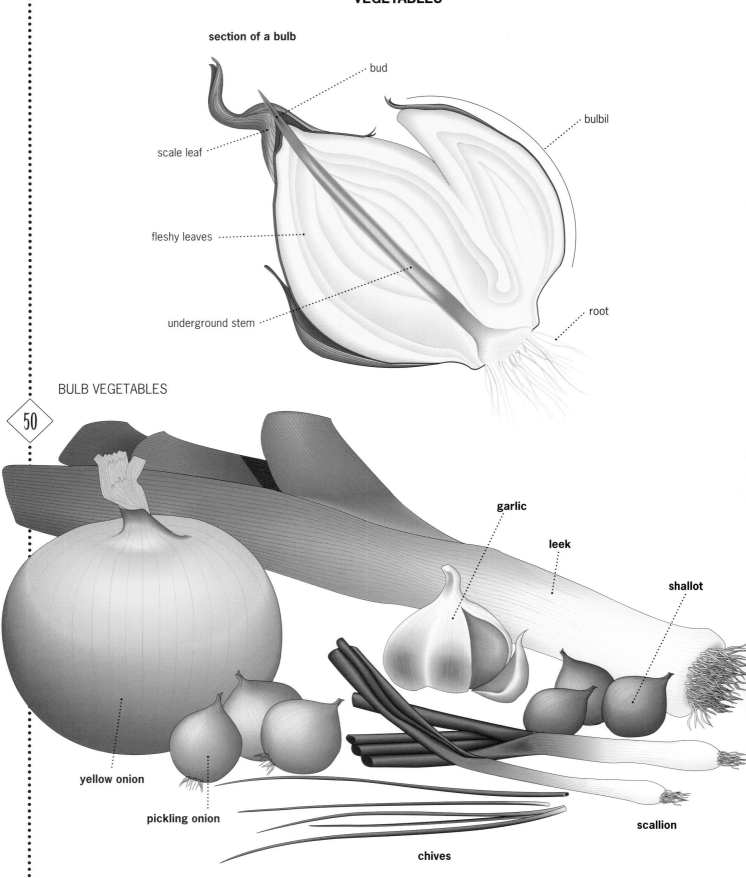

section of a bulb

bud

bulbil

scale leaf

fleshy leaves

underground stem

root

BULB VEGETABLES

garlic

leek

shallot

yellow onion

pickling onion

chives

scallion

TUBER VEGETABLES

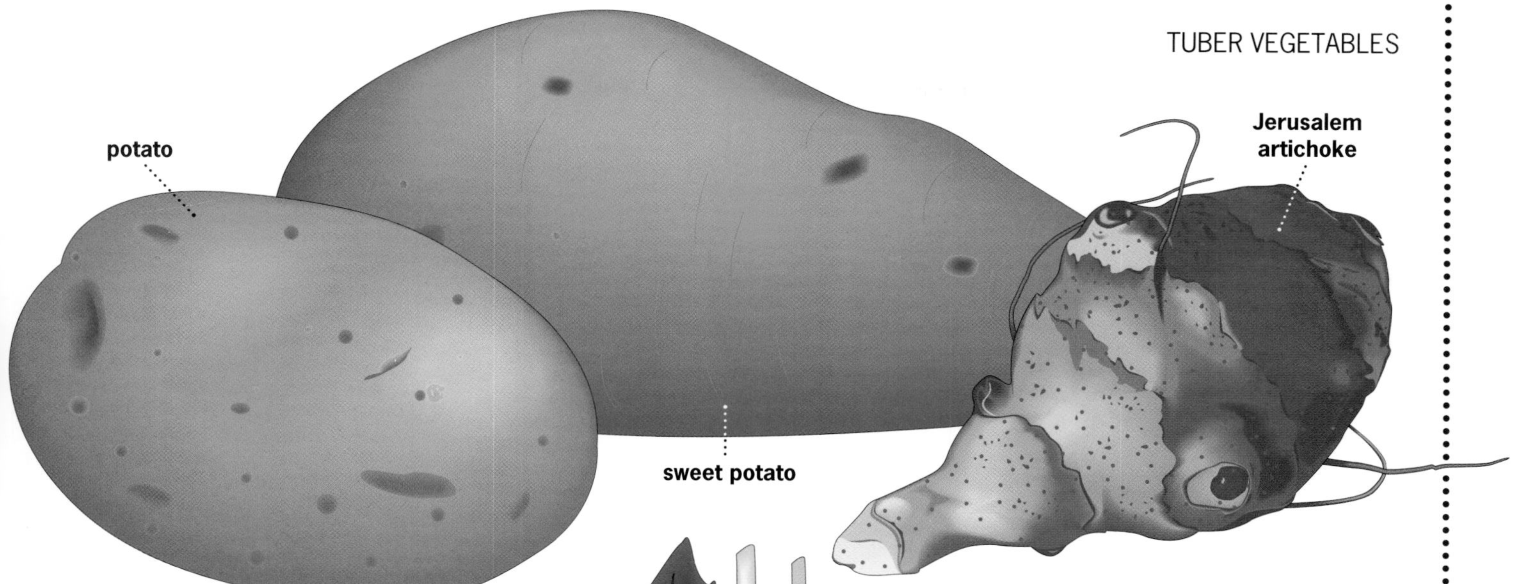

potato

Jerusalem artichoke

sweet potato

ROOT VEGETABLES

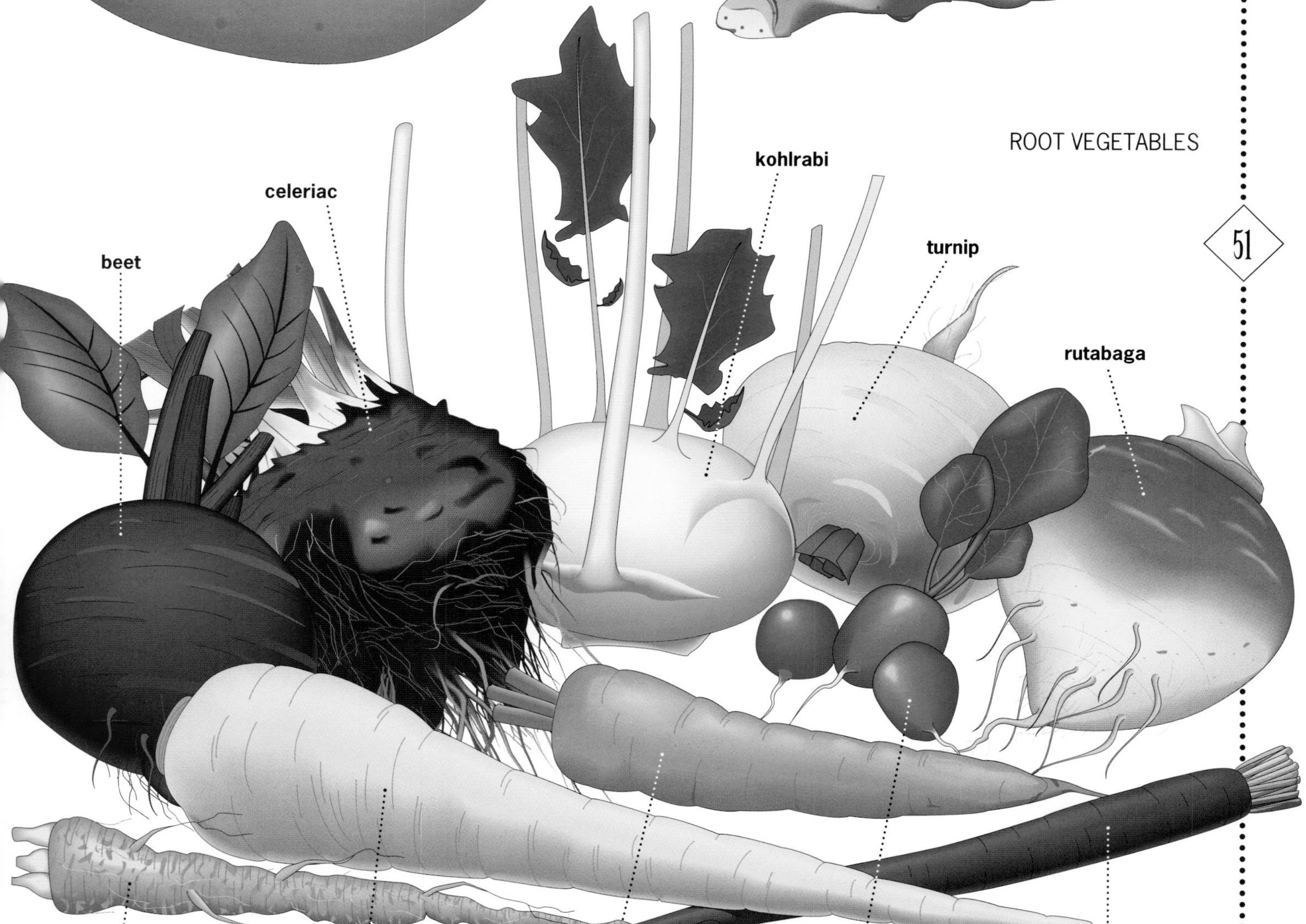

51

celeriac

kohlrabi

beet

turnip

rutabaga

horseradish

parsnip

carrot

radish

salsify

VEGETABLES

STALK VEGETABLES

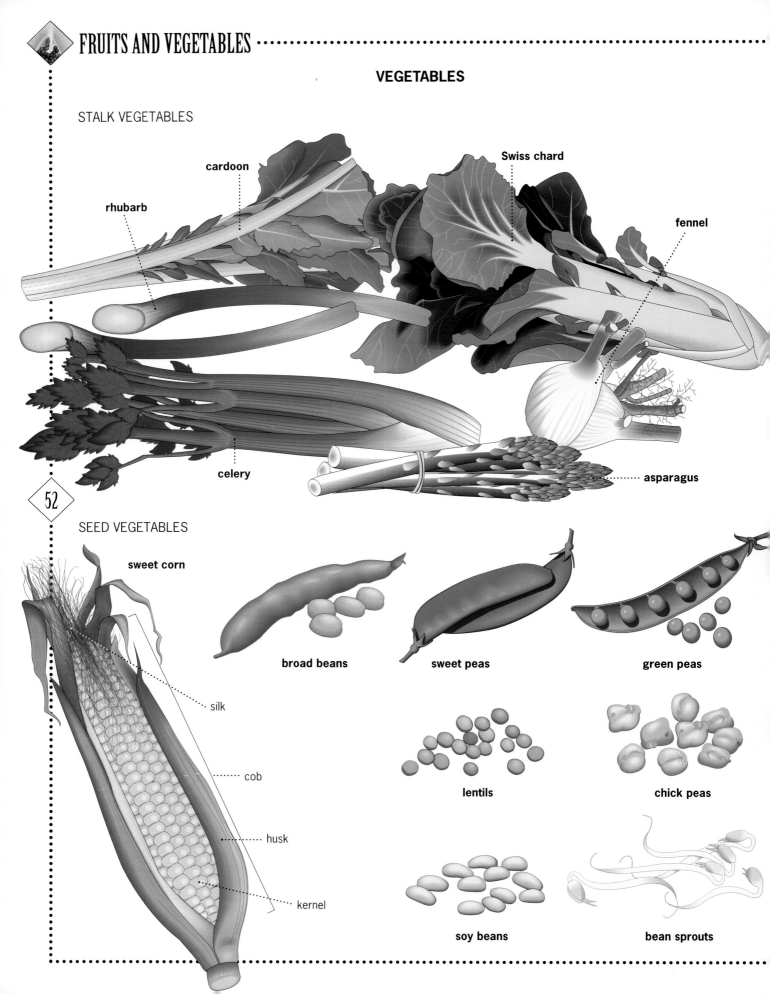

cardoon

rhubarb

Swiss chard

fennel

celery

asparagus

52

SEED VEGETABLES

sweet corn

silk

cob

husk

kernel

broad beans

sweet peas

green peas

lentils

chick peas

soy beans

bean sprouts

LEAF VEGETABLES

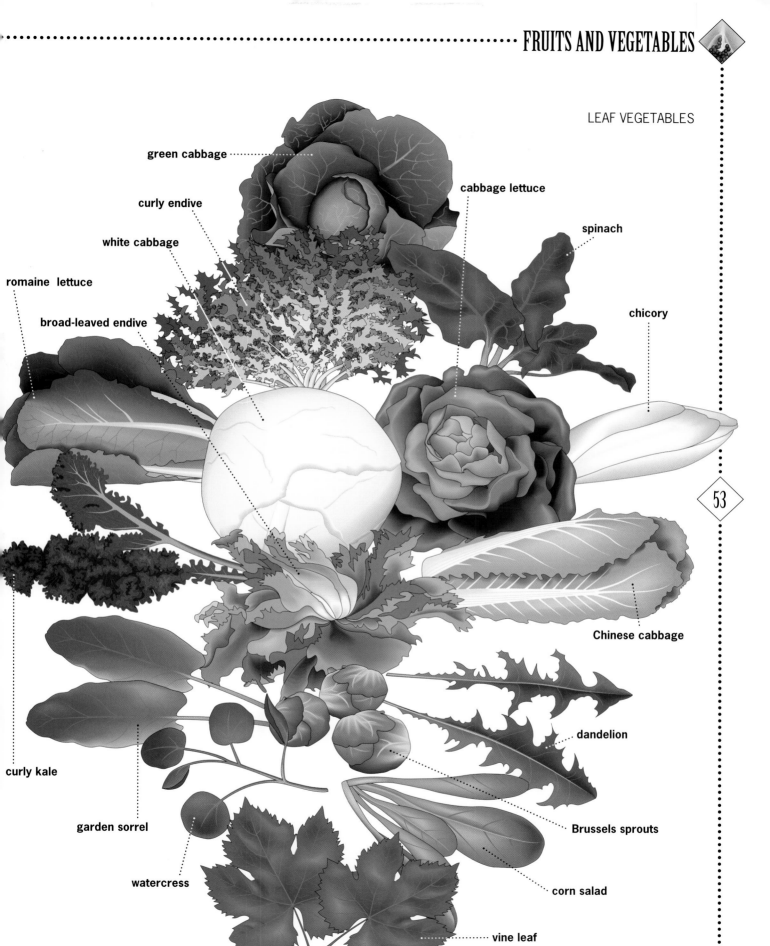

green cabbage

cabbage lettuce

curly endive

spinach

white cabbage

romaine lettuce

chicory

broad-leaved endive

Chinese cabbage

curly kale

dandelion

garden sorrel

Brussels sprouts

watercress

corn salad

vine leaf

53

GARDENING

trowel

hand fork

hand cultivator

pruning shears

lawnmower

speed control

ignition key

handle

safety handle

watering can

grassbox

starter

motor

deflector

casing

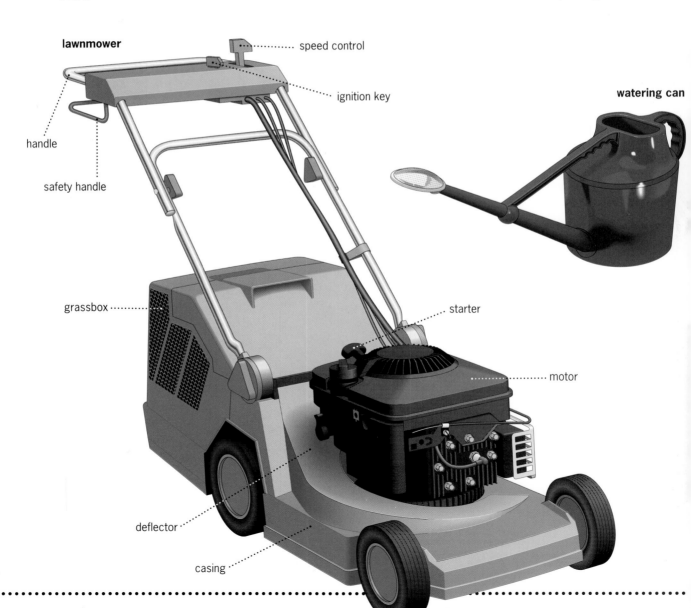

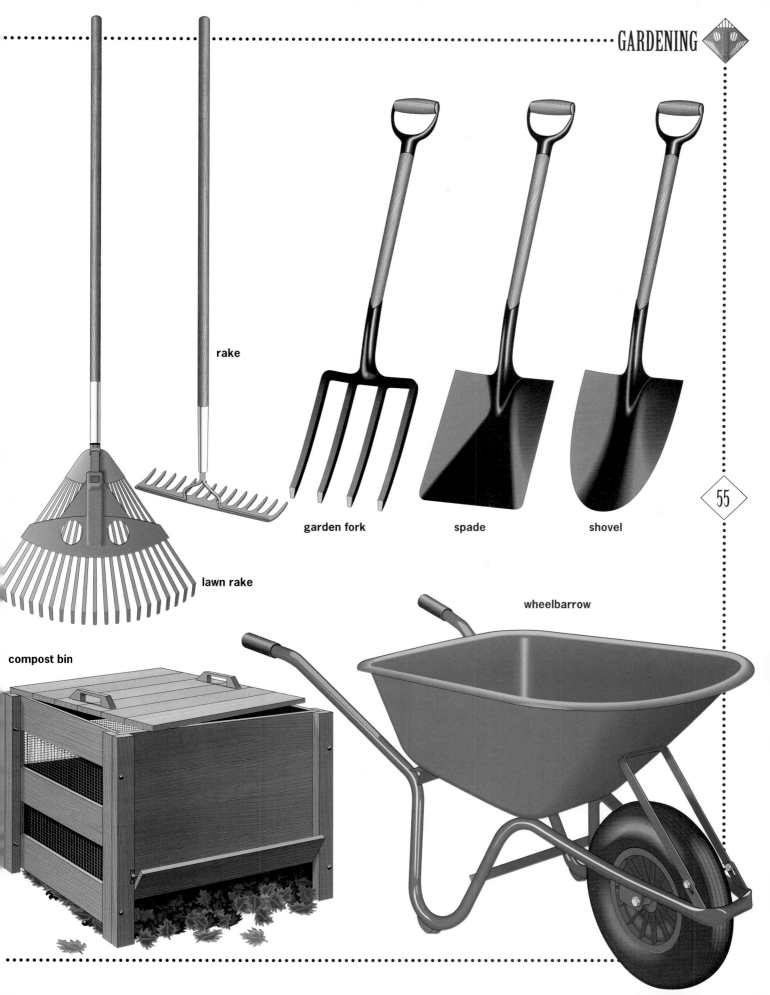

rake

garden fork

spade

shovel

lawn rake

wheelbarrow

compost bin

INSECTS AND SPIDER

ant

ladybug

fly

spider

grasshopper

dragonfly

BUTTERFLY

caterpillar

head

simple eye

mandible

walking leg

proleg

forewing

chrysalis

wing vein

cell

hind wing

thorax

head

antenna

labial palp

compound eye

proboscis

foreleg

middle leg

claw

abdomen

hind leg

HONEYBEE

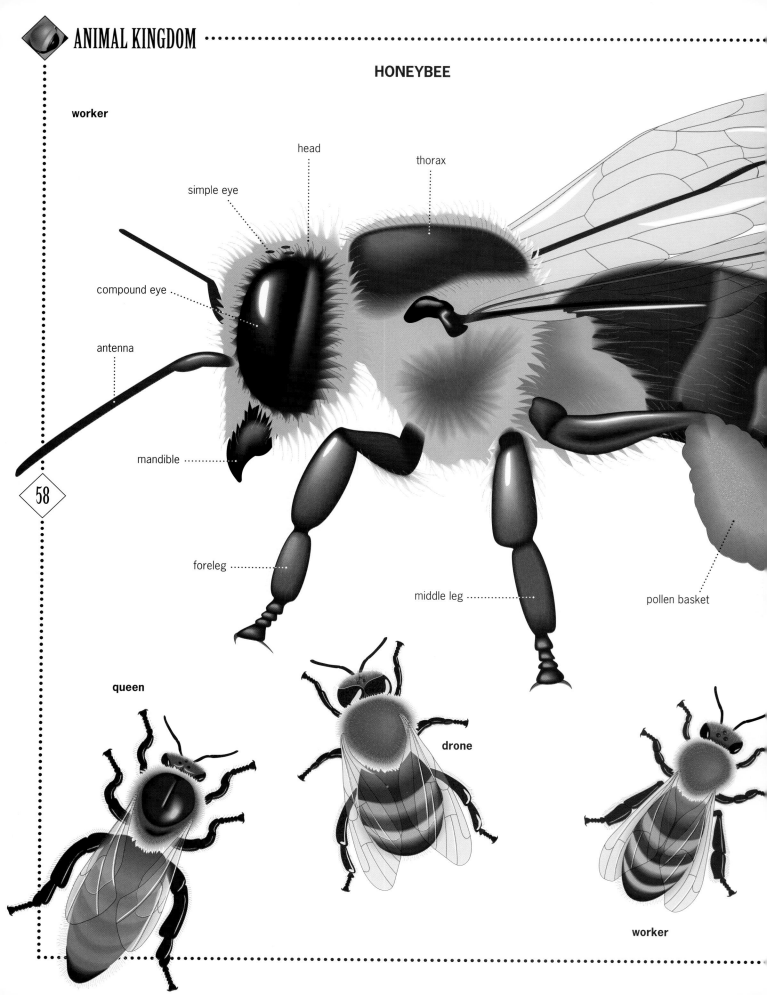

worker

simple eye

head

thorax

compound eye

antenna

mandible

foreleg

middle leg

pollen basket

58

queen

drone

worker

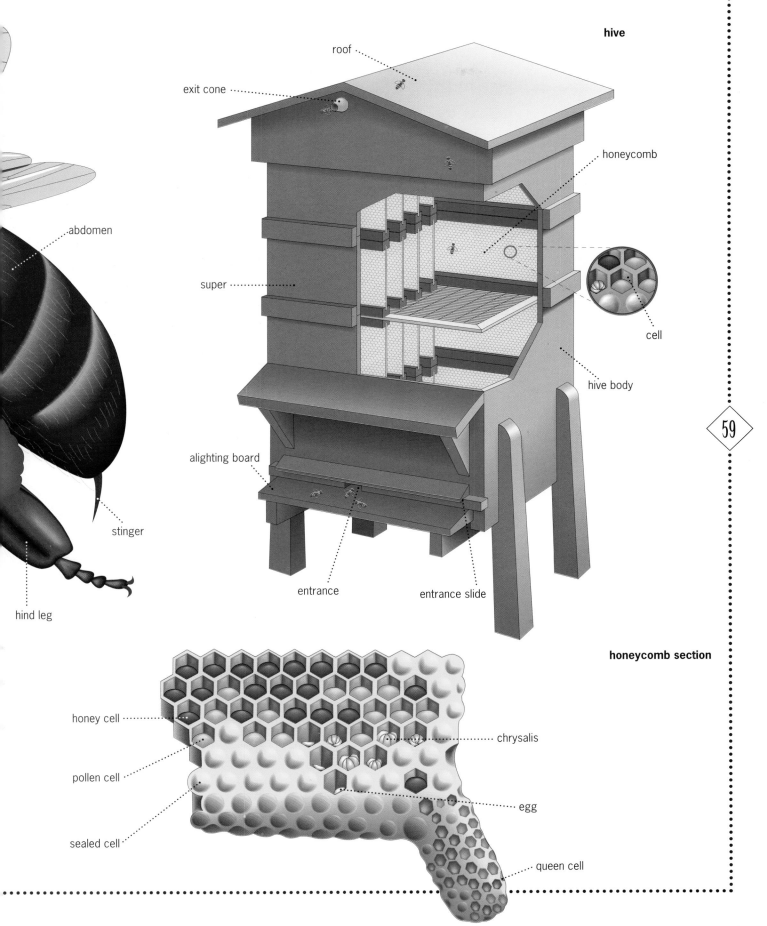

hive

roof

exit cone

abdomen

honeycomb

super

cell

hive body

alighting board

stinger

hind leg

entrance

entrance slide

honeycomb section

honey cell

chrysalis

pollen cell

sealed cell

egg

queen cell

AMPHIBIANS

frog

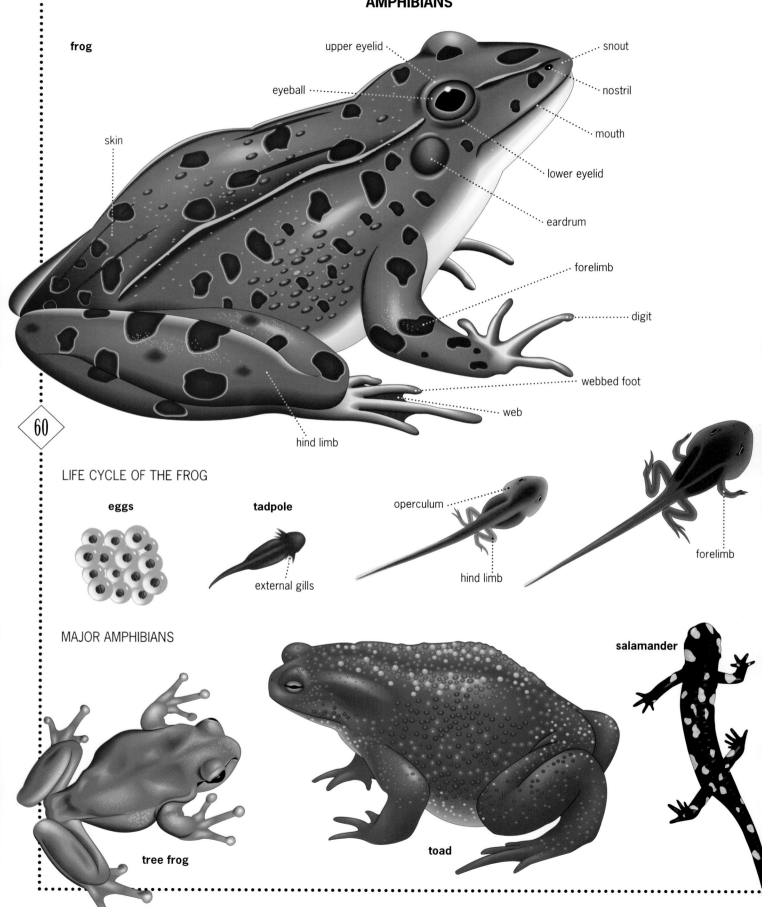

upper eyelid

snout

eyeball

nostril

mouth

lower eyelid

skin

eardrum

forelimb

digit

webbed foot

web

hind limb

LIFE CYCLE OF THE FROG

eggs

tadpole

operculum

external gills

hind limb

forelimb

MAJOR AMPHIBIANS

salamander

tree frog

toad

CRUSTACEANS

thoracic legs

lobster

antenna

eye

carapace

antennule

maxillipeds

claw

swimmerets

cephalothorax

abdomen

tail

MAJOR EDIBLE CRUSTACEANS

shrimp

crayfish

crab

scampi

spiny lobster

FISH

MORPHOLOGY

gills

sea horse

first dorsal fin

nostril

mandible

maxilla

pectoral fin

pelvic fin

trout

swordfish

tuna

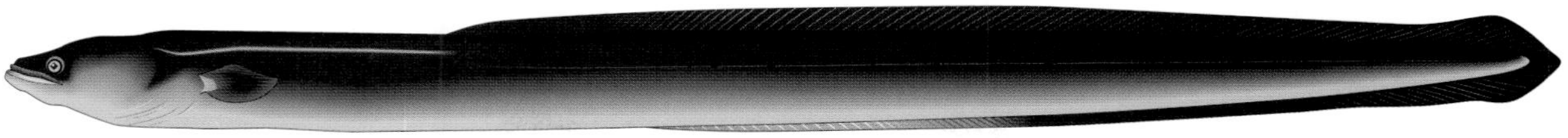

eel

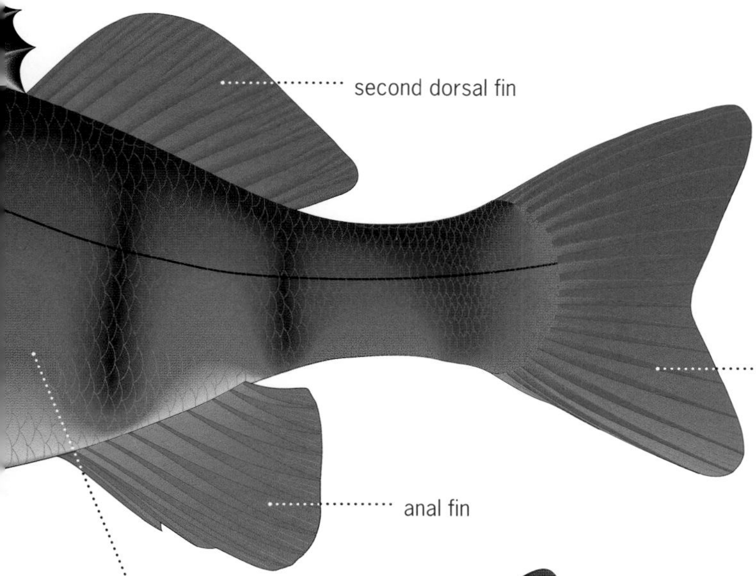

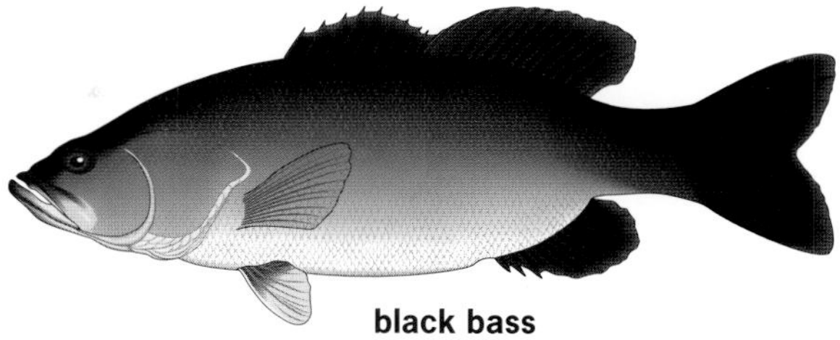

second dorsal fin

black bass

caudal fin

anal fin

flounder

scale

63

shark

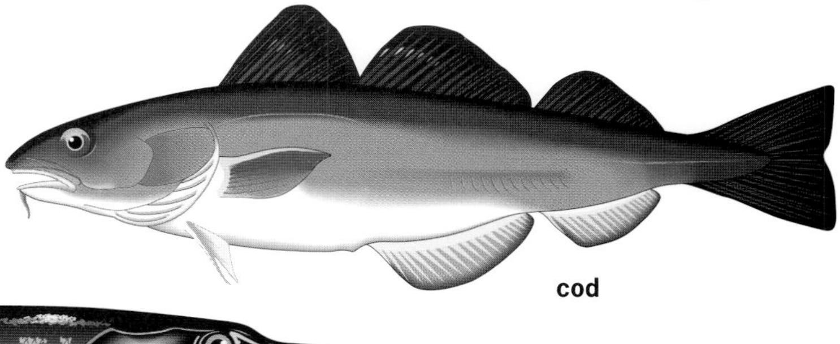

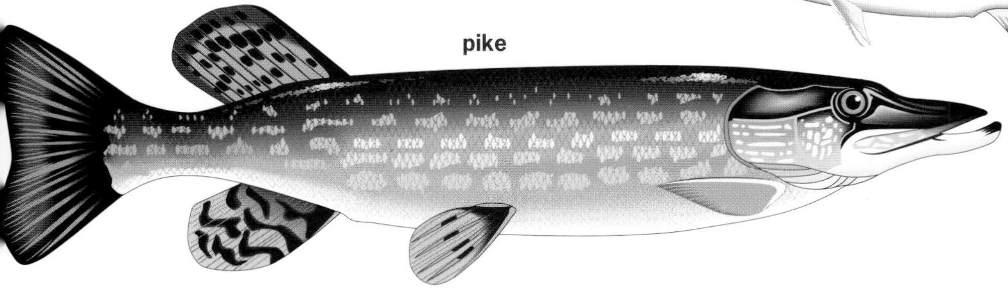

pike

cod

REPTILES

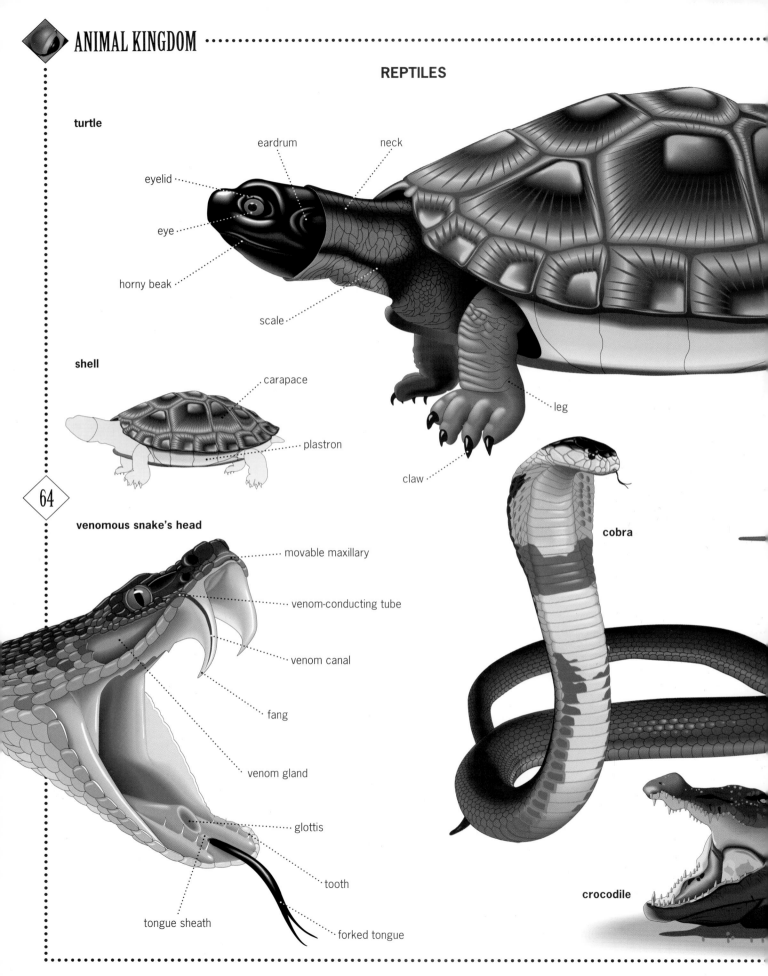

turtle

eardrum

neck

eyelid

eye

horny beak

scale

leg

shell

carapace

plastron

claw

64

venomous snake's head

movable maxillary

venom-conducting tube

venom canal

fang

venom gland

glottis

tooth

tongue sheath

forked tongue

cobra

crocodile

shield

tail

chameleon

lizard

rattlesnake

CAT

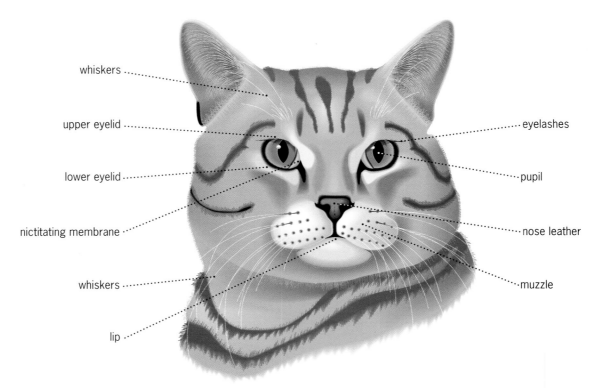

whiskers

upper eyelid

lower eyelid

nictitating membrane

whiskers

lip

eyelashes

pupil

nose leather

muzzle

66

DOG

MORPHOLOGY

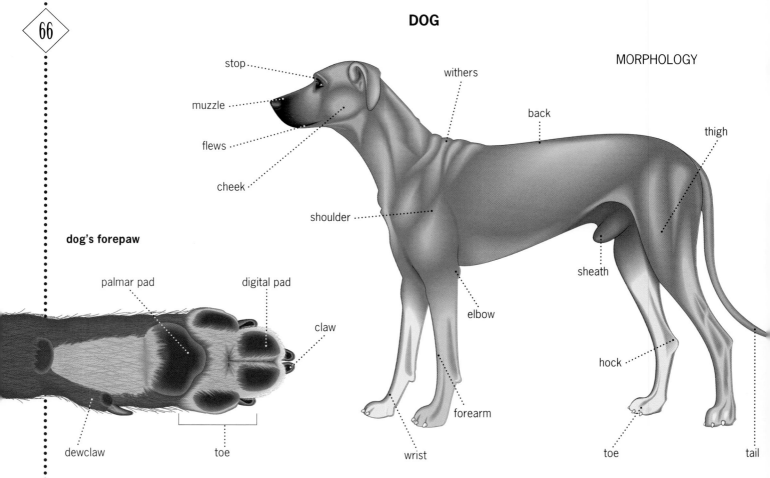

stop

muzzle

flews

cheek

withers

back

thigh

shoulder

sheath

dog's forepaw

palmar pad

digital pad

claw

elbow

hock

dewclaw

toe

forearm

wrist

toe

tail

HORSE

forelock

nose

nostril

muzzle

lip

mane

withers

back

loin

tail

flank

croup

neck

shoulder

chest

arm

elbow

knee

chestnut

fetlock joint

coronet

fetlock

belly

sheath

thigh

gaskin

pastern

hoof

hock

cannon

FARM ANIMALS

hen

chick

rooster; cock

duck

goose

turkey

cow

calf

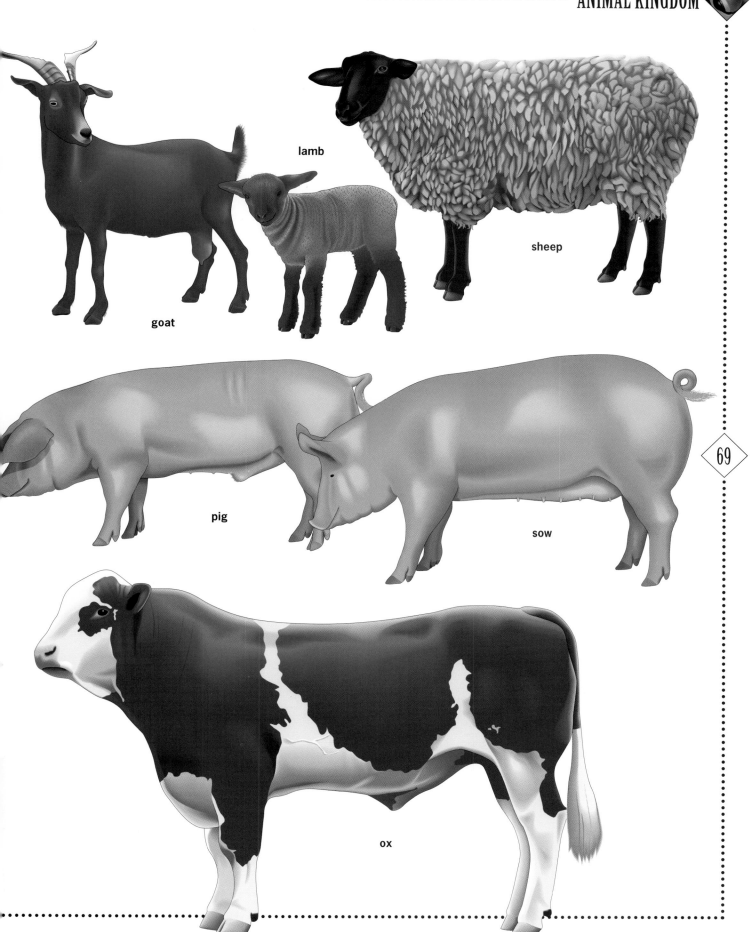

lamb

sheep

goat

pig

sow

ox

TYPES OF JAWS

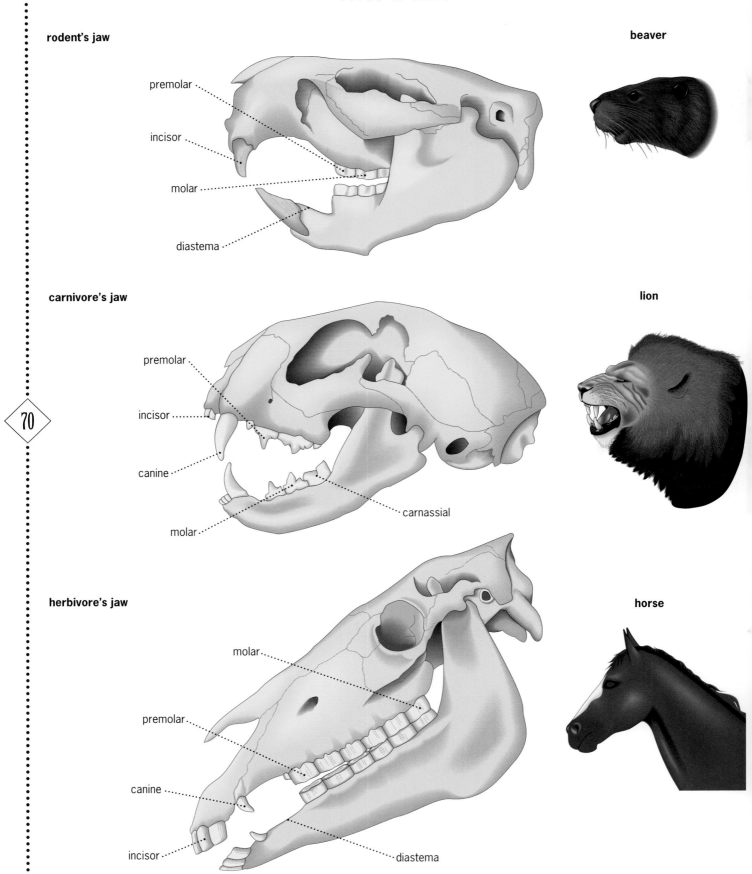

rodent's jaw

beaver

premolar

incisor

molar

diastema

carnivore's jaw

lion

premolar

incisor

canine

carnassial

molar

herbivore's jaw

horse

molar

premolar

canine

incisor

diastema

70

MAJOR TYPES OF HORNS

horns of mouflon

horns of giraffe

horns of rhinoceros

MAJOR TYPES OF TUSKS

tusks of walrus

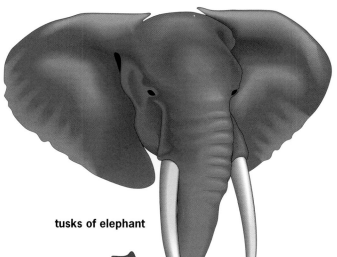

tusks of elephant

tusks of wart hog

TYPES OF HOOFS

one-toe hoof

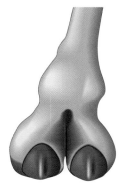

two-toed hoof

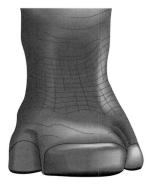

three-toed hoof

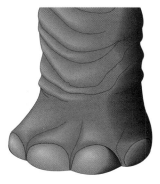

four-toed hoof

WILD ANIMALS

giraffe

polar bear

monkey

lion

dolphin

whale

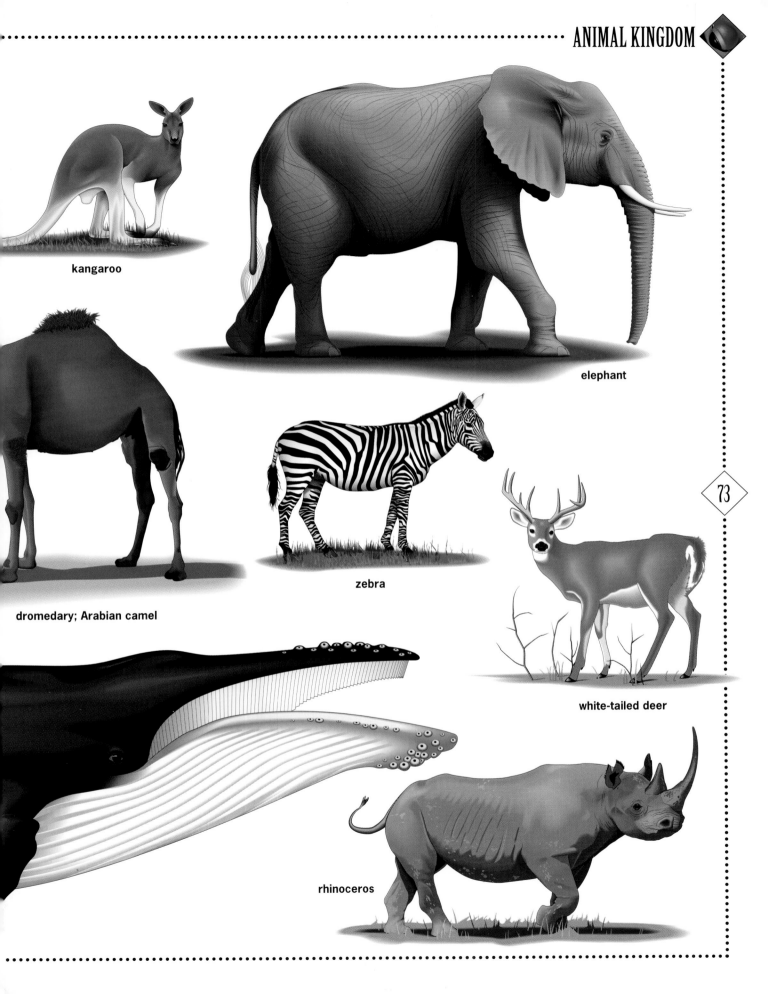

kangaroo

elephant

dromedary; Arabian camel

zebra

white-tailed deer

rhinoceros

BIRD

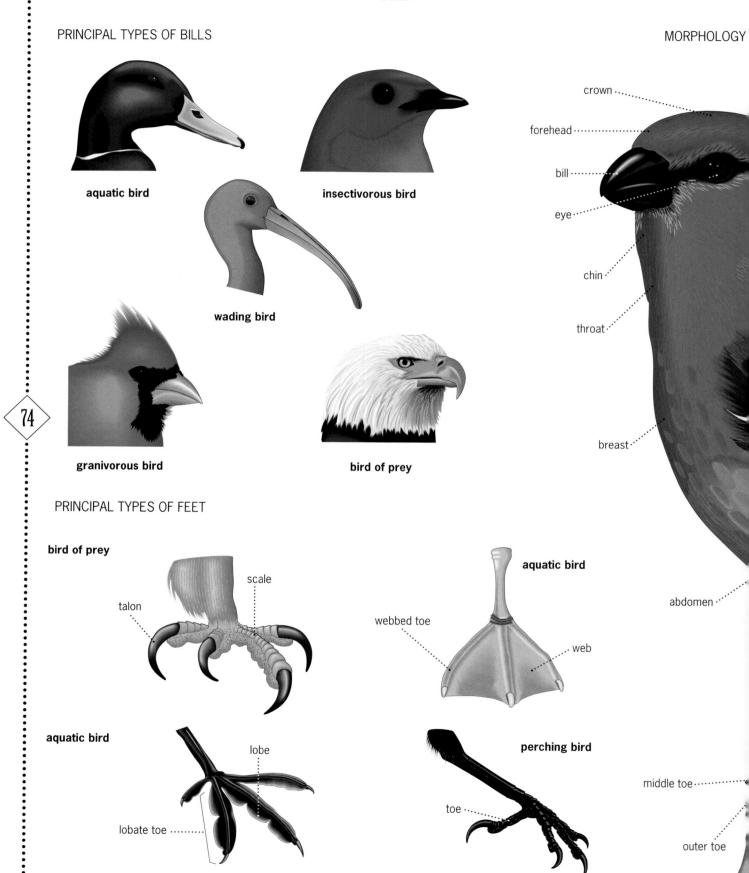

PRINCIPAL TYPES OF BILLS

aquatic bird

insectivorous bird

wading bird

granivorous bird

bird of prey

MORPHOLOGY

crown
forehead
bill
eye
chin
throat
breast
abdomen
middle toe
outer toe

PRINCIPAL TYPES OF FEET

bird of prey

talon
scale

aquatic bird

webbed toe
web

aquatic bird

lobe
lobate toe

perching bird

toe

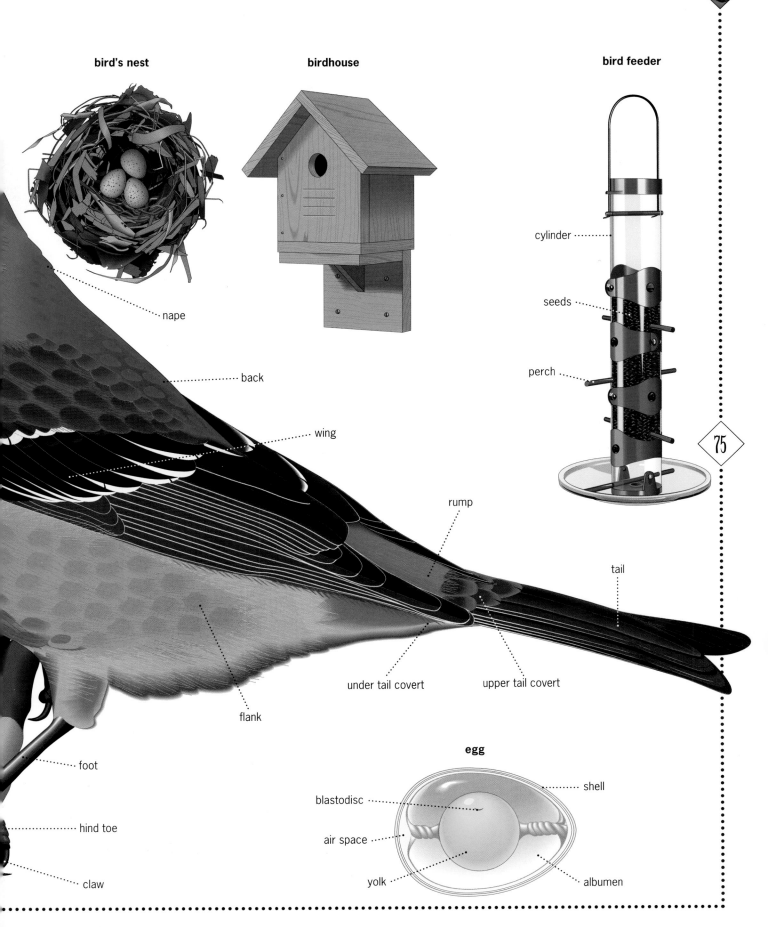

bird's nest

birdhouse

bird feeder

cylinder

seeds

perch

nape

back

wing

rump

tail

under tail covert

upper tail covert

flank

foot

hind toe

claw

egg

blastodisc

air space

shell

yolk

albumen

75

EXAMPLES OF BIRDS

crow

parrot

stork

swallow

flamingo

ostrich

robin

blue jay

owl

nightingale

hummingbird

peacock

HUMAN BODY, ANTERIOR VIEW

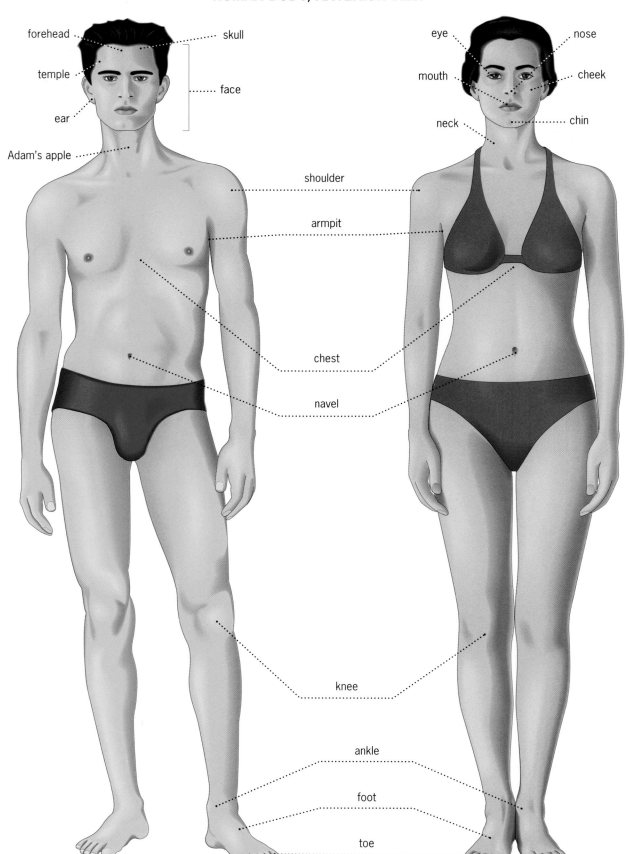

forehead

skull

temple

face

ear

Adam's apple

eye

nose

mouth

cheek

neck

chin

shoulder

armpit

chest

navel

knee

ankle

foot

toe

78

HUMAN BODY, POSTERIOR VIEW

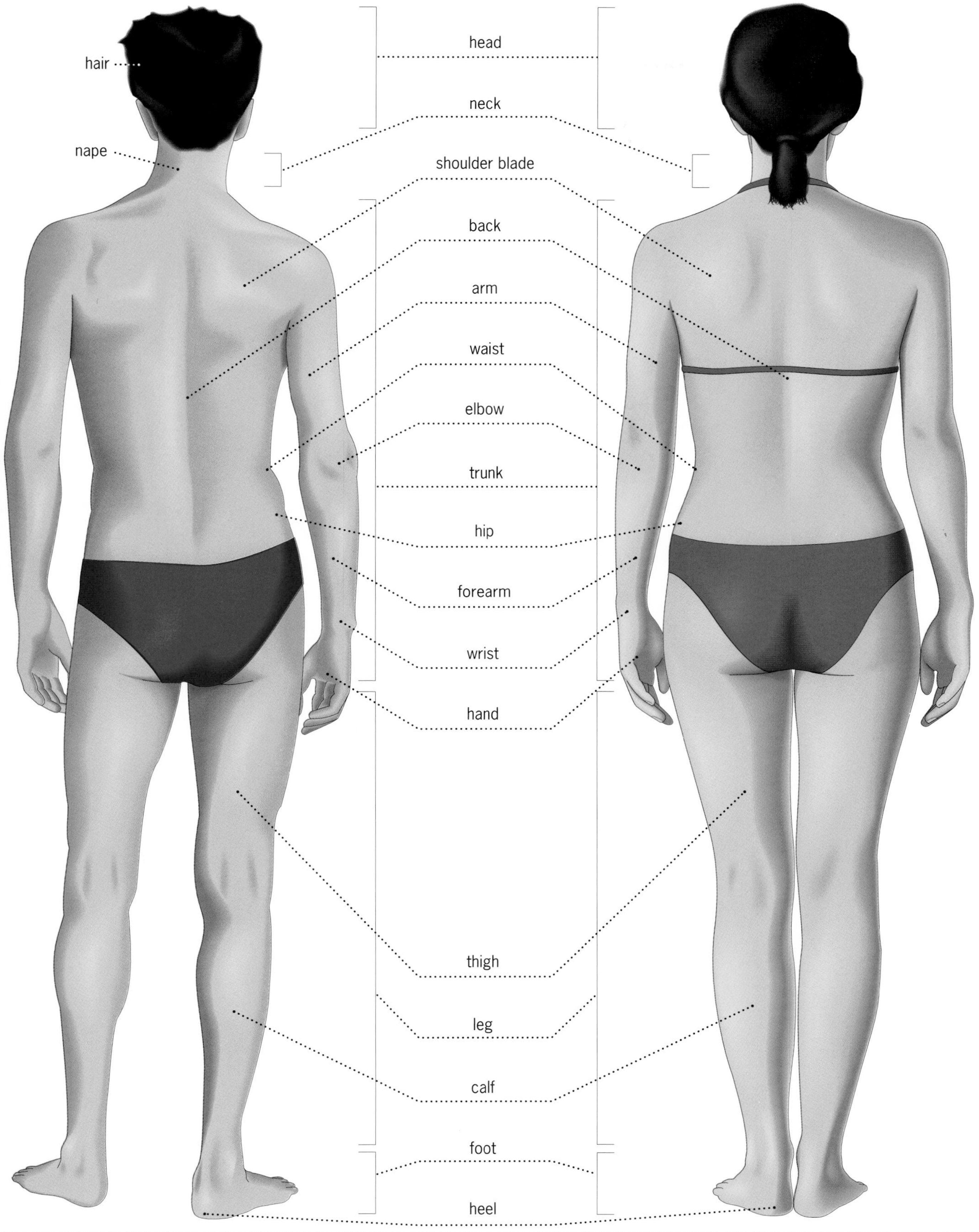

hair

nape

head

neck

shoulder blade

back

arm

waist

elbow

trunk

hip

forearm

wrist

hand

thigh

leg

calf

foot

heel

SKELETON

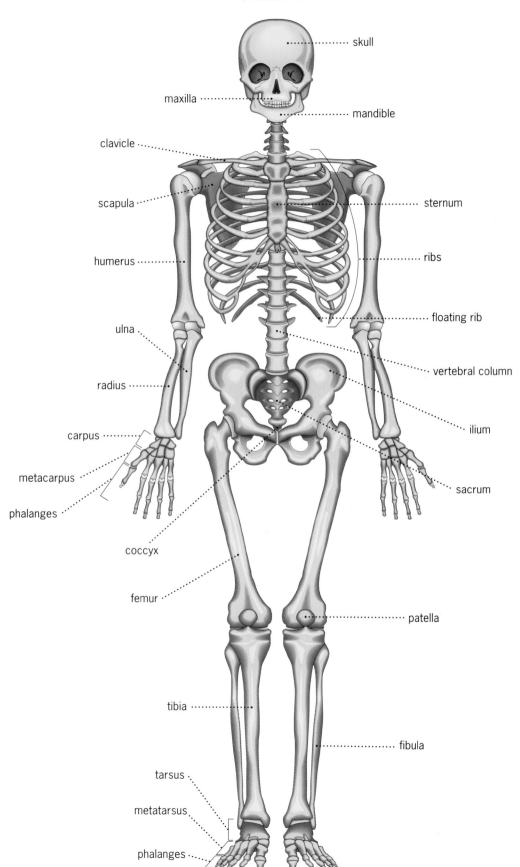

skull

maxilla

mandible

clavicle

sternum

scapula

humerus

ribs

floating rib

ulna

radius

vertebral column

ilium

carpus

metacarpus

phalanges

sacrum

coccyx

femur

patella

tibia

fibula

tarsus

metatarsus

phalanges

HUMAN ANATOMY

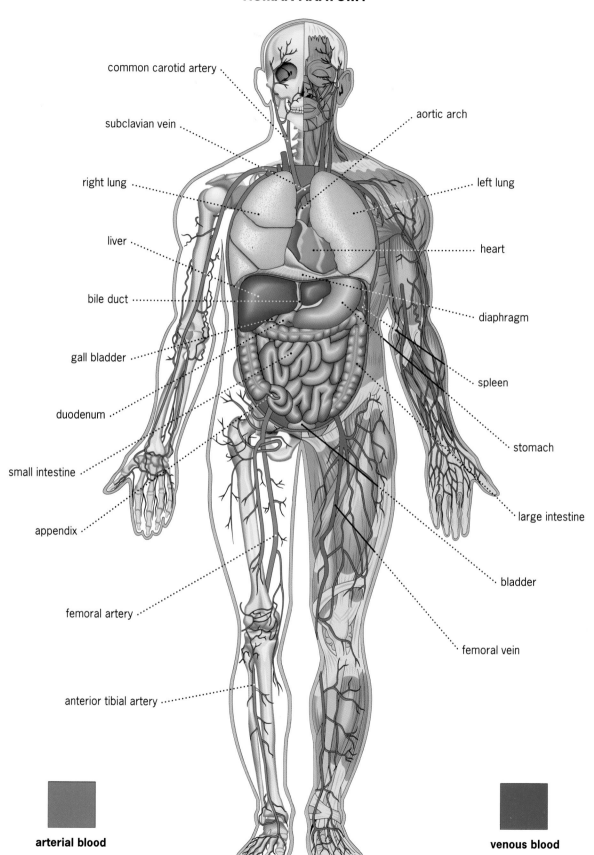

common carotid artery

subclavian vein

right lung

liver

bile duct

gall bladder

duodenum

small intestine

appendix

femoral artery

anterior tibial artery

aortic arch

left lung

heart

diaphragm

spleen

stomach

large intestine

bladder

femoral vein

arterial blood

venous blood

EYE: THE ORGAN OF SIGHT

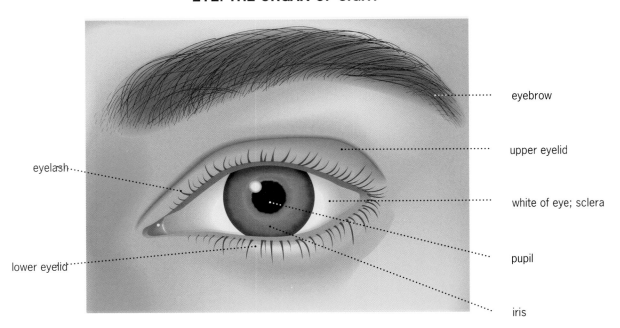

eyebrow

upper eyelid

eyelash

white of eye; sclera

pupil

lower eyelid

iris

HAND: THE ORGAN OF TOUCH

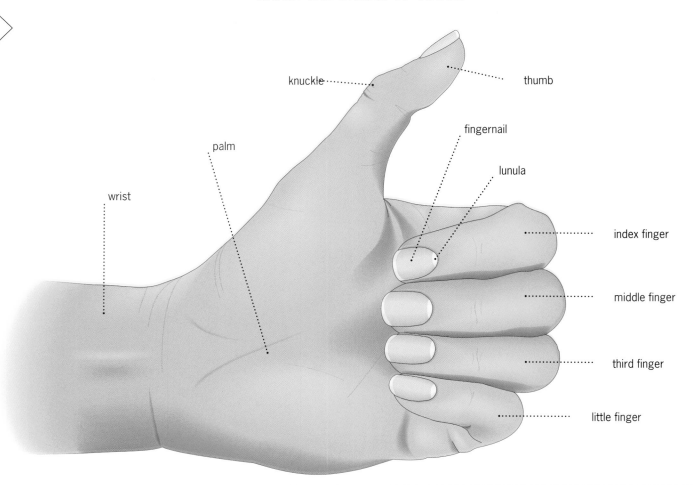

knuckle

thumb

fingernail

palm

lunula

wrist

index finger

middle finger

third finger

little finger

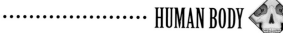

EAR: THE ORGAN OF HEARING

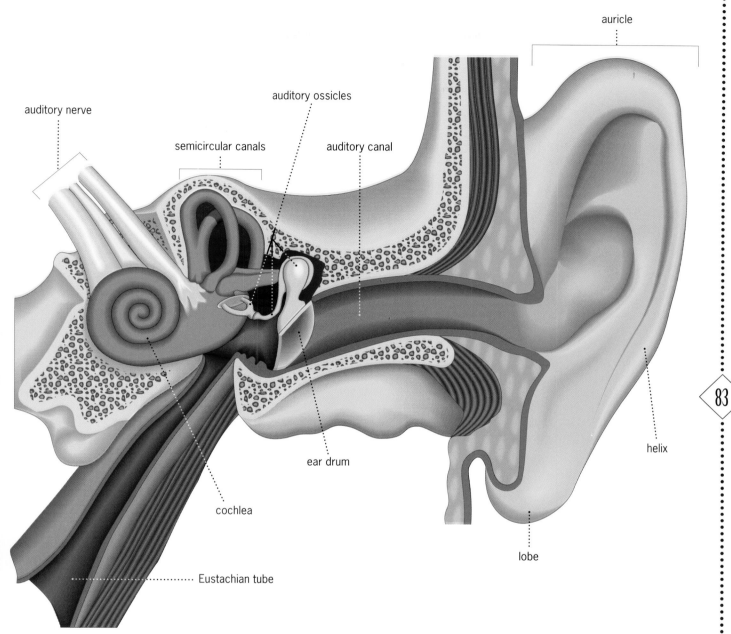

auricle

auditory nerve

auditory ossicles

semicircular canals

auditory canal

helix

ear drum

cochlea

lobe

Eustachian tube

PARTS OF THE EAR

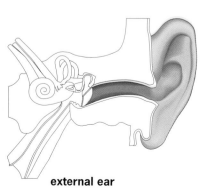

external ear

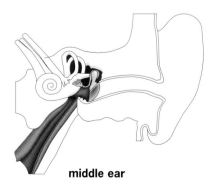

middle ear

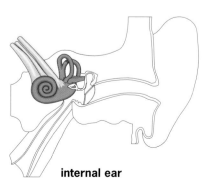

internal ear

NOSE: THE ORGAN OF SMELL

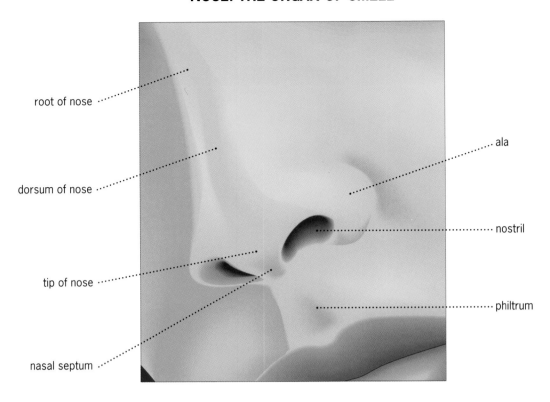

root of nose

dorsum of nose

tip of nose

nasal septum

ala

nostril

philtrum

84

MOUTH: THE ORGAN OF TASTE

taste sensations

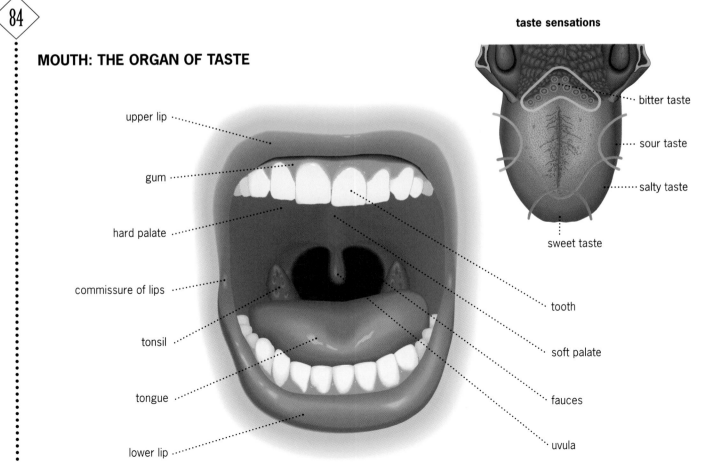

upper lip

gum

hard palate

commissure of lips

tonsil

tongue

lower lip

bitter taste

sour taste

salty taste

sweet taste

tooth

soft palate

fauces

uvula

HUMAN DENTURE

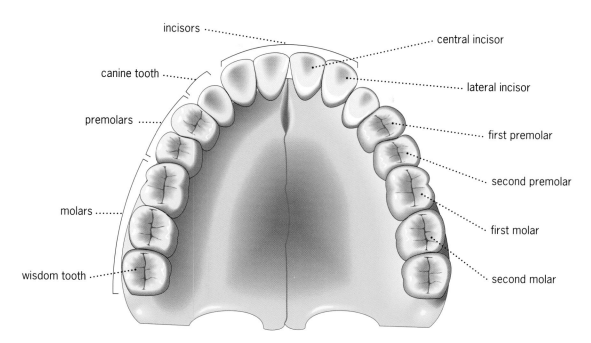

incisors

canine tooth

premolars

molars

wisdom tooth

central incisor

lateral incisor

first premolar

second premolar

first molar

second molar

cross section of a molar

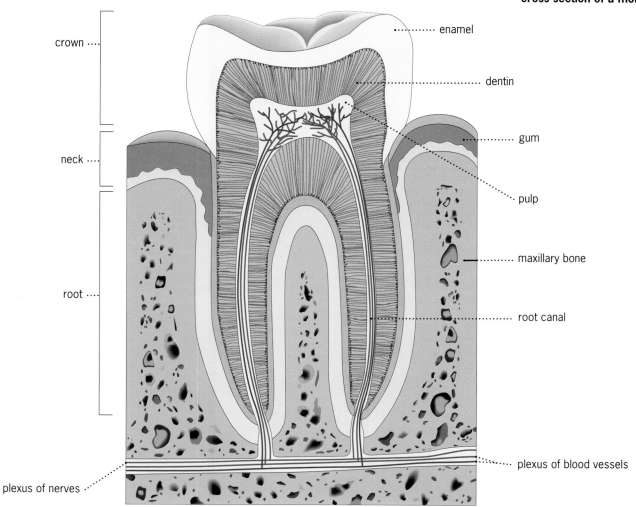

crown

neck

root

enamel

dentin

gum

pulp

maxillary bone

root canal

plexus of blood vessels

plexus of nerves

TRADITIONAL HOUSES

igloo

wigwam

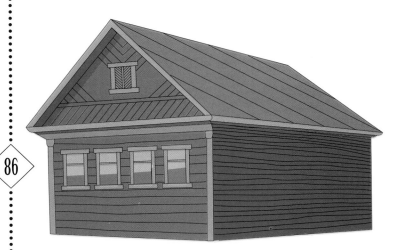

log cabin

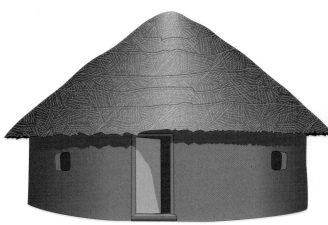

mud hut

house on stilts

tepee

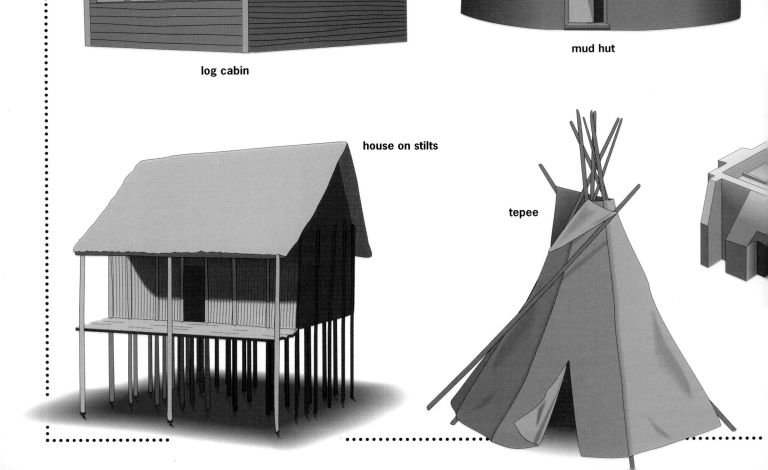

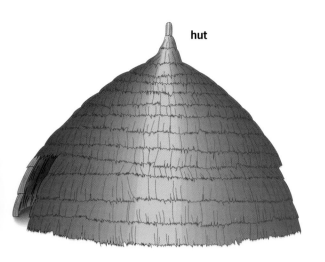

hut

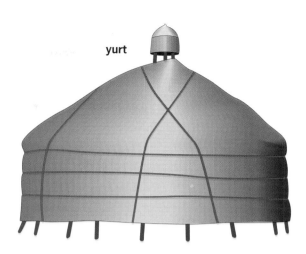

yurt

MOSQUE

direction of Mecca

prayer hall   central nave   Mihrab dome

shady arcades

Qibla wall

minaret

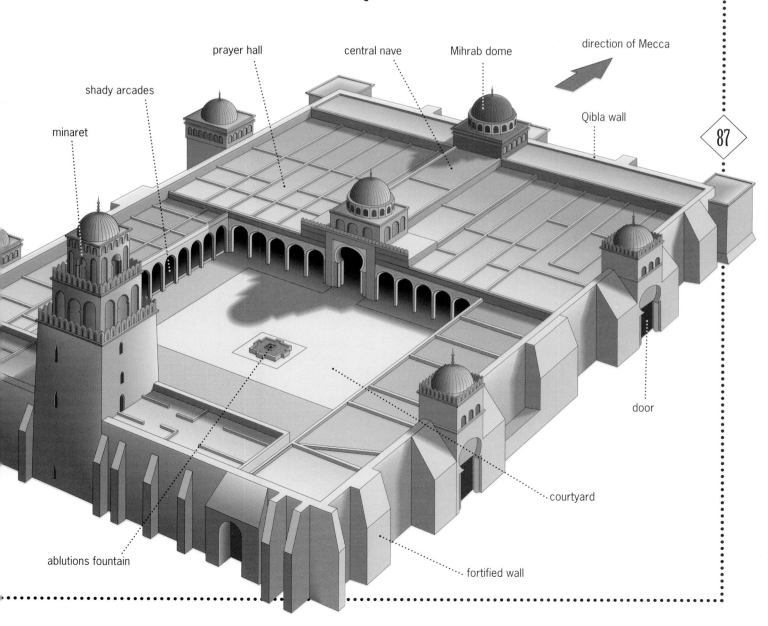

87

door

courtyard

ablutions fountain

fortified wall

CASTLE

machicolation

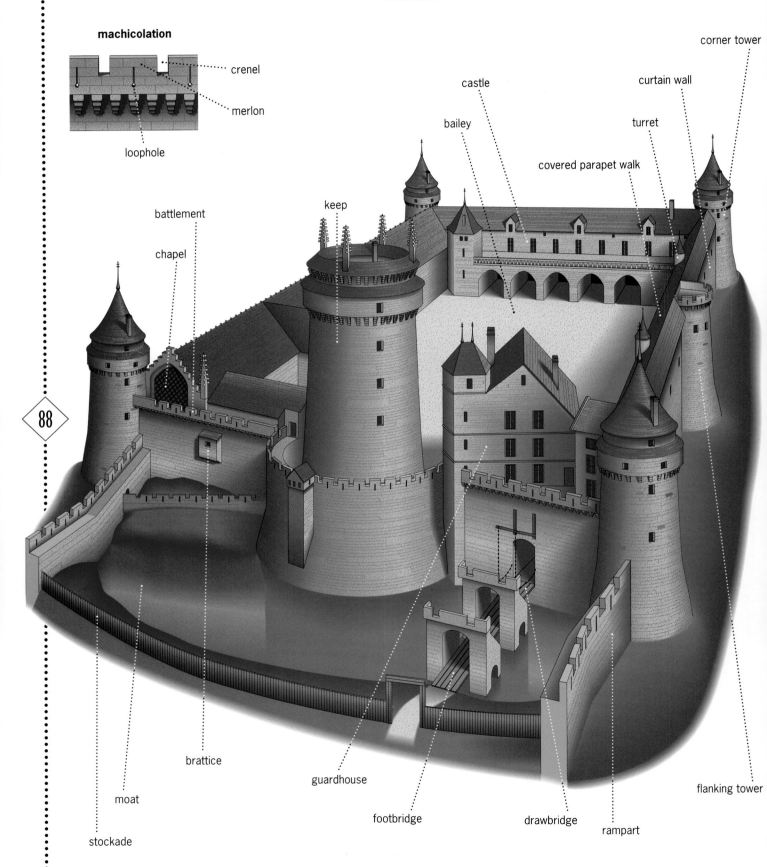

crenel

merlon

loophole

corner tower

castle

curtain wall

bailey

turret

covered parapet walk

keep

battlement

chapel

88

brattice

moat

stockade

guardhouse

footbridge

drawbridge

rampart

flanking tower

GOTHIC CATHEDRAL

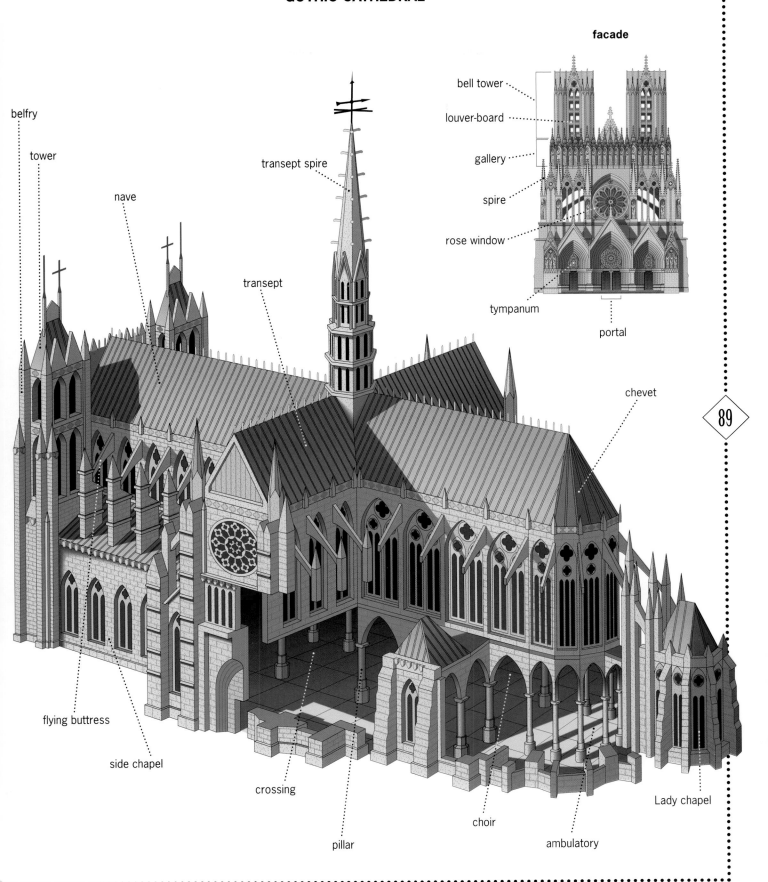

facade

bell tower

louver-board

gallery

spire

rose window

tympanum

portal

belfry

tower

nave

transept spire

transept

chevet

flying buttress

side chapel

crossing

pillar

choir

ambulatory

Lady chapel

DOWNTOWN

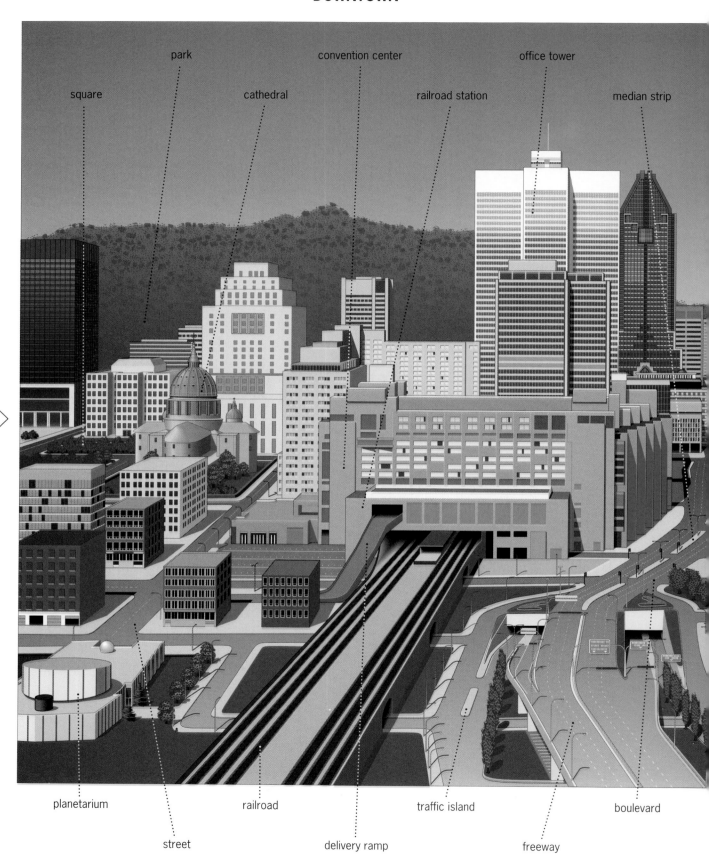

square
park
cathedral
convention center
railroad station
office tower
median strip

planetarium
street
railroad
delivery ramp
traffic island
freeway
boulevard

hotel

restaurant

skyscraper

church

high-rise apartment

street lamp

parking lot

office building

museum

commercial building

stadium

HOUSE

exterior of a house

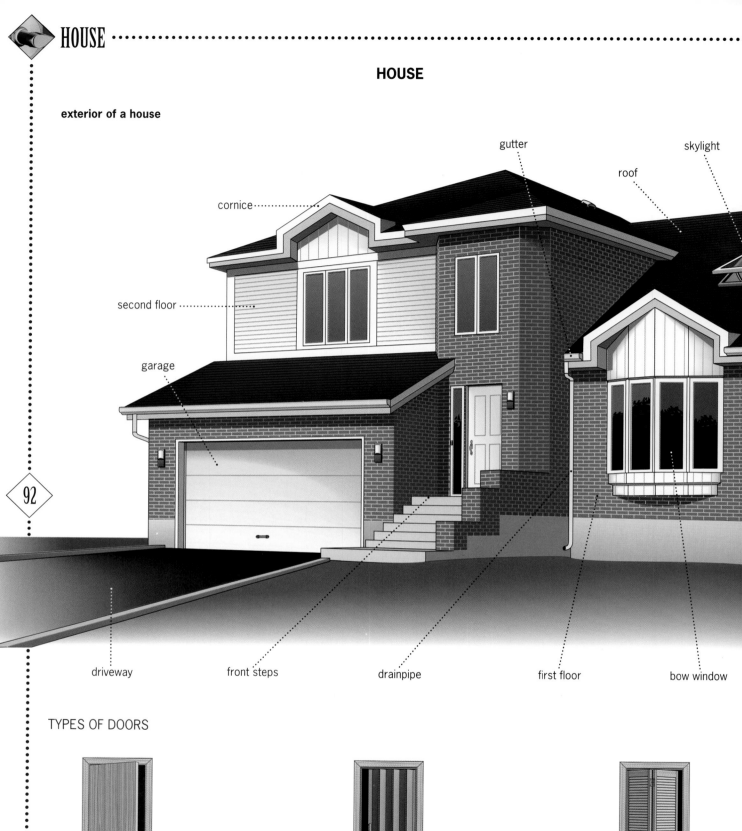

gutter

skylight

roof

cornice

second floor

garage

driveway

front steps

drainpipe

first floor

bow window

TYPES OF DOORS

conventional door

sliding folding door

folding door

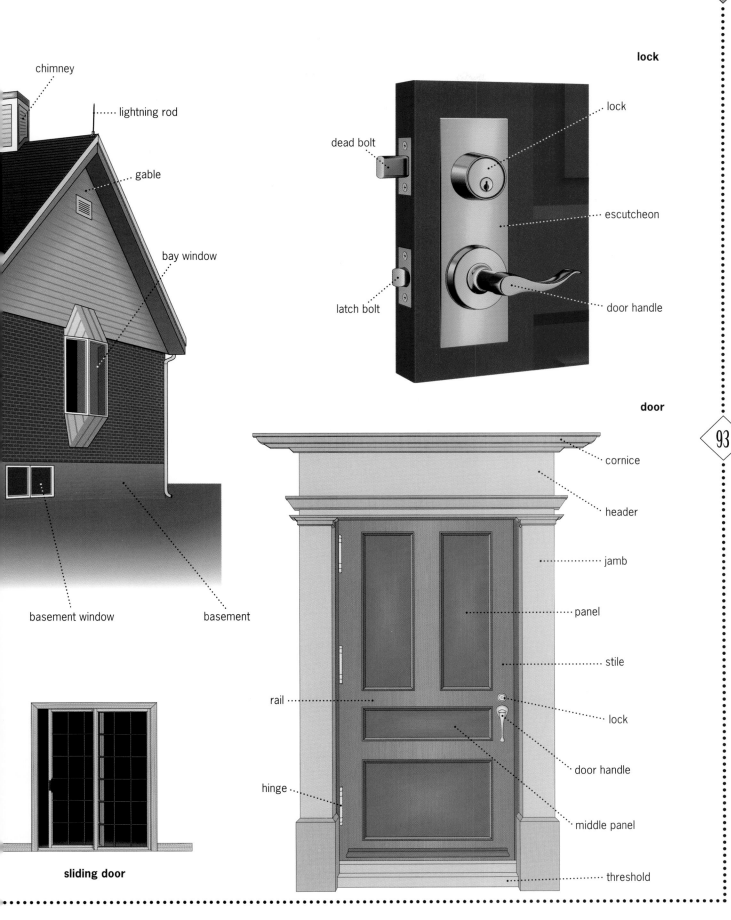

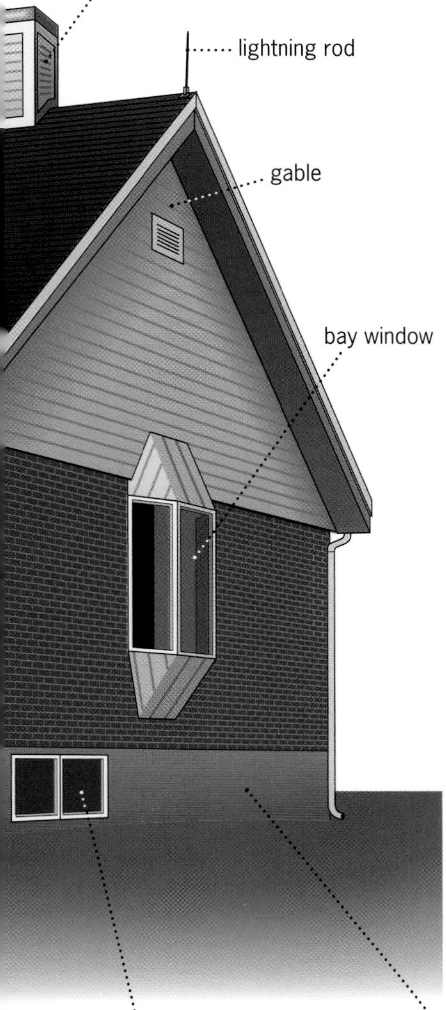
chimney
lightning rod
gable
bay window
basement window
basement

lock

lock
dead bolt
escutcheon
latch bolt
door handle

door

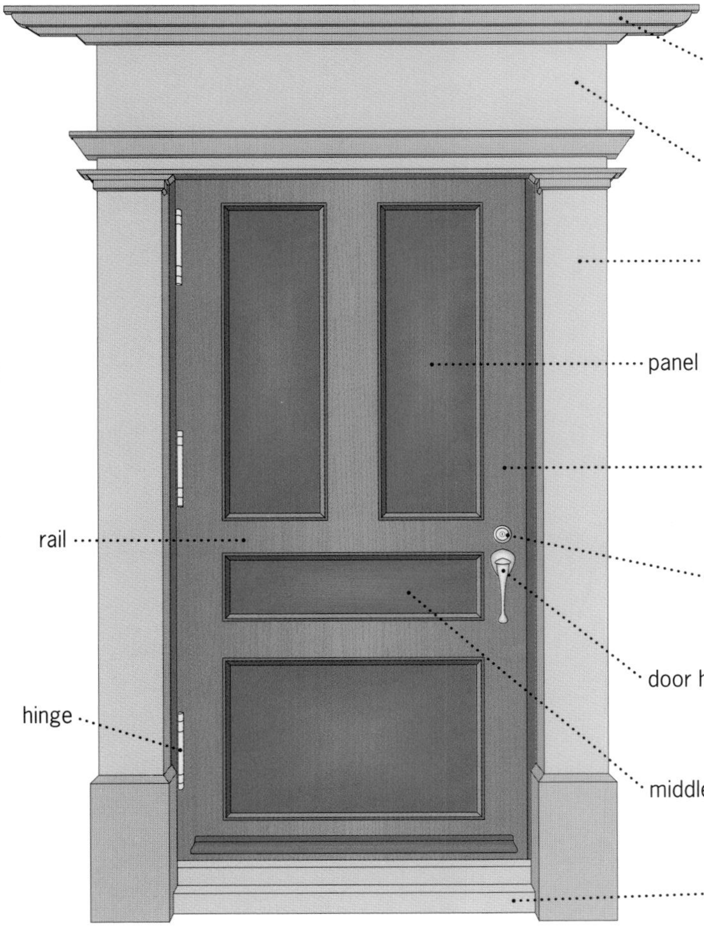
cornice
header
jamb
panel
stile
rail
lock
door handle
hinge
middle panel
threshold

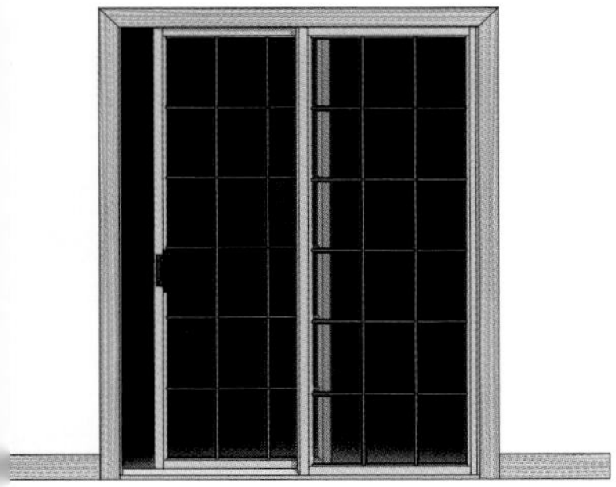

sliding door

WINDOW

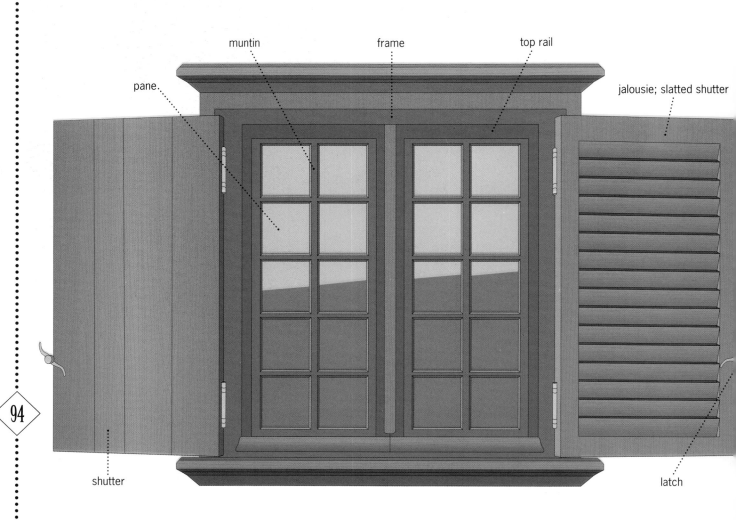

muntin

frame

top rail

pane

jalousie; slatted shutter

shutter

latch

TYPES OF WINDOWS

**casement window
(inward opening)**

**casement window
(outward opening)**

horizontal pivoting window

sliding window

sliding folding window

vertical pivoting window

sash window

louvred window

BED

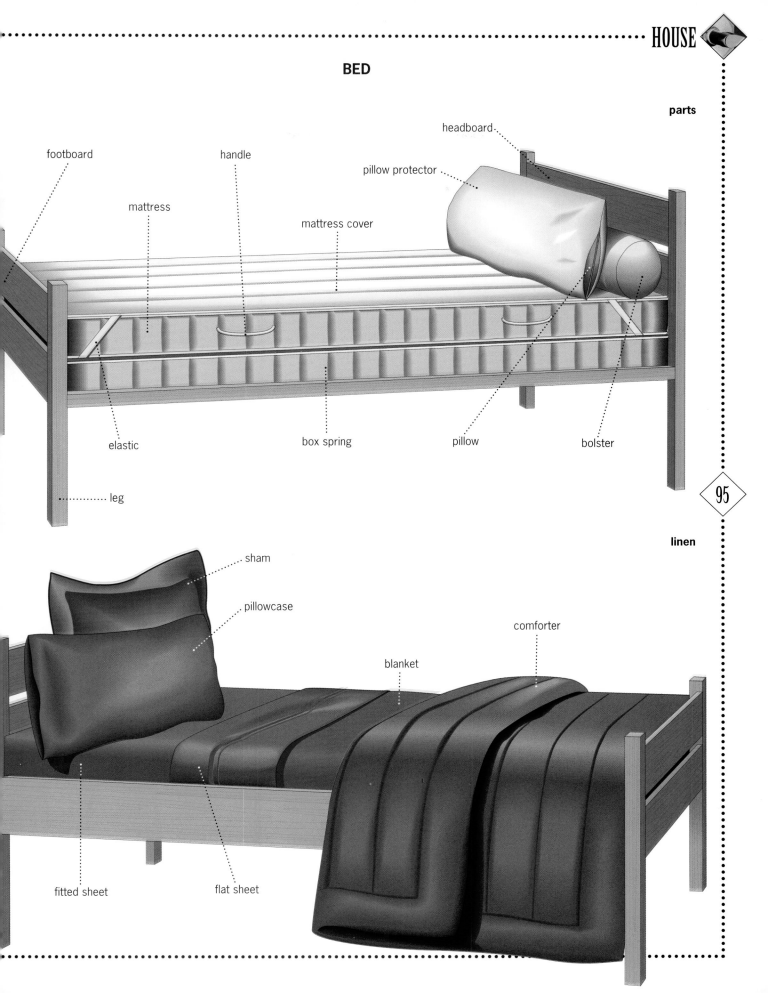

headboard

footboard

handle

pillow protector

mattress

mattress cover

elastic

box spring

pillow

bolster

leg

sham

pillowcase

comforter

blanket

fitted sheet

flat sheet

SEATS

sofa

loveseat

armchair

footstool

bench

bar stool

stool

chaise longue

folding chair

rocking chair

stacking chairs

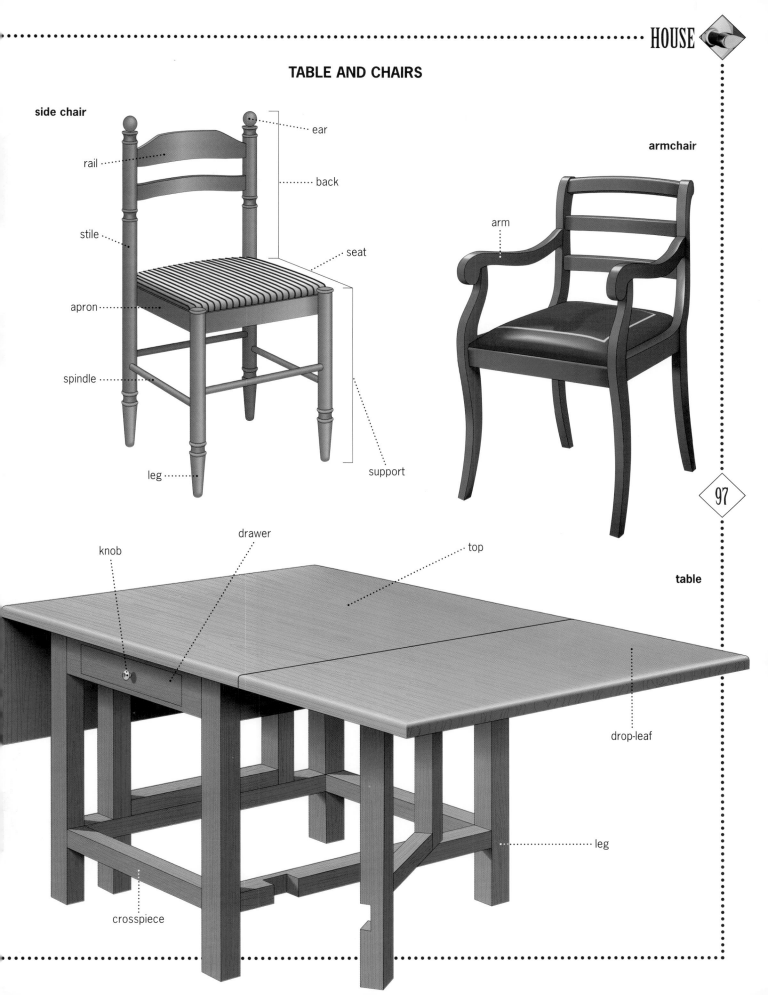

TABLE AND CHAIRS

side chair

ear

rail

back

stile

seat

apron

spindle

leg

support

armchair

arm

table

knob

drawer

top

drop-leaf

leg

crosspiece

LIGHTS

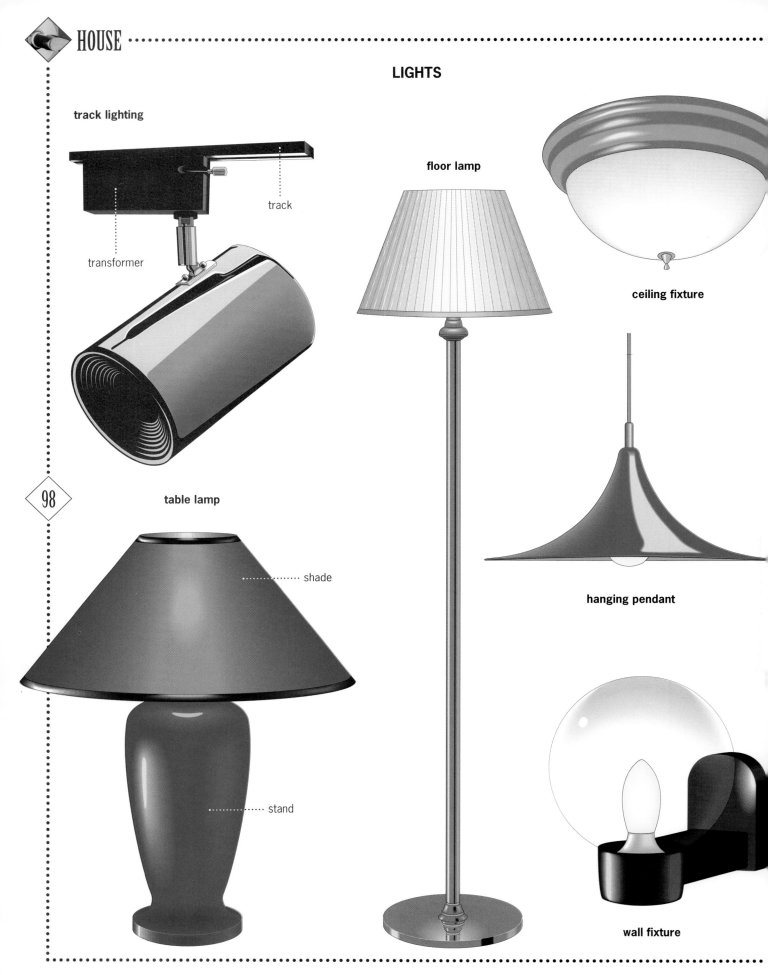

track lighting

track

transformer

floor lamp

ceiling fixture

table lamp

shade

stand

hanging pendant

wall fixture

LIGHTING

incandescent lamp

inert gas

filament

lead-in wire

base

contact

bulb

screw base

bayonet base

energy saving bulb

bulb

fluorescent tube

housing

base

tungsten-halogen lamp

pin

base

fluorescent tube

pin base

gas

phosphorescent coating

pin

bulb

switch

outlet

European plug

cover

pin

American plug

pin

grounding terminal

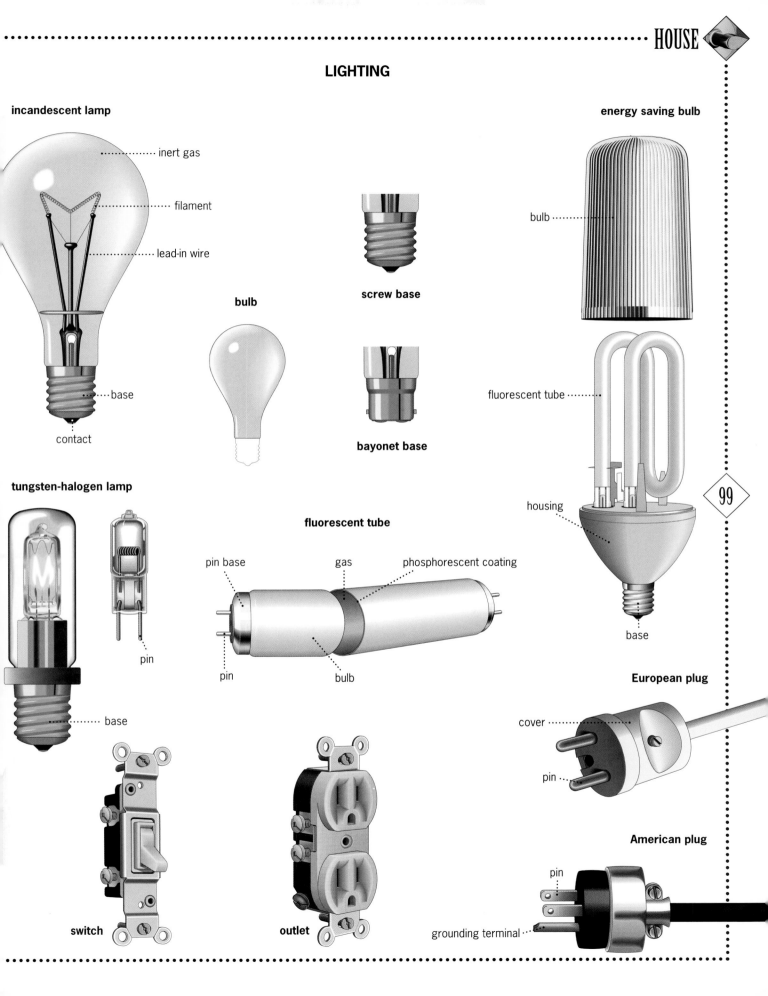

GLASSWARE

champagne glass

white wine glass

red wine glass

champagne flute

tumbler; glass

beer mug

carafe

decanter

DINNERWARE

coffee cup

cup

mug

creamer

sugar bowl

pepper shaker

salt shaker

butter dish

cereal bowl

soup bowl

dinner plate

salad plate

bread and butter plate; side plate

salad dish

salad bowl

teapot

coffee plunger

soup tureen

water pitcher

SILVERWARE

knife

back

blade

handle

cutting edge

TYPES OF KNIVES

butter knife

cheese knife

dinner knife

steak knife

fork

handle

tine

point

TYPES OF FORKS

dinner fork

fondue fork

spoon

handle

TYPES OF SPOONS

coffee spoon

teaspoon

soup spoon

inside

bowl

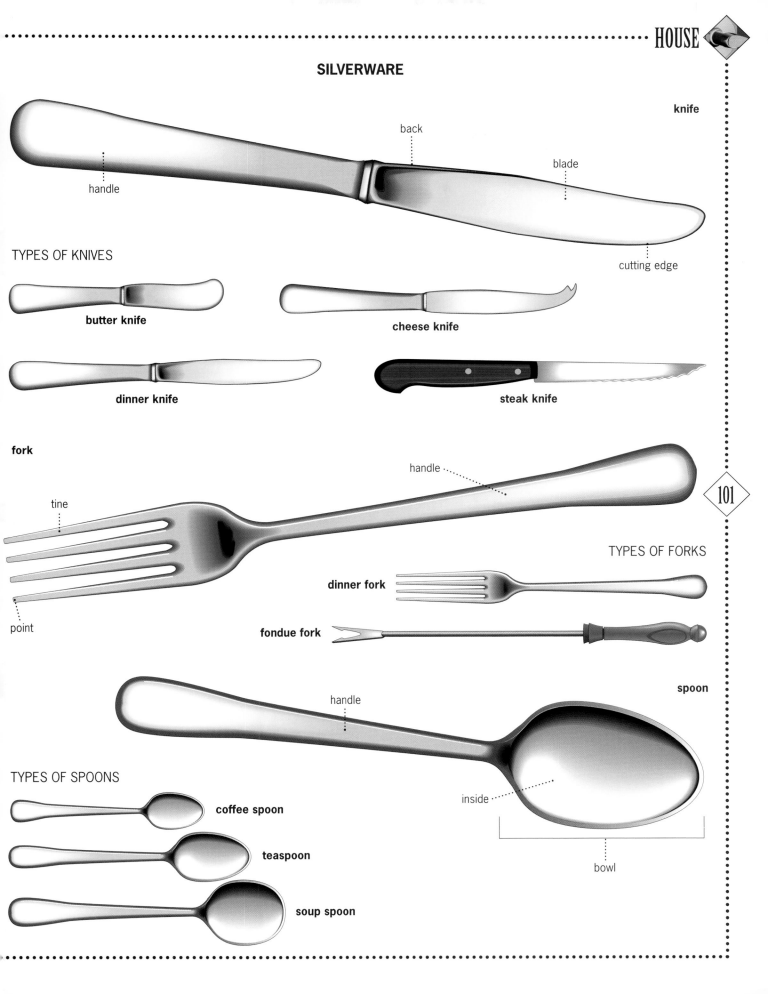

KITCHEN UTENSILS

ladle

potato masher

spatula

whisk

egg beater

measuring spoons

nutcracker

lever corkscrew

bottle opener

peeler

can opener

rolling pin

spaghetti tongs

funnel

ice–cream scoop

colander

lemon squeezer

salad spinner

strainer

grater

COOKING UTENSILS

sauté pan

frying pan

stockpot; casserole

fondue set

wok

fondue pot

burner

double boiler

vegetable steamer

saucepan

roasting pans

pressure cooker

pressure regulator

safety valve

KITCHEN APPLIANCES

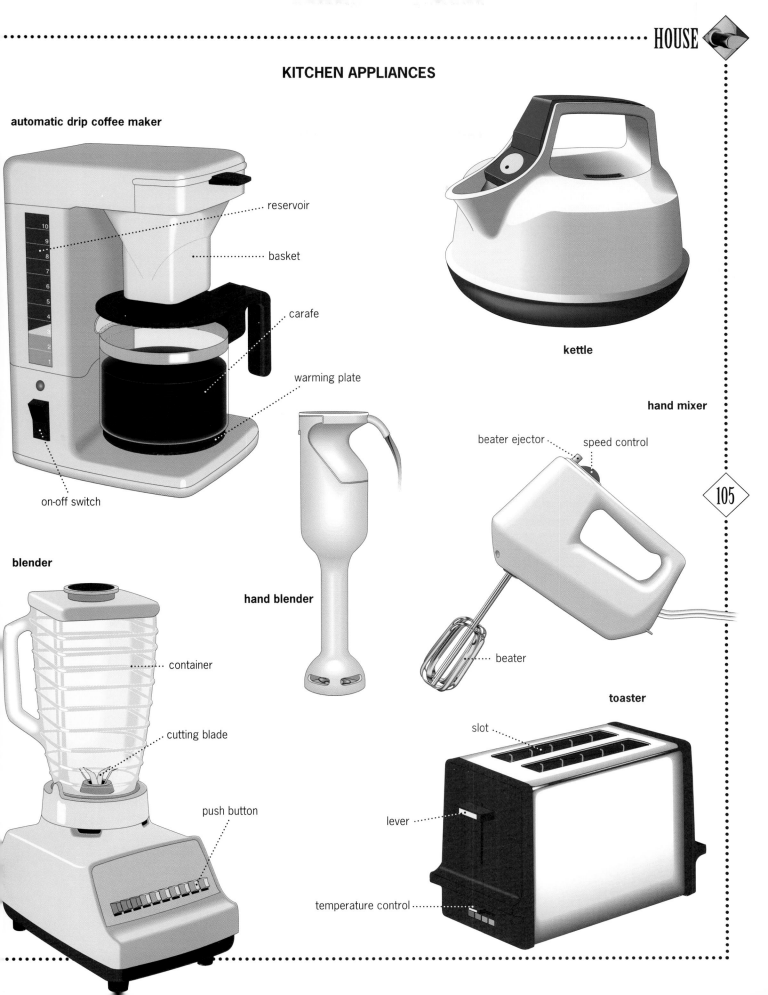

automatic drip coffee maker

reservoir

basket

carafe

warming plate

on-off switch

kettle

hand mixer

beater ejector

speed control

hand blender

beater

blender

container

cutting blade

push button

toaster

slot

lever

temperature control

REFRIGERATOR

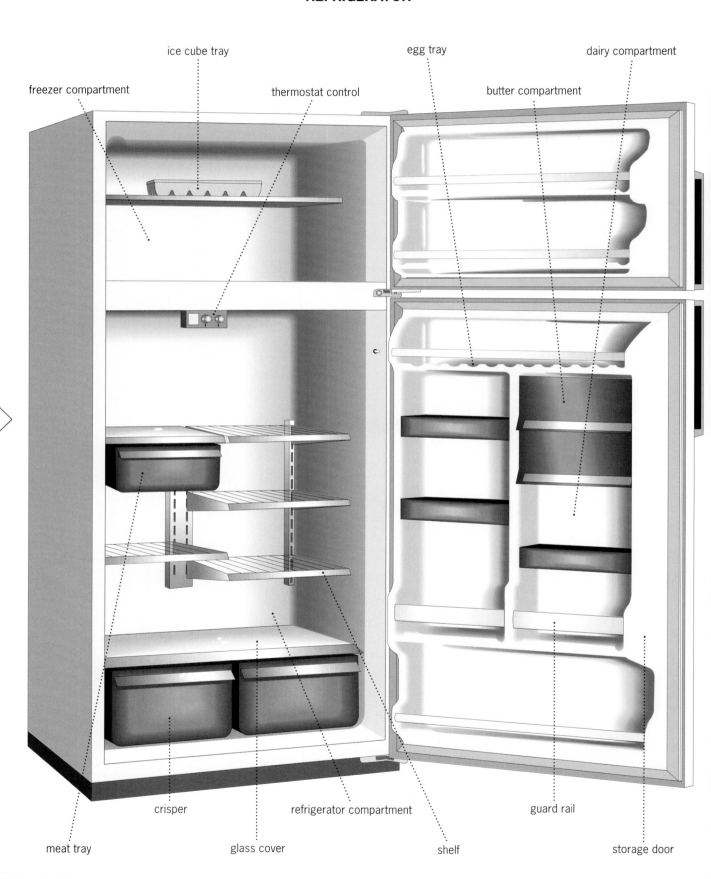

ice cube tray

egg tray

dairy compartment

freezer compartment

thermostat control

butter compartment

crisper

refrigerator compartment

guard rail

meat tray

glass cover

shelf

storage door

COOKING APPLIANCES

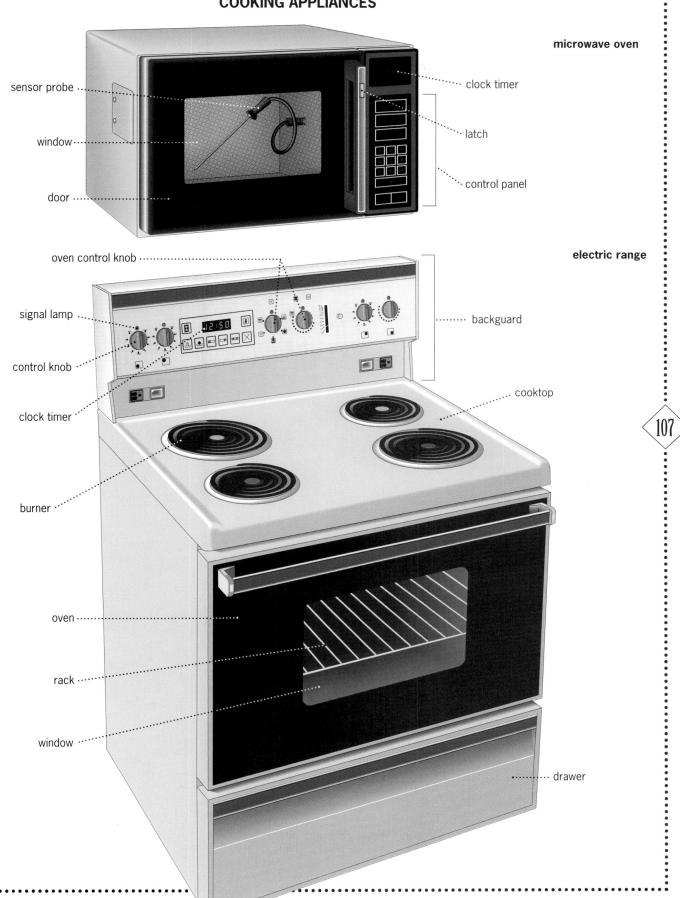

microwave oven

sensor probe

window

door

clock timer

latch

control panel

electric range

oven control knob

signal lamp

control knob

clock timer

burner

backguard

cooktop

oven

rack

window

drawer

CARPENTRY TOOLS

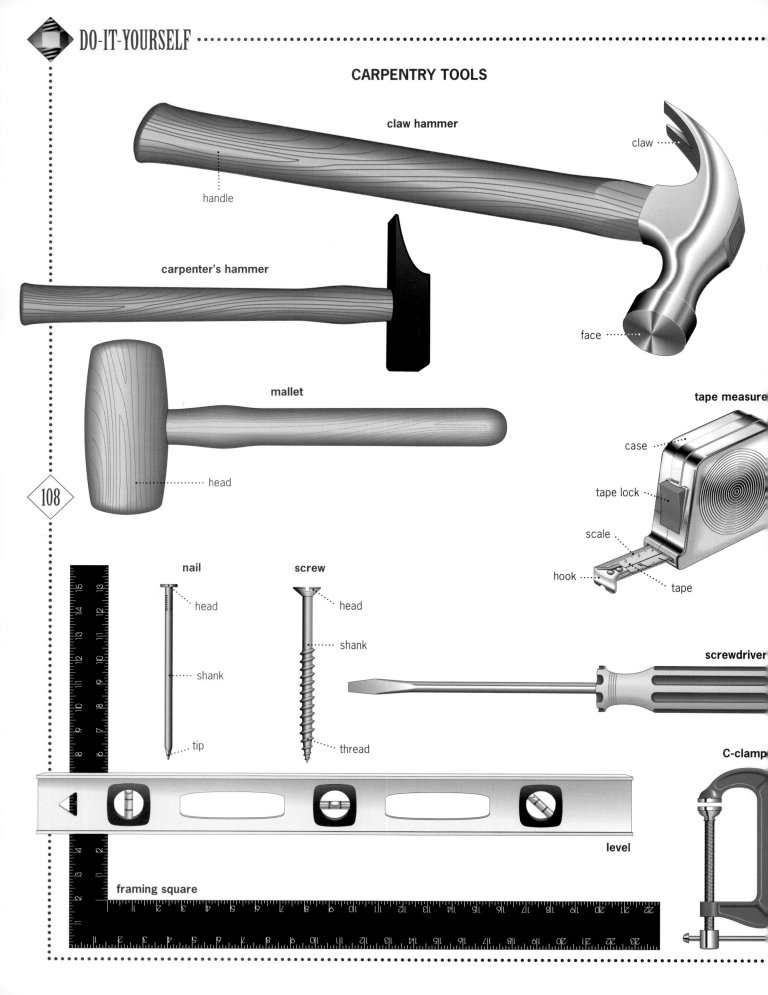

claw hammer

claw

handle

face

carpenter's hammer

mallet

head

tape measure

case

tape lock

scale

hook

tape

108

nail

head

shank

tip

screw

head

shank

thread

screwdriver

C-clamp

level

framing square

handsaw

blade

tooth

handle

adjustable wrench

fixed jaw

thumbscrew

handle

movable jaw

locking pliers

lever

spring

adjusting screw

release lever

jaw

rib joint pliers

adjustable channel

bolt

nut

head

threaded rod

long-nose pliers

slip joint pliers

handle

slip joint

ELECTRIC TOOLS

electric drill

housing

chuck

jaw

switch lock

auger bit

twist drill

auxiliary handle

switch

pistol grip handle

chuck key

cable

plug

110

circular saw

handle

trigger switch

blade guard

circular saw blade

blade tilting mechanism

tip

motor

knob handle

blade

base plate

tooth

PAINTING UPKEEP

paint roller

tray

scraper

blade

roller frame

roller cover

brush

handle

bristles

extension ladder

side rail

pulley

locking device

rung

stepladder

platform ladder

hoisting rope

anti-slip shoe

111

MEN'S CLOTHING

shirt

collar

collar point

placket

breast pocket

front

button

cuff

shirttail

suspenders

adjustment slide

button loop

leather end

suspender clip

tie

rear apron

neck end

loop

front apron

belt

frame

punch hole

belt carrier

tongue

pants

waistband

pocket

fly

crease

cuff

boxer shorts

undershirt

briefs

fly

crotch

waistband

112

double-breasted jacket

collar

lining

breast welt pocket

sleeve

concealed pocket

flap

patch pocket

duffle coat

hood

frog

toggle fastening

cap

crown

peak

stocking cap

hunting cap

ear flap

jacket

snap fastener

elastic waistband

windbreaker

waistband

drawstring

113

WOMEN'S CLOTHING

toque

knitted hat

balaclava

peak

beret

blouse

double-breasted jacket

suit

jacket

skirt

overcoat

poncho

dress

114

jeans

ski pants

shorts

footstrap

Bermuda shorts

straight skirt

culottes

pleated skirt

WOMEN'S CLOTHING

pajamas

bra

shoulder strap

cup

briefs

half-slip

bathrobe

116

SWEATERS

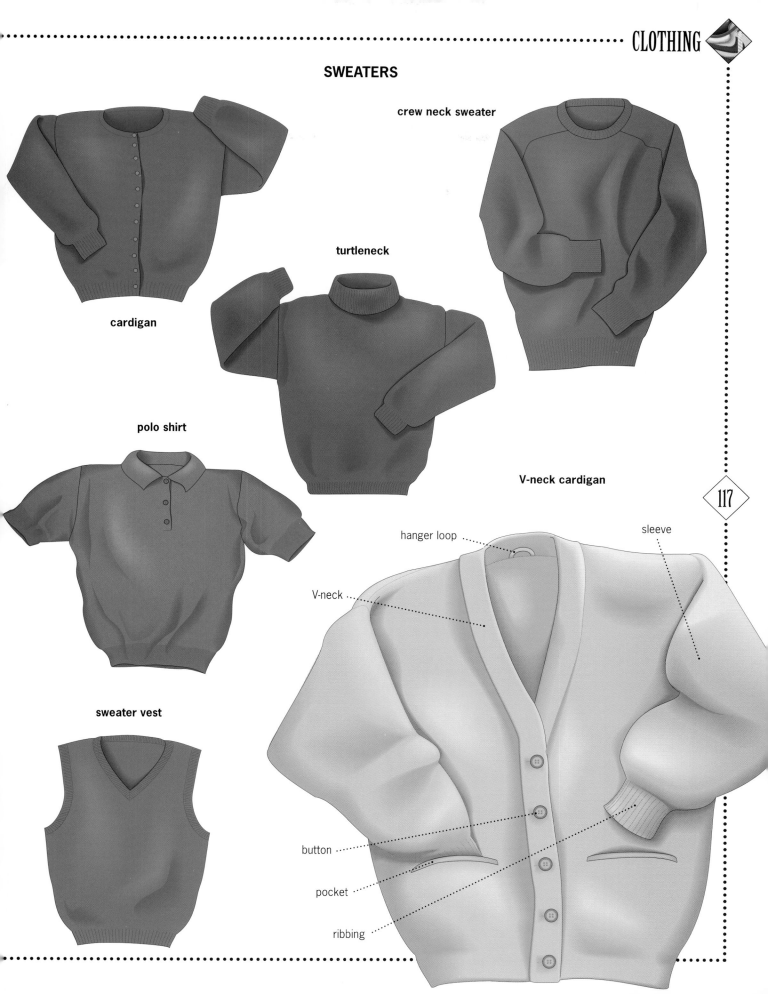

crew neck sweater

turtleneck

cardigan

polo shirt

V-neck cardigan

hanger loop

sleeve

V-neck

sweater vest

button

pocket

ribbing

GLOVES AND STOCKINGS

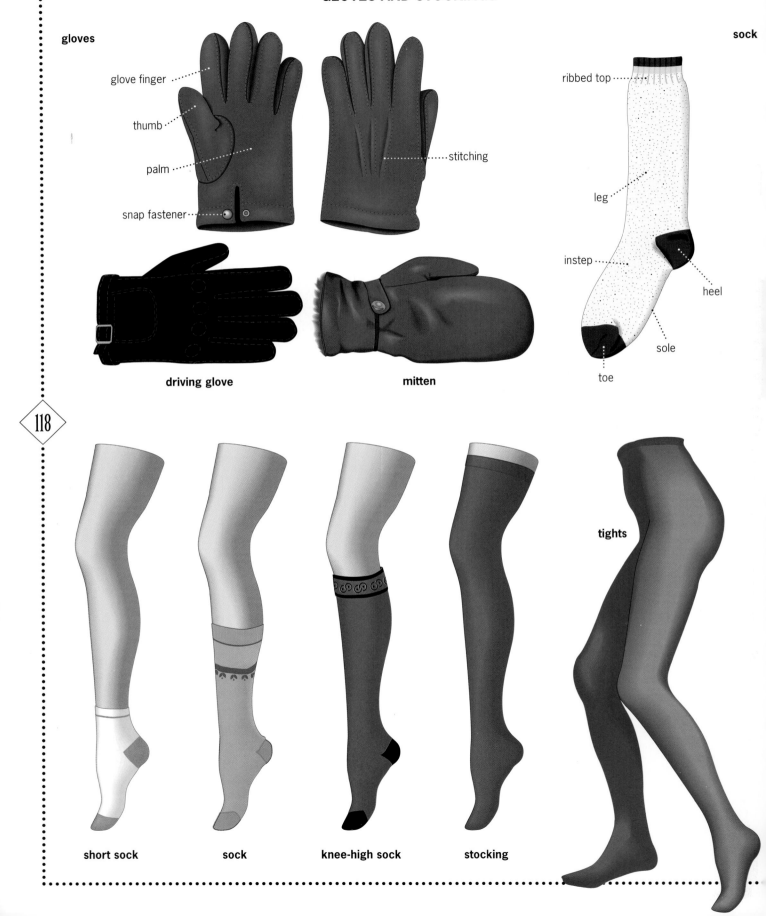

gloves

glove finger

thumb

palm

snap fastener

stitching

sock

ribbed top

leg

instep

heel

sole

toe

driving glove

mitten

tights

short sock

sock

knee-high sock

stocking

SHOES

heavy duty boot

slingback

ballerina

thigh-boot

pump

tennis shoe

espadrille

loafer

moccasin

sandal

boot

ankle boot

SPORTSWEAR

EXERCISE WEAR

tank top

swimsuit

leotard

TRACK SUIT

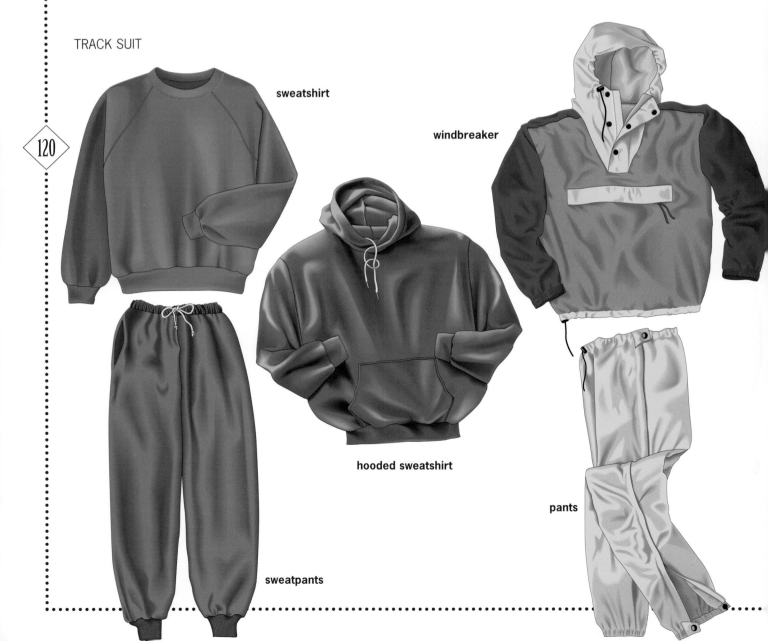

sweatshirt

windbreaker

hooded sweatshirt

pants

sweatpants

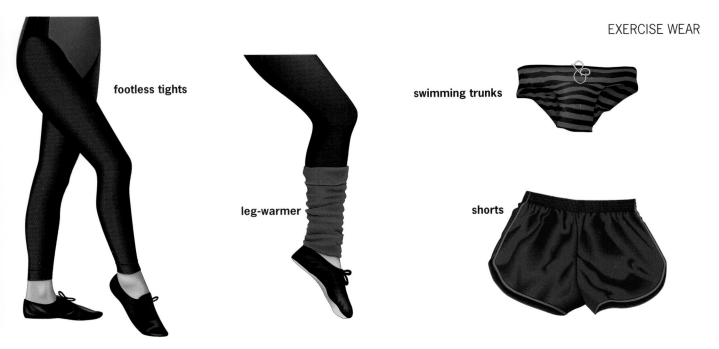

EXERCISE WEAR

footless tights

leg-warmer

swimming trunks

shorts

running shoe

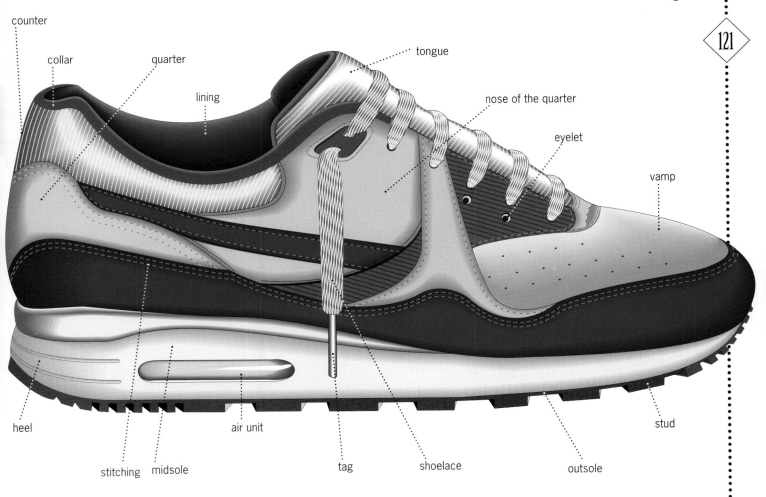

counter

collar

quarter

lining

tongue

nose of the quarter

eyelet

vamp

heel

stitching

midsole

air unit

tag

shoelace

outsole

stud

DENTAL CARE

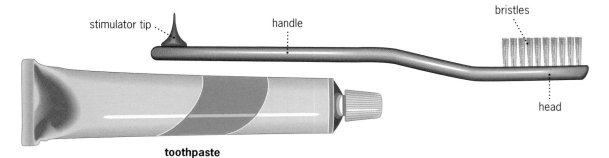

toothbrush

stimulator tip

handle

bristles

dental floss

toothpaste

head

HAIRDRESSING

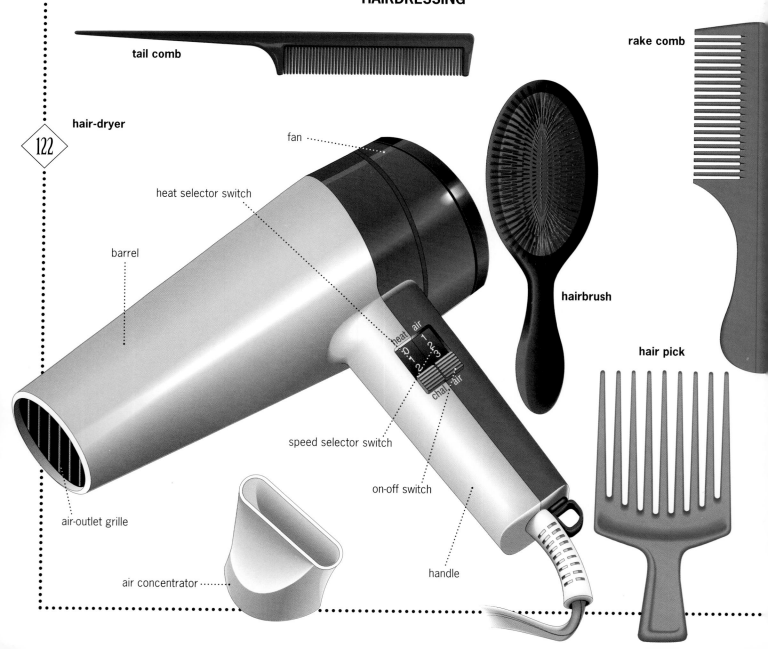

tail comb

rake comb

hair-dryer

fan

heat selector switch

barrel

hairbrush

hair pick

heat   air

speed selector switch

on-off switch

air-outlet grille

handle

air concentrator

LEATHER GOODS

drawstring bag

drawstring

knapsack

key case

wallet

shoulder strap

purse

front pocket

GLASSES

glass lens

bridge

bar

rim

nose pad

temple

UMBRELLA

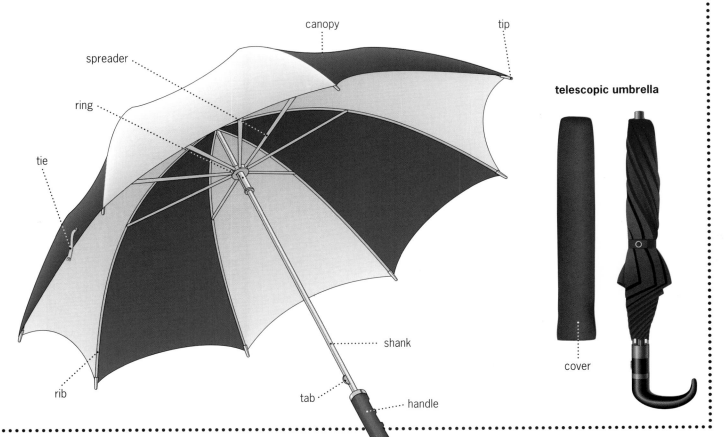

canopy

tip

spreader

ring

tie

rib

tab

handle

shank

telescopic umbrella

cover

COMMUNICATION BY TELEPHONE

telephone set

telephone answering machine

handset

earpiece

display

mouthpiece

function selectors

789·3456

automatic dialer

handset cord

push buttons

telephone index

outgoing announcement cassette

incoming message cassette

speaker

listen button

record announcement button

volume control

cassette player controls

pay phone

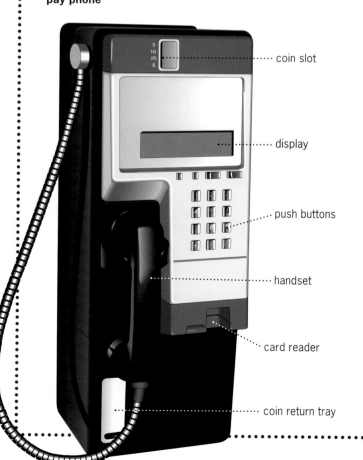

coin slot

display

push buttons

handset

card reader

coin return tray

push-button telephone

portable cellular telephone

cordless telephone

393 1452

PHOTOGRAPHY

single lens reflex (slr) camera

accessory shoe

film rewind button

hot-shoe contact

control panel

film advance button

control dial

exposure button

film speed

remote control terminal

camera body

focus setting ring

shutter release button

objective lens

electronic flash

flashtube

photoelectric cell

mounting foot

rangefinder; compact camera

perforation

cassette film

film leader

Polaroid® Land camera

pocket camera

cartridge film

film pack

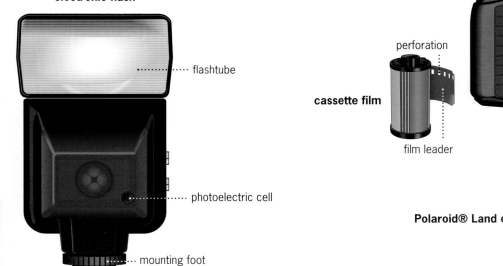

TELEVISION

television set

cabinet

screen

remote control sensor

on/off button

indicators

tuning controls

remote control

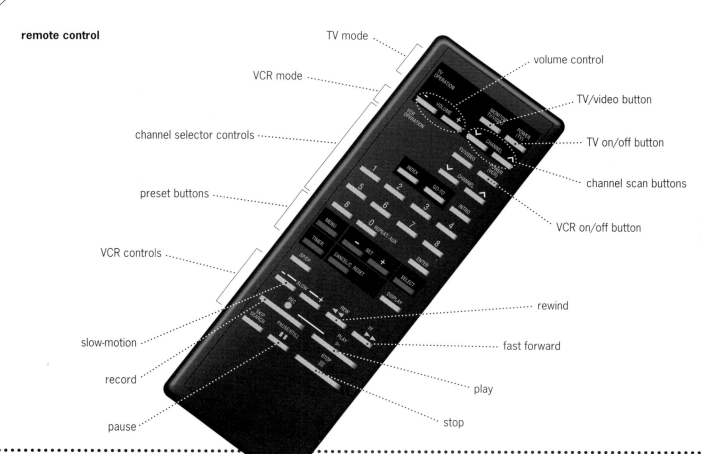

TV mode

VCR mode

channel selector controls

preset buttons

VCR controls

slow-motion

record

pause

volume control

TV/video button

TV on/off button

channel scan buttons

VCR on/off button

rewind

fast forward

play

stop

VIDEO

videocassette recorder (VCR)

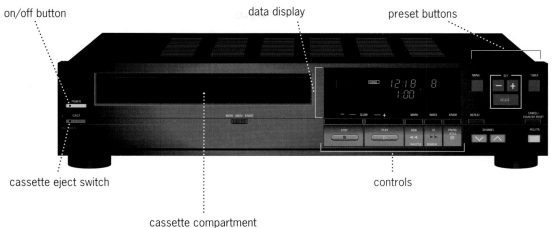

on/off button

data display

preset buttons

cassette eject switch

controls

cassette compartment

video camera

accessory shoe

eyepiece

power zoom button

electronic viewfinder

cassette eject switch

videotape operation controls

viewfinder adjustment keys

built-in microphone

battery

DATA SET

ZERO MEM.

ADJUST

RESET

SELECT

BATT

00425

SPEED

EXPOSURE

EDIT SEARCH

AUTO LOCK

FOCUS

WHITE BAL.

FADER

battery eject switch

zoom lens

shooting adjustment keys

cassette compartment

data display

edit/search buttons

STEREO SYSTEM

SYSTEM COMPONENTS

tuner

FM antenna

AM antenna

899

turntable

compact disc player

amplifier

cassette tape deck

graphic equalizer

loudspeakers

left channel

right channel

tweeter

midrange

woofer

diaphragm; cone

speaker cover

headphones

headband

ear cushion

adjusting band

earphone

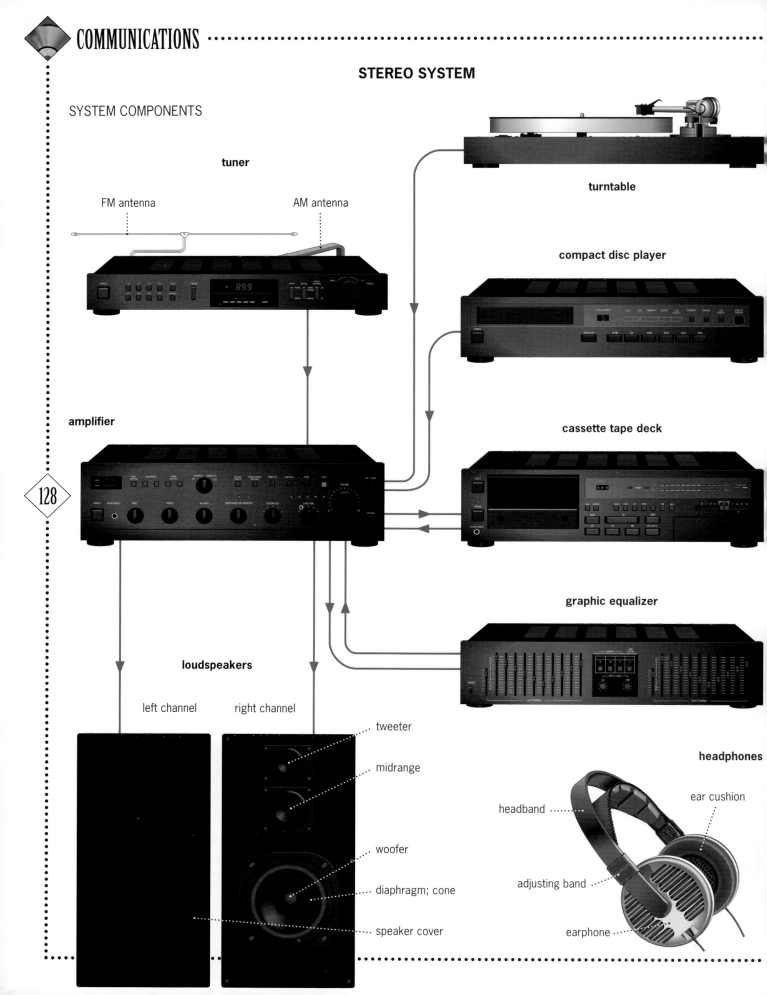

PORTABLE SOUND SYSTEMS

portable CD AM/FM cassette recorder

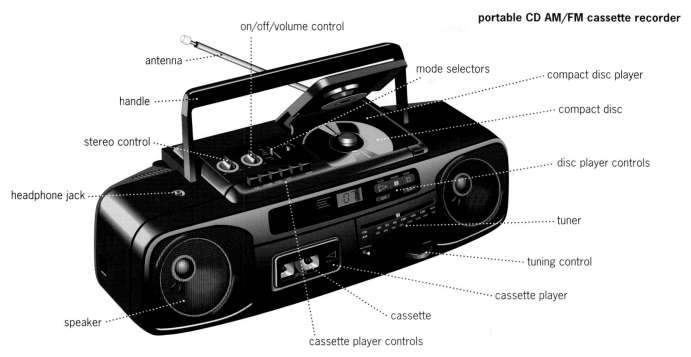

on/off/volume control

antenna

handle

stereo control

headphone jack

speaker

mode selectors

compact disc player

compact disc

disc player controls

tuner

tuning control

cassette player

cassette

cassette player controls

personal AM/FM cassette player; Walkman®

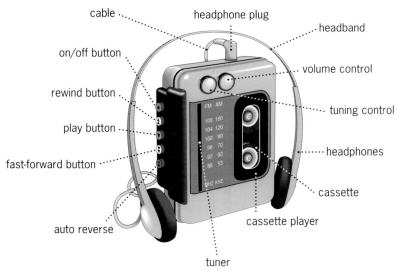

cable

headphone plug

headband

on/off button

volume control

rewind button

play button

tuning control

fast-forward button

headphones

cassette

auto reverse

cassette player

tuner

compact disc

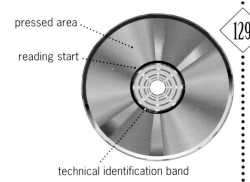

pressed area

reading start

129

technical identification band

record

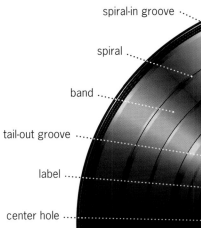

spiral-in groove

spiral

band

tail-out groove

label

center hole

cassette

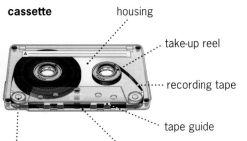

housing

take-up reel

recording tape

tape guide

guide roller

playing window

CAR

body

windshield

windshield wiper

outside mirror

washer nozzle

hood

headlight

grille

bumper

fender

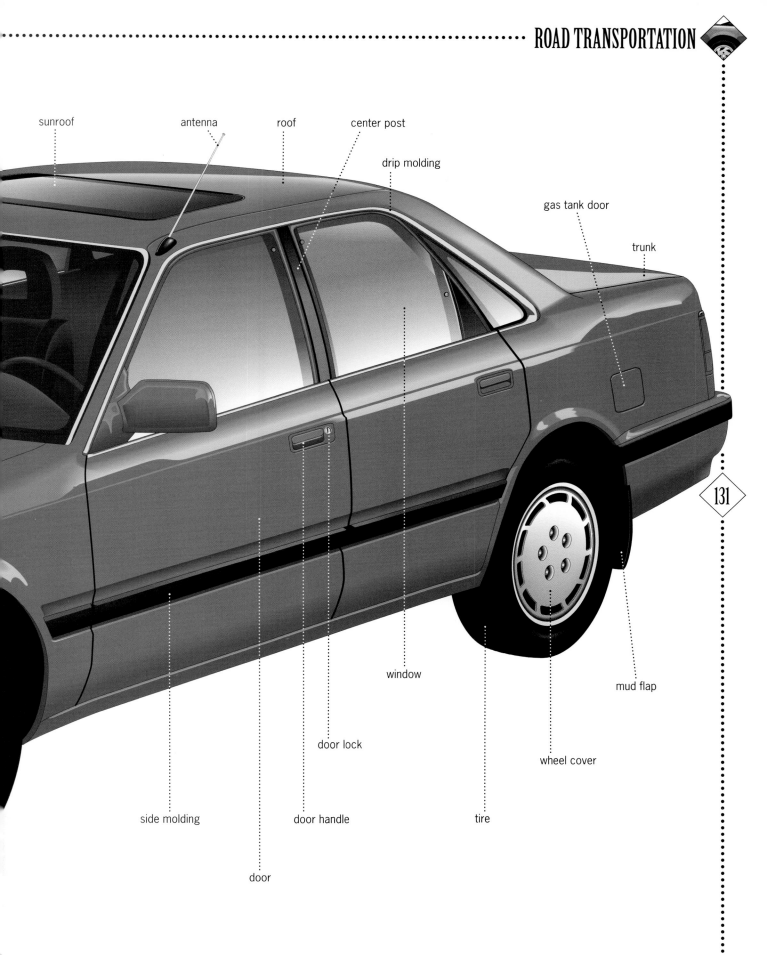

sunroof

antenna

roof

center post

drip molding

gas tank door

trunk

side molding

door

door handle

door lock

window

tire

wheel cover

mud flap

131

CAR

dashboard

- wiper switch
- rearview mirror
- vanity mirror
- instrument panel
- sun visor
- ignition switch
- clock
- horn
- air vent
- steering wheel
- glove compartment
- headlight/turn signal
- heater control
- clutch pedal
- audio system
- brake pedal
- accelerator pedal
- gearshift lever
- handbrake
- center console

instrument panel

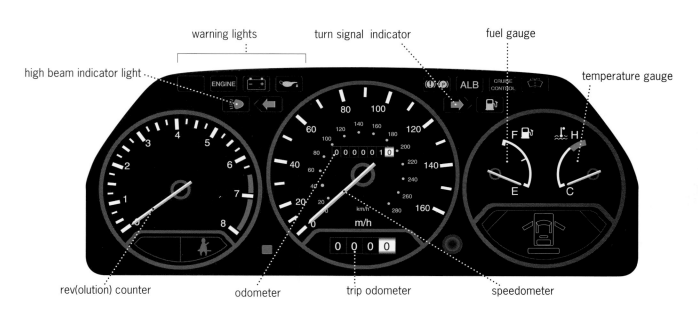

- warning lights
- turn signal indicator
- fuel gauge
- high beam indicator light
- temperature gauge
- rev(olution) counter
- odometer
- trip odometer
- speedometer

CAR LIGHTS

front lights

low beam

turn signal

side light

high beam

fog light

rear lights

turn signal

tail light

side light

brake light

backup light

license plate light

brake light

TYPES OF CAR BODIES

sports car

two-door sedan

hatchback

convertible

pickup truck

four-door sedan

station wagon

multipurpose vehicle

minivan

limousine

TRUCK

tractor unit

wind deflector

exhaust stack ⋯⋯

mirror

marker light

sleeping cab

air horn

grab handle

storage compartment

fifth wheel

step

mud flap

fog light

radiator grille

fuel tank

service station

maintenance

ice dispenser

air pump

mechanics

office

soft-drink dispenser

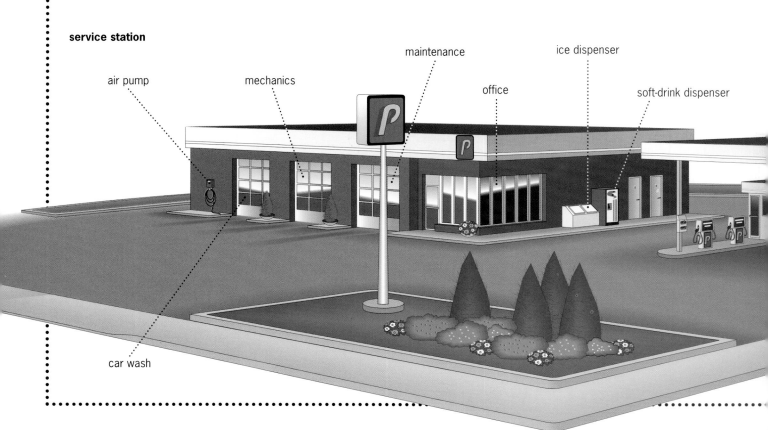

car wash

⟨134⟩

MOTORCYCLE

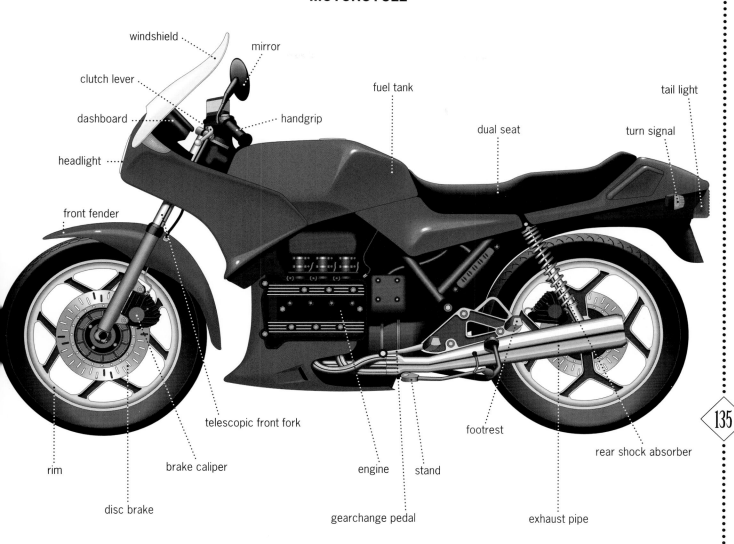

windshield

mirror

clutch lever

dashboard

headlight

front fender

rim

disc brake

telescopic front fork

brake caliper

handgrip

fuel tank

dual seat

tail light

turn signal

engine

gearchange pedal

stand

footrest

exhaust pipe

rear shock absorber

135

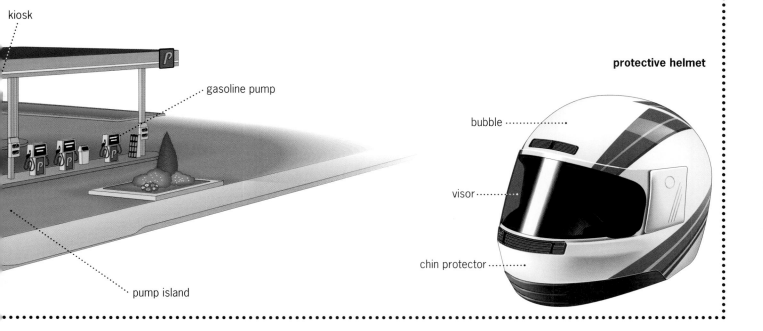

kiosk

gasoline pump

pump island

protective helmet

bubble

visor

chin protector

BICYCLE

seat

seat post

tire pump

crossbar

carrier

rear brake

generator

water bottle clip

reflector

front derailleur

rear light

water bottle

136

chain wheel

crank

mudguard

chain guide

toe clip

rear derailleur

pedal

drive chain

bicycle bag

lock

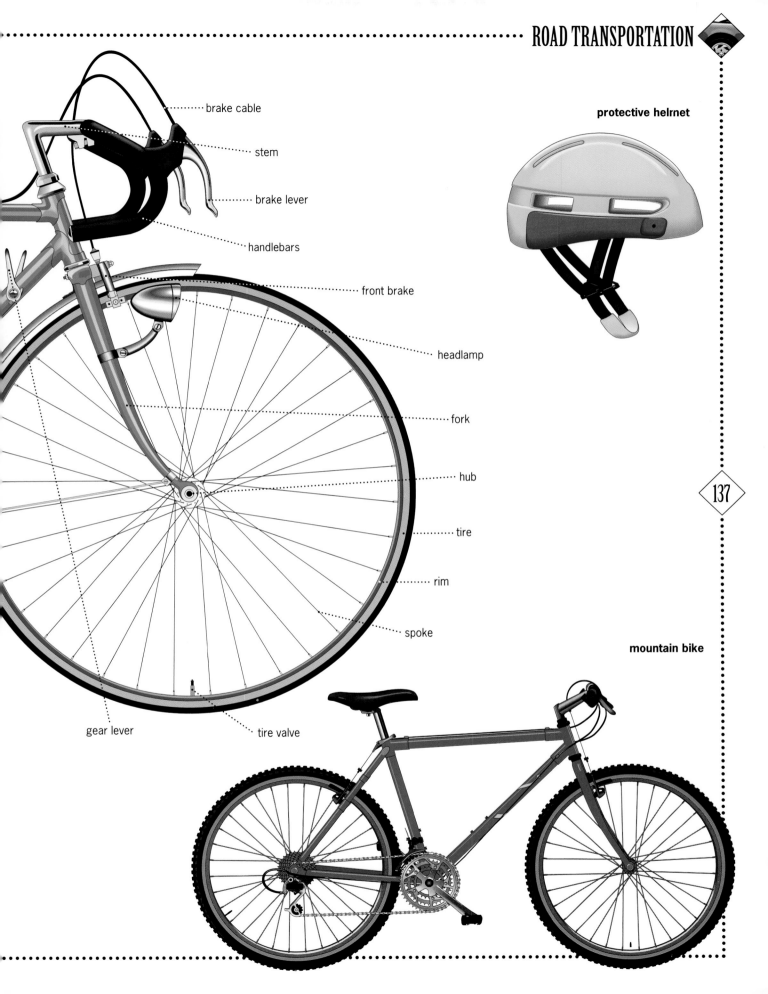

brake cable

stem

brake lever

handlebars

front brake

headlamp

fork

hub

tire

rim

spoke

gear lever

tire valve

protective helrnet

mountain bike

137

DIESEL-ELECTRIC LOCOMOTIVE

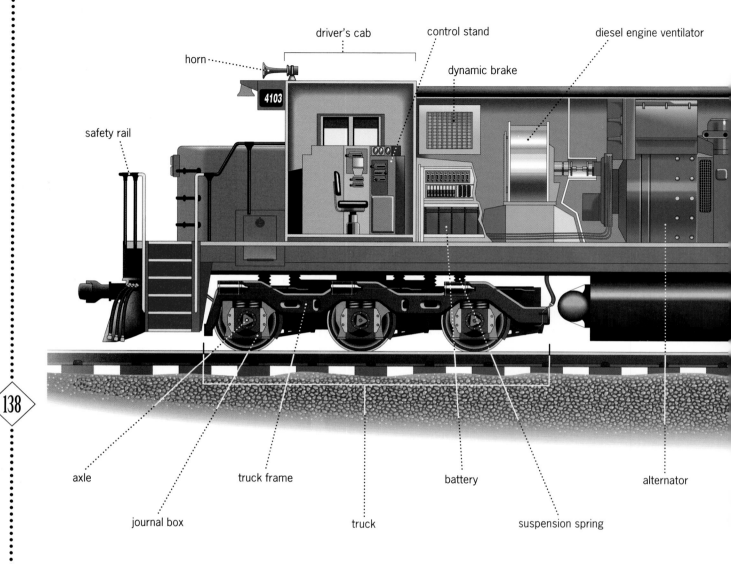

driver's cab

horn ····

control stand

diesel engine ventilator

dynamic brake

safety rail

4103

axle

journal box

truck frame

truck

battery

suspension spring

alternator

TYPES OF FREIGHT CARS

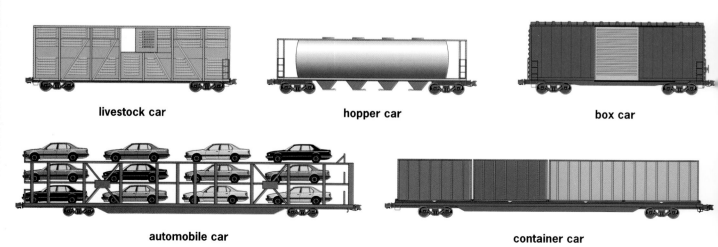

livestock car

hopper car

box car

automobile car

container car

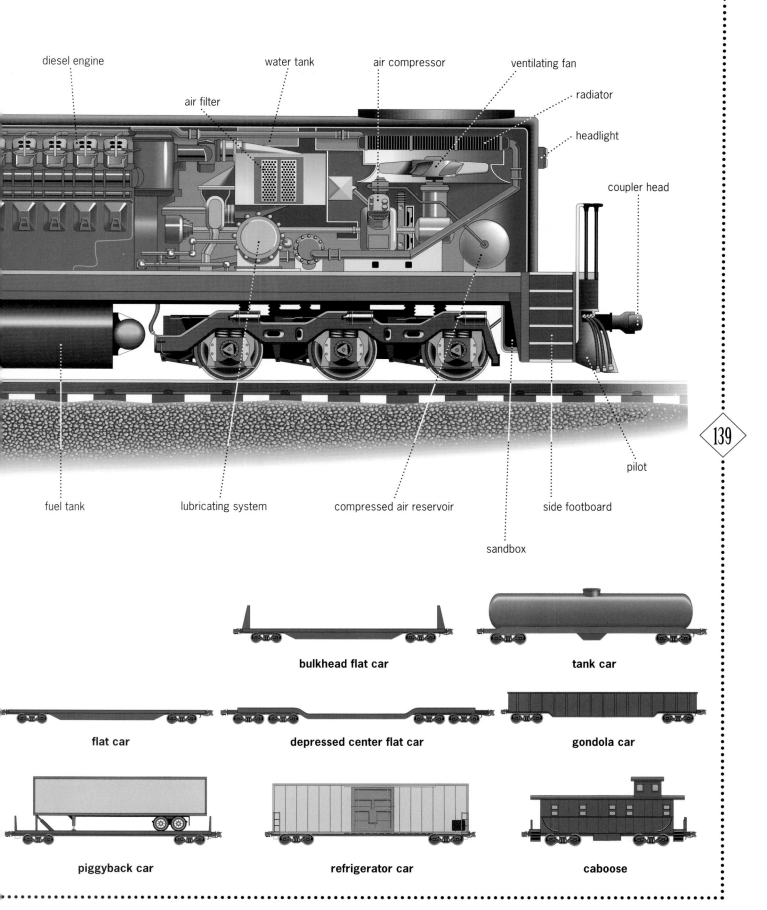

diesel engine

water tank

air compressor

ventilating fan

air filter

radiator

headlight

coupler head

fuel tank

lubricating system

compressed air reservoir

side footboard

pilot

sandbox

139

bulkhead flat car

tank car

flat car

depressed center flat car

gondola car

piggyback car

refrigerator car

caboose

HIGHWAY CROSSING

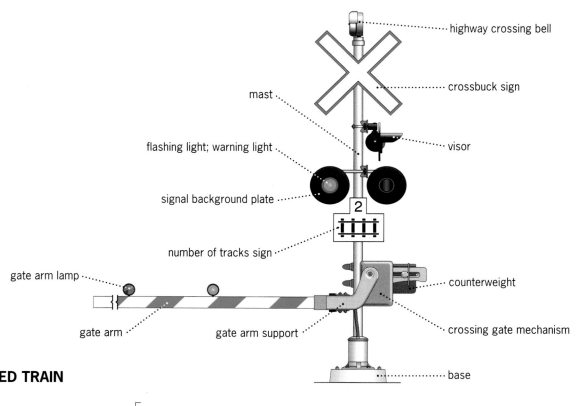

highway crossing bell

crossbuck sign

mast

visor

flashing light; warning light

signal background plate

2

number of tracks sign

gate arm lamp

counterweight

gate arm

gate arm support

crossing gate mechanism

base

HIGH-SPEED TRAIN

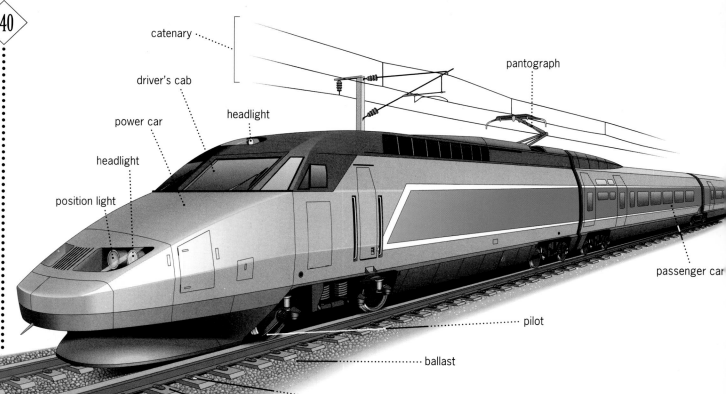

catenary

pantograph

driver's cab

power car

headlight

headlight

position light

passenger car

pilot

ballast

tie plate

tie

rail

FOUR-MASTED BARK

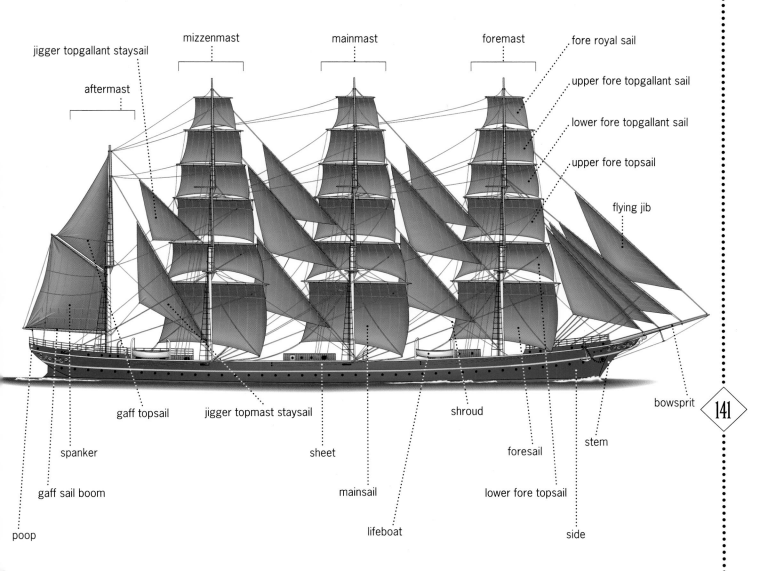

jigger topgallant staysail

mizzenmast

mainmast

foremast

fore royal sail

aftermast

upper fore topgallant sail

lower fore topgallant sail

upper fore topsail

flying jib

bowsprit

gaff topsail

jigger topmast staysail

shroud

stem

spanker

sheet

foresail

side

gaff sail boom

mainsail

lower fore topsail

lifeboat

poop

HOVERCRAFT

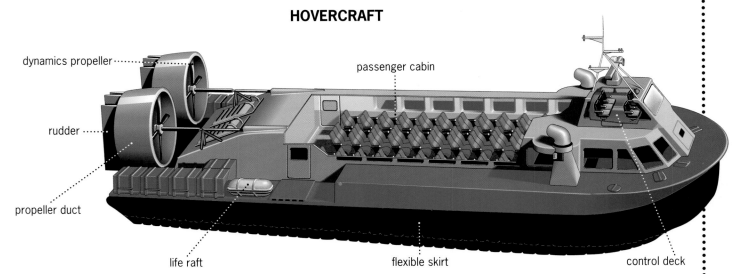

dynamics propeller

passenger cabin

rudder

propeller duct

life raft

flexible skirt

control deck

CRUISE LINER

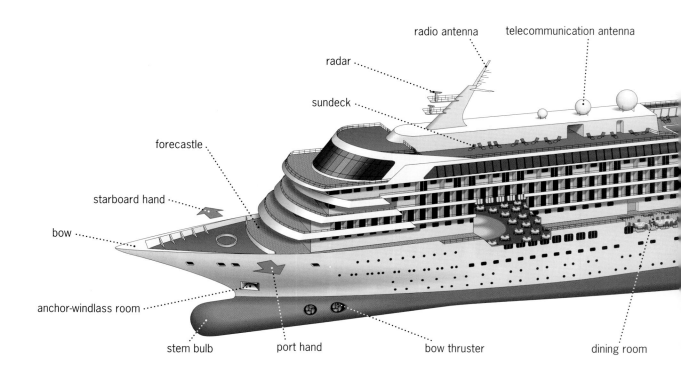

radio antenna

telecommunication antenna

radar

sundeck

forecastle

starboard hand

bow

anchor-windlass room

stem bulb

port hand

bow thruster

dining room

HARBOR

bulk terminal

container-loading bridge

dry dock

quay

grain terminal

canal lock

silos

floating crane

container ship

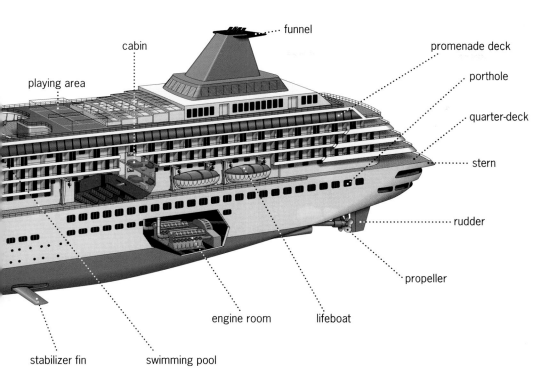

funnel

cabin

playing area

promenade deck

porthole

quarter-deck

stern

rudder

propeller

engine room

lifeboat

stabilizer fin

swimming pool

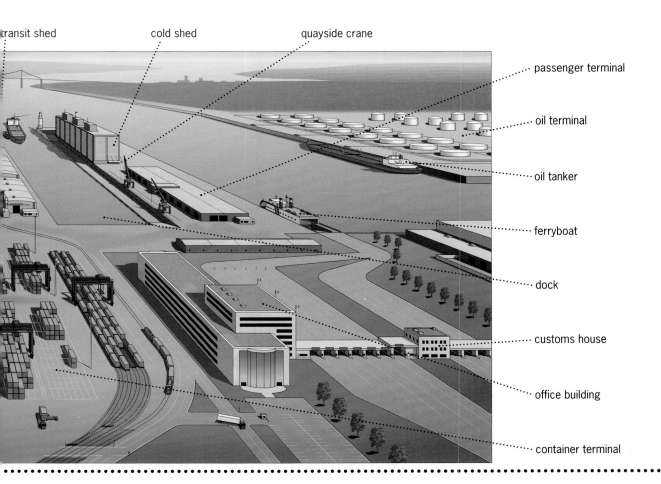

transit shed

cold shed

quayside crane

passenger terminal

oil terminal

oil tanker

ferryboat

dock

customs house

office building

container terminal

PLANE

TYPES OF WING SHAPES

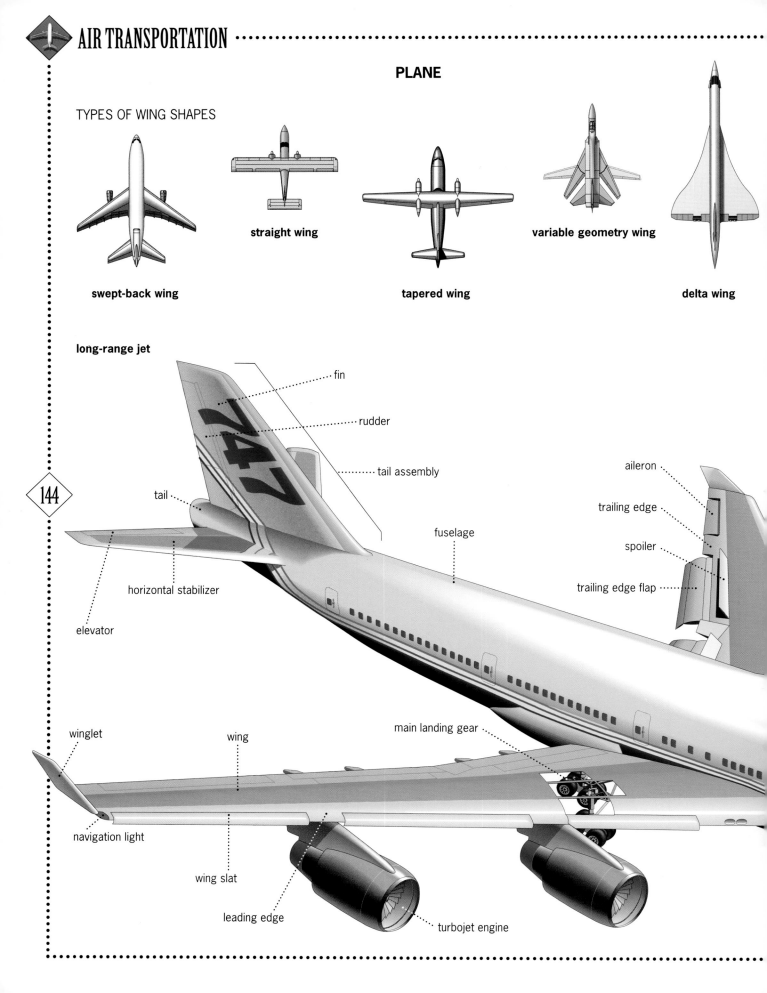

straight wing

variable geometry wing

swept-back wing

tapered wing

delta wing

long-range jet

fin

rudder

tail assembly

aileron

trailing edge

spoiler

trailing edge flap

tail

fuselage

horizontal stabilizer

elevator

winglet

wing

main landing gear

navigation light

wing slat

leading edge

turbojet engine

HELICOPTER

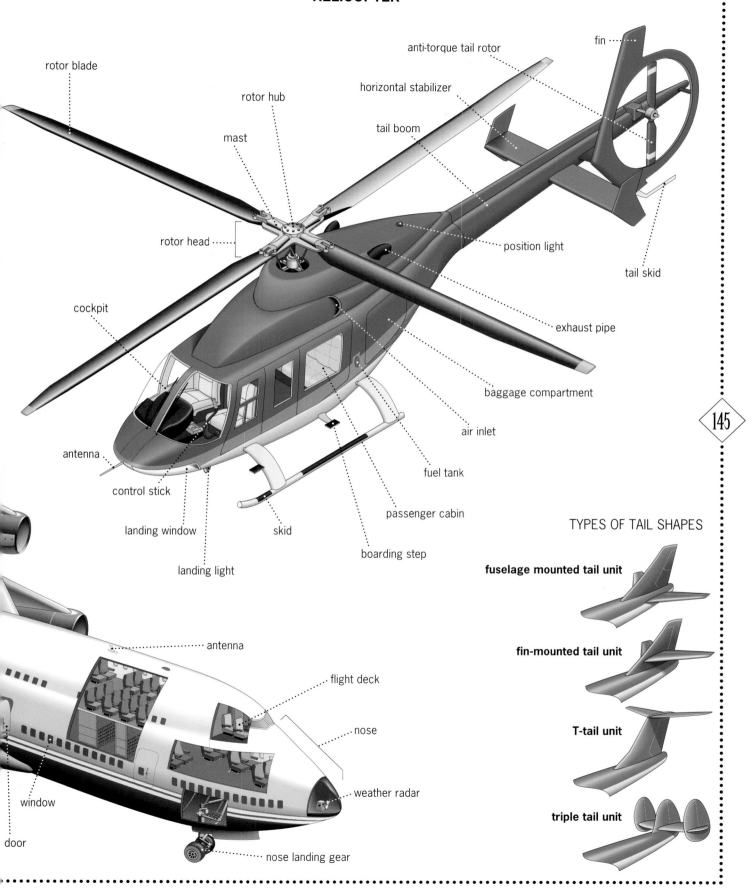

rotor blade

rotor hub

mast

anti-torque tail rotor

fin

horizontal stabilizer

tail boom

rotor head

position light

tail skid

cockpit

exhaust pipe

baggage compartment

air inlet

antenna

fuel tank

control stick

passenger cabin

landing window

skid

boarding step

landing light

antenna

flight deck

nose

weather radar

window

door

nose landing gear

TYPES OF TAIL SHAPES

fuselage mounted tail unit

fin-mounted tail unit

T-tail unit

triple tail unit

AIRPORT

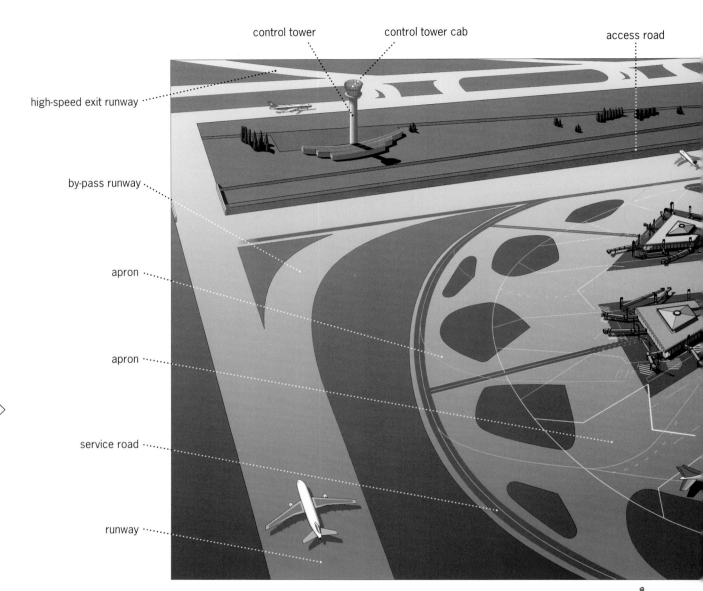

control tower   control tower cab   access road

high-speed exit runway

by-pass runway

apron

apron

service road

runway

AIRPORT GROUND EQUIPMENT

tow bar

tow tractor

container/pallet loader

universal step

baggage conveyor

wheel chock

127

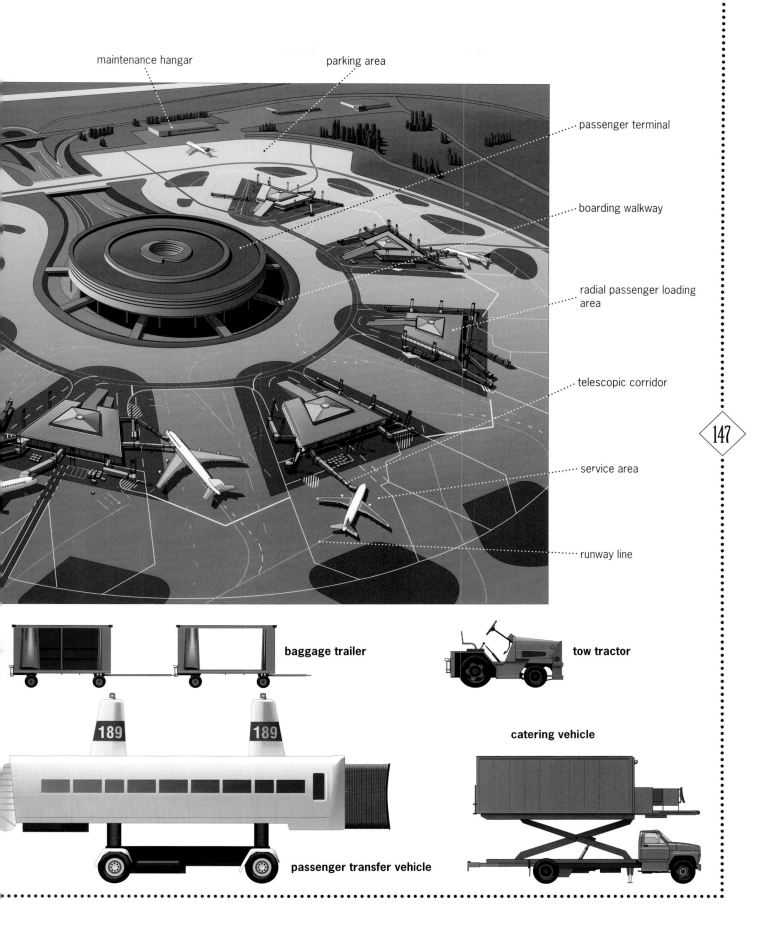

maintenance hangar

parking area

passenger terminal

boarding walkway

radial passenger loading area

telescopic corridor

service area

runway line

baggage trailer

tow tractor

catering vehicle

189

189

passenger transfer vehicle

147

SPACE SHUTTLE

space shuttle at takeoff

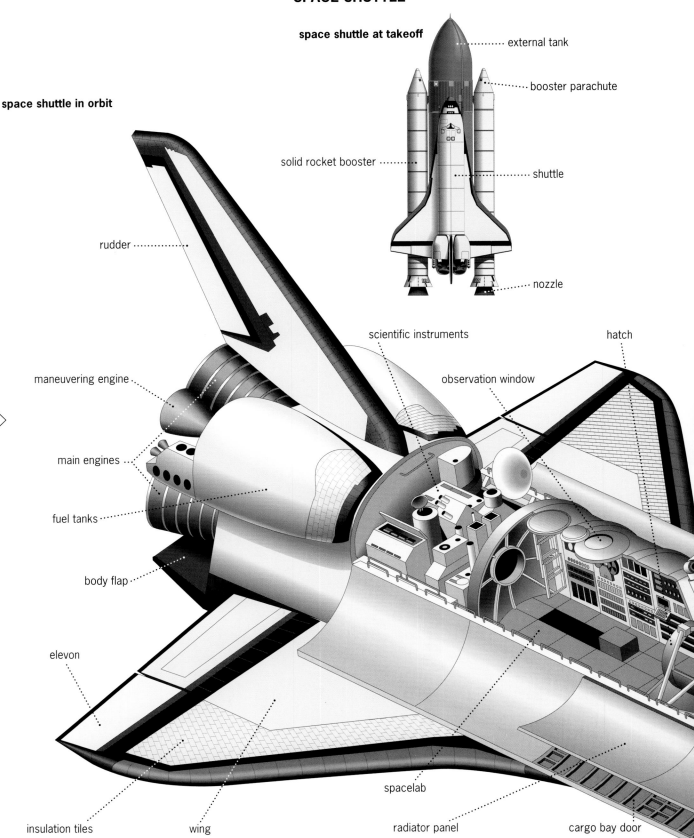

external tank

booster parachute

solid rocket booster

shuttle

nozzle

space shuttle in orbit

rudder

scientific instruments

hatch

observation window

maneuvering engine

main engines

fuel tanks

body flap

elevon

insulation tiles

wing

spacelab

radiator panel

cargo bay door

SPACESUIT

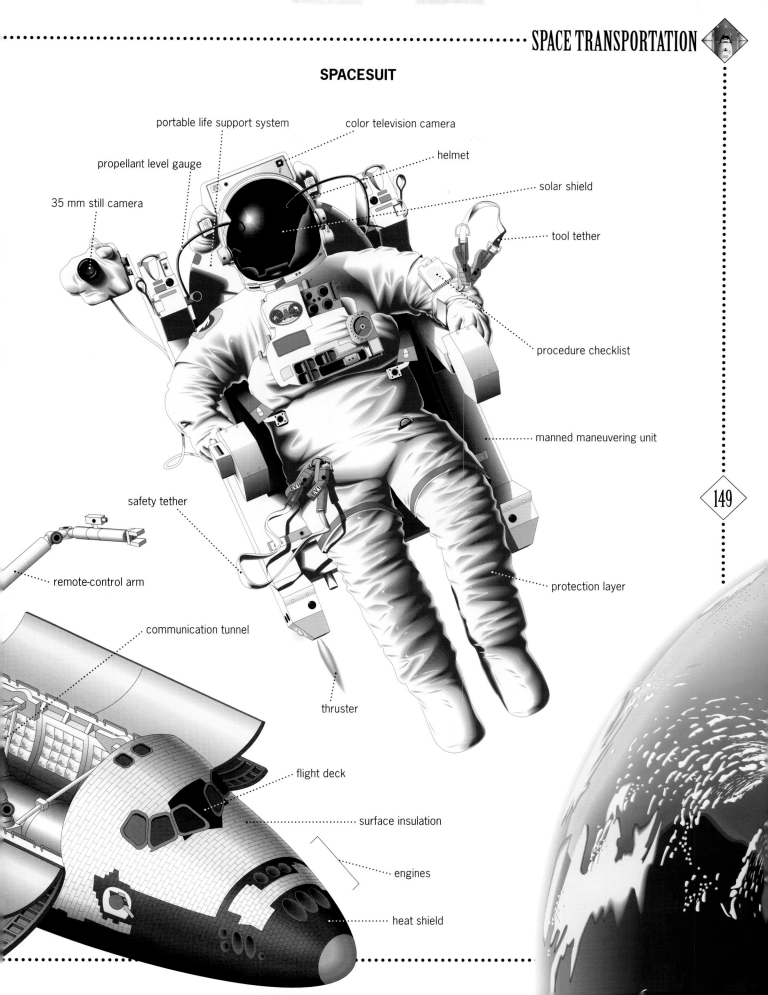

portable life support system

color television camera

propellant level gauge

helmet

solar shield

35 mm still camera

tool tether

procedure checklist

manned maneuvering unit

safety tether

remote-control arm

protection layer

communication tunnel

thruster

flight deck

surface insulation

engines

heat shield

SCHOOL SUPPLIES

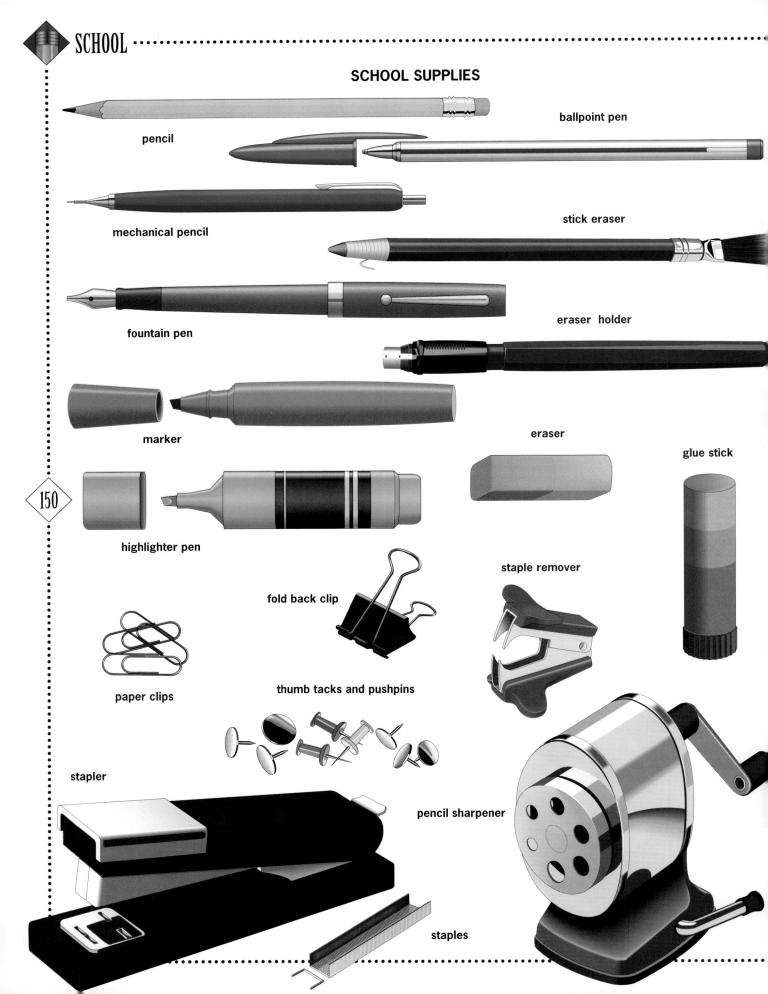

pencil

ballpoint pen

mechanical pencil

stick eraser

fountain pen

eraser holder

marker

eraser

glue stick

highlighter pen

staple remover

fold back clip

paper clips

thumb tacks and pushpins

stapler

pencil sharpener

staples

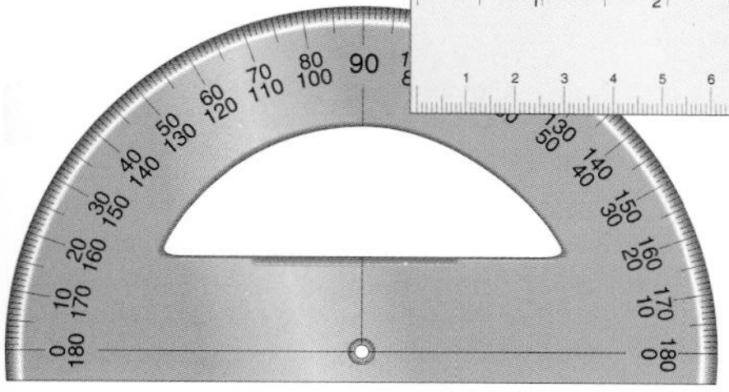

ruler

protractor

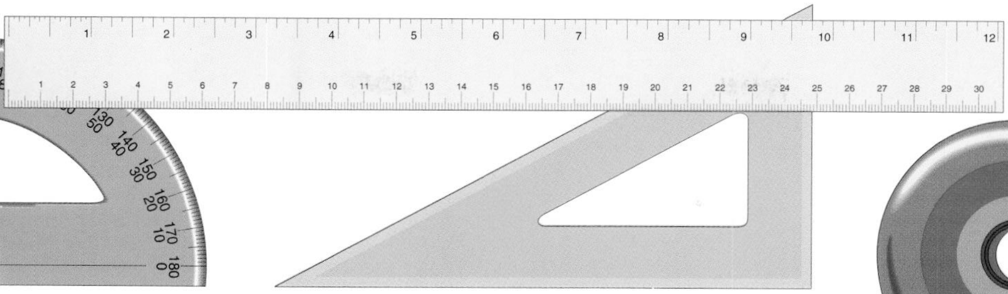

set square

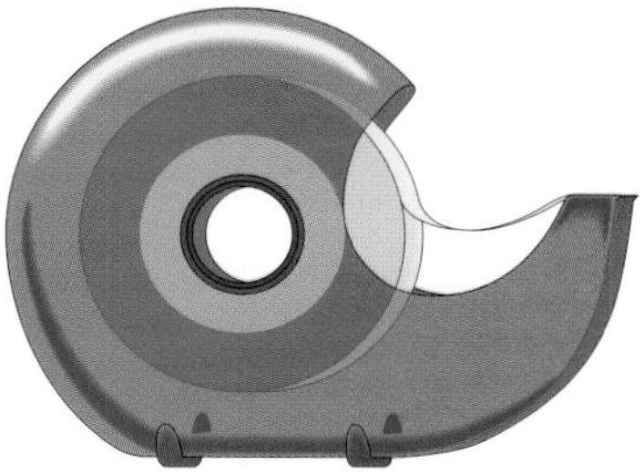

tape dispenser

ring binder

spiral bound notebook

loose-leaf paper

notebook

notepad

briefcase

book bag

SCHOOL EQUIPMENT

blackboard

a b c

1 2 3

152

overhead projector

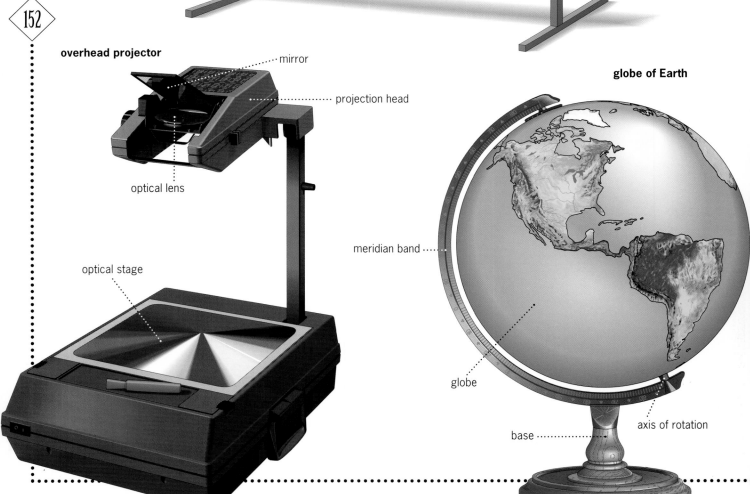

mirror

projection head

optical lens

globe of Earth

meridian band

optical stage

globe

base

axis of rotation

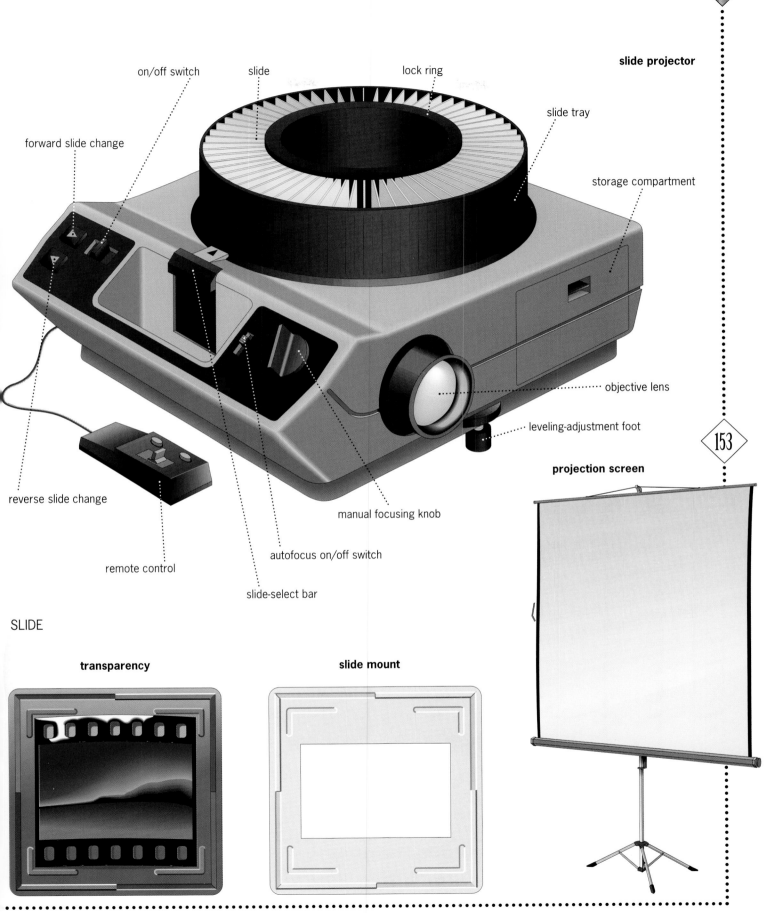

slide projector

on/off switch

slide

lock ring

slide tray

forward slide change

storage compartment

objective lens

leveling-adjustment foot

reverse slide change

projection screen

manual focusing knob

autofocus on/off switch

remote control

slide-select bar

SLIDE

transparency

slide mount

SCHOOL EQUIPMENT

pocket calculator

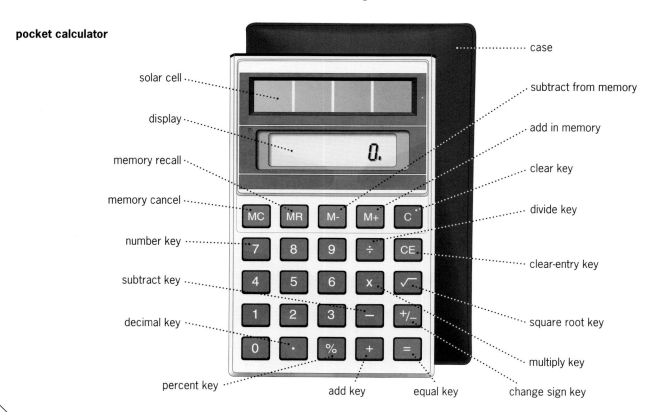

solar cell

display

memory recall

memory cancel

number key

subtract key

decimal key

percent key

add key

equal key

case

subtract from memory

add in memory

clear key

divide key

clear-entry key

square root key

multiply key

change sign key

MC · MR · M- · M+ · C · 7 · 8 · 9 · ÷ · CE · 4 · 5 · 6 · x · √ · 1 · 2 · 3 · − · +/− · 0 · · · % · + · =

personal computer

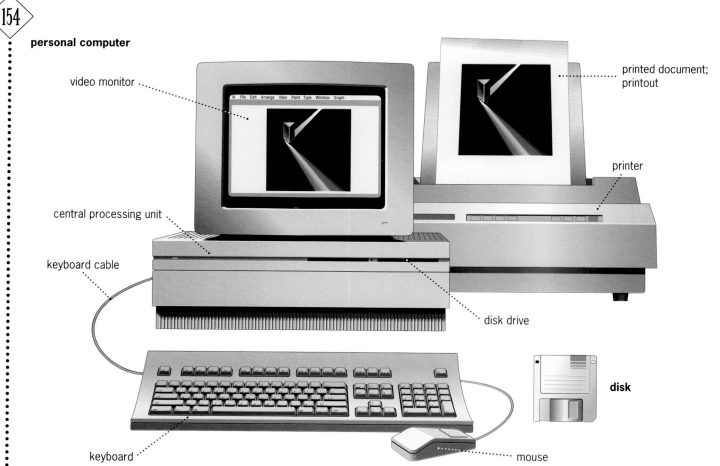

video monitor

central processing unit

keyboard cable

printed document; printout

printer

disk drive

keyboard

mouse

disk

magnifying glass

microscope

eyepiece

draw tube

coarse adjustment knob

fine adjustment knob

revolving nosepiece

objective

arm

test tube

stage clip

glass slide

stage

condenser

mirror

base

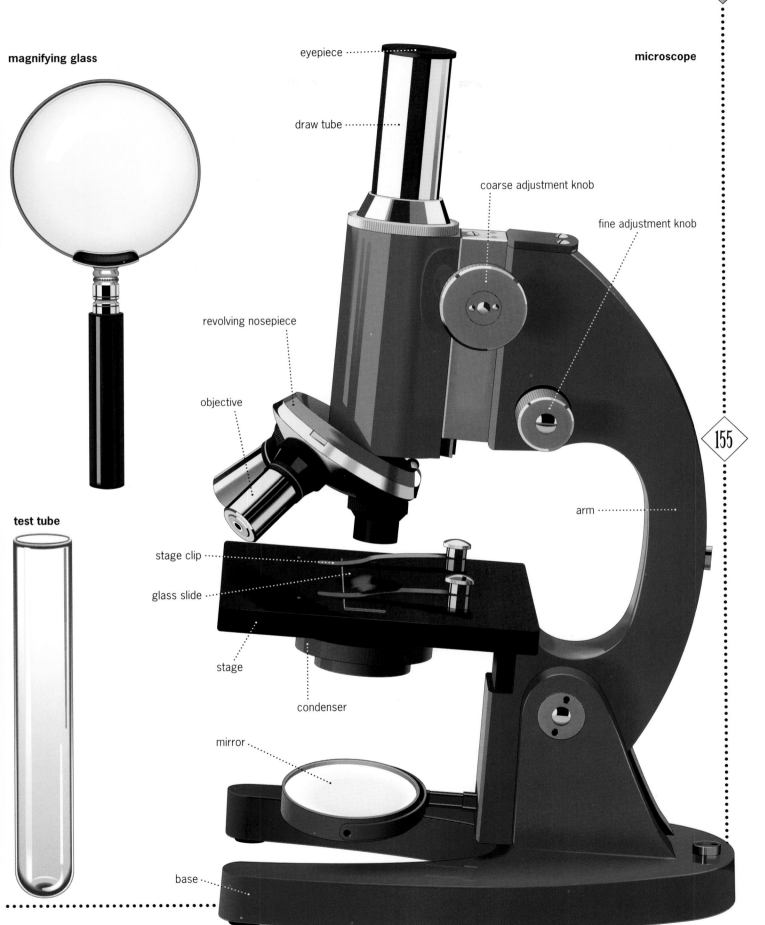

GEOMETRY

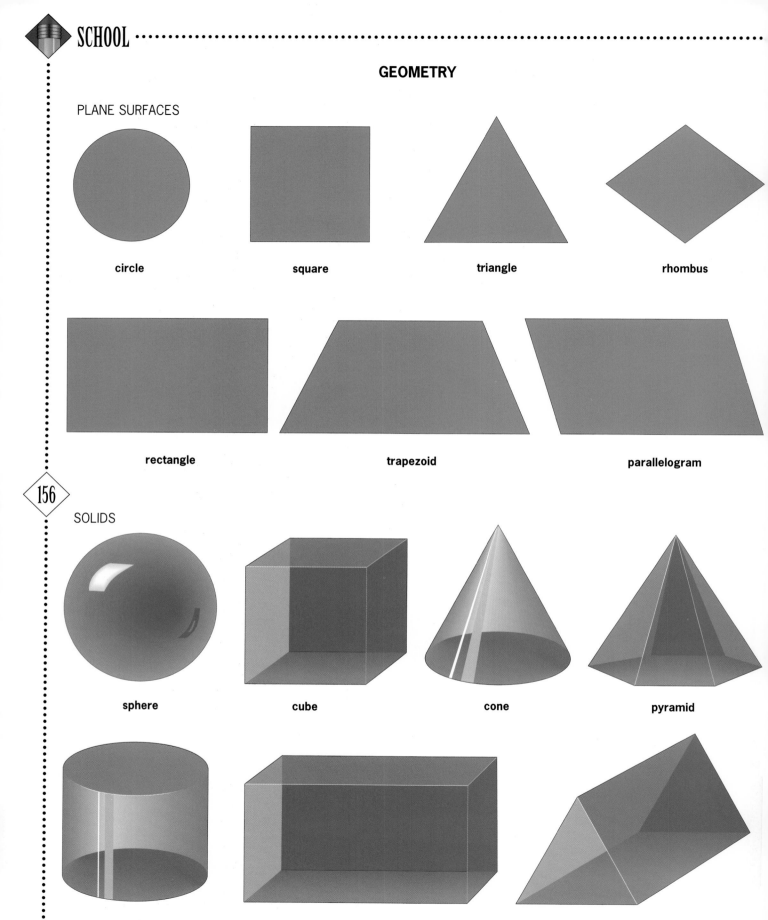

PLANE SURFACES

circle

square

triangle

rhombus

rectangle

trapezoid

parallelogram

156

SOLIDS

sphere

cube

cone

pyramid

cylinder

parallelepiped

prism

DRAWING

primary colors

secondary colors

tertiary colors

COLOR CIRCLE

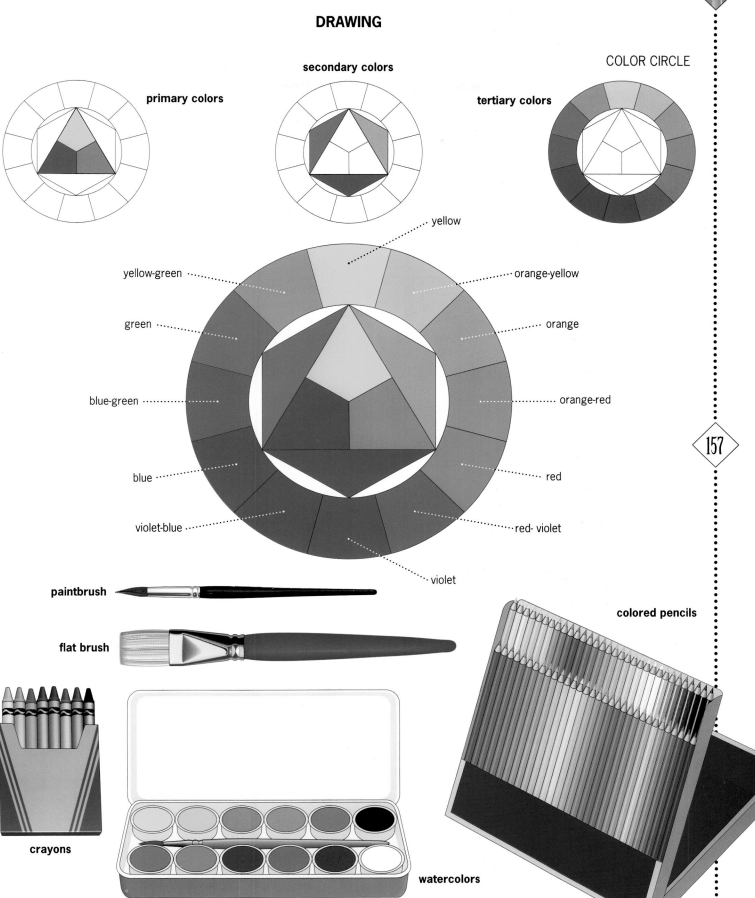

- yellow
- yellow-green
- orange-yellow
- green
- orange
- blue-green
- orange-red
- blue
- red
- violet-blue
- red-violet
- violet

paintbrush

flat brush

crayons

watercolors

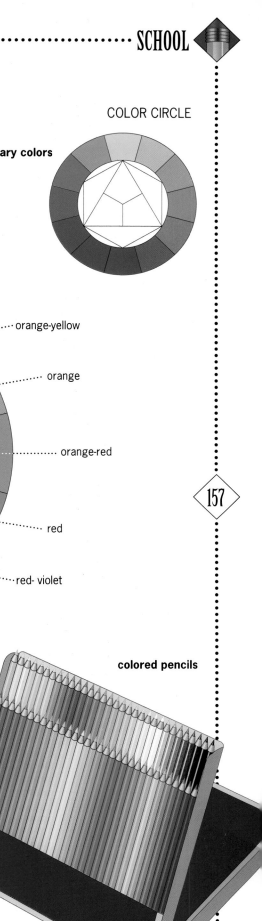

colored pencils

TRADITIONAL MUSICAL INSTRUMENTS

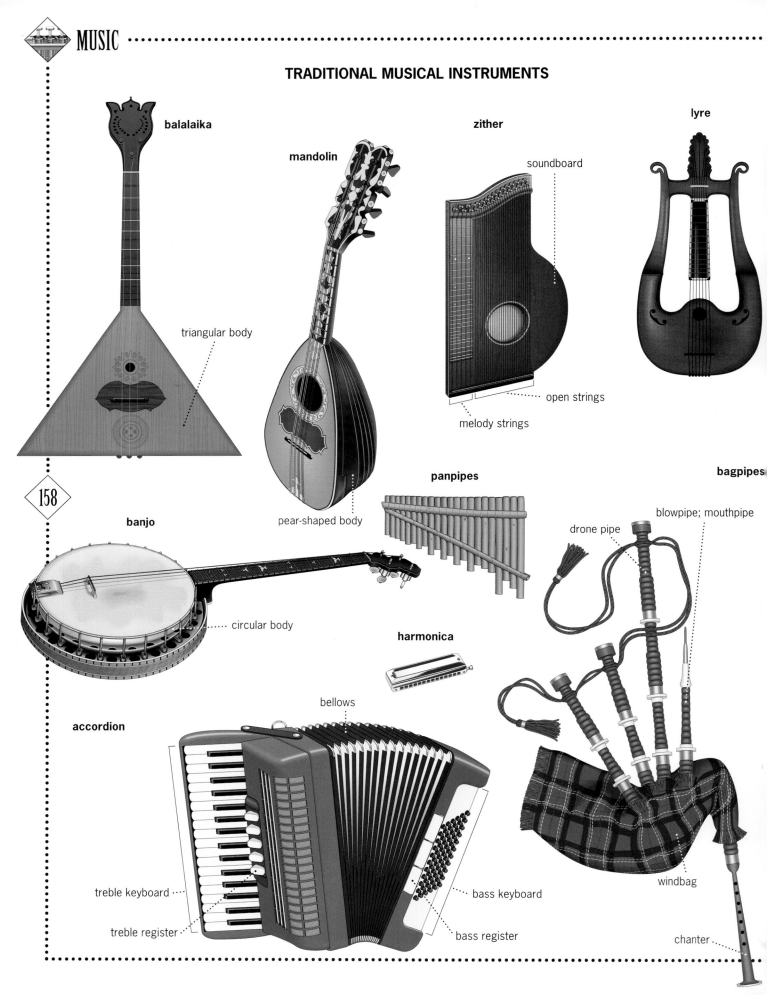

balalaika

triangular body

mandolin

pear-shaped body

zither

soundboard

open strings

melody strings

lyre

banjo

circular body

panpipes

harmonica

bagpipes

drone pipe

blowpipe; mouthpipe

windbag

accordion

bellows

treble keyboard

treble register

bass keyboard

bass register

chanter

KEYBOARD INSTRUMENT

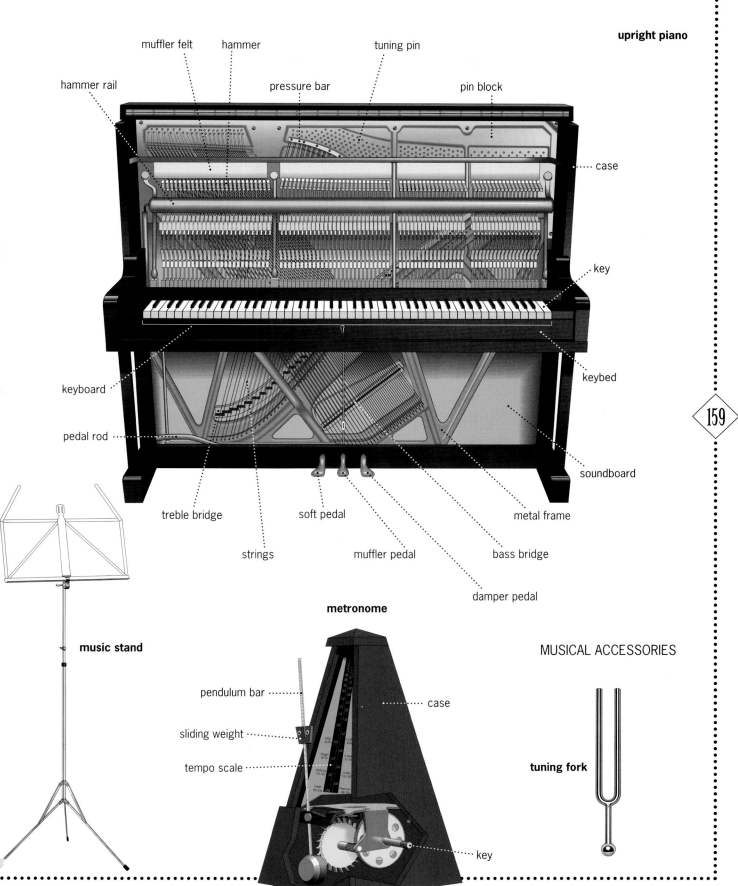

upright piano

muffler felt

hammer

tuning pin

hammer rail

pressure bar

pin block

case

key

keybed

keyboard

pedal rod

soundboard

treble bridge

soft pedal

metal frame

strings

muffler pedal

bass bridge

damper pedal

metronome

music stand

MUSICAL ACCESSORIES

pendulum bar

case

sliding weight

tempo scale

tuning fork

key

MUSICAL NOTATION

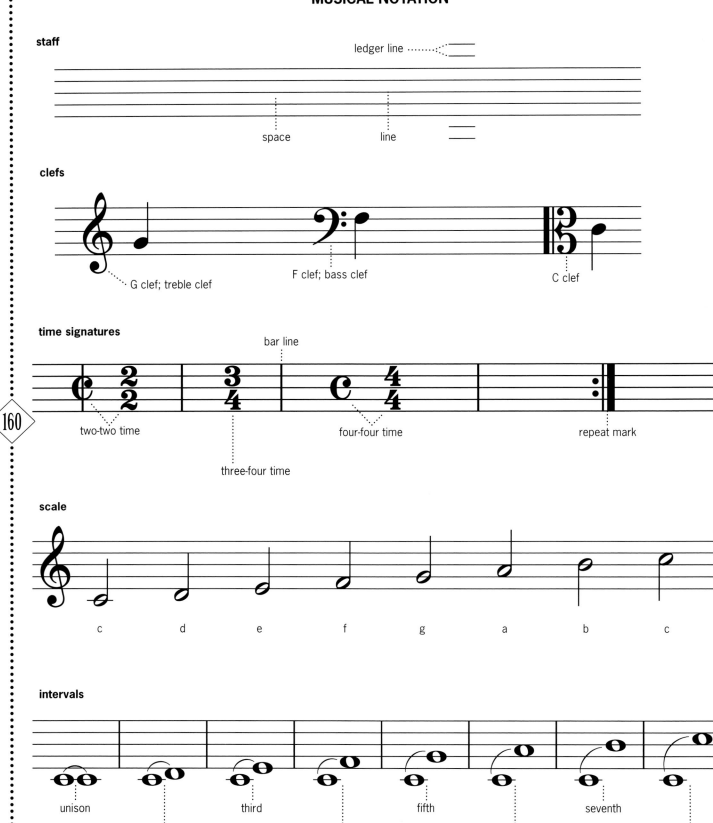

note symbols

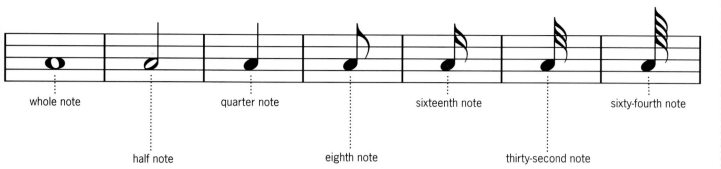

whole note

half note

quarter note

eighth note

sixteenth note

thirty-second note

sixty-fourth note

rest symbols

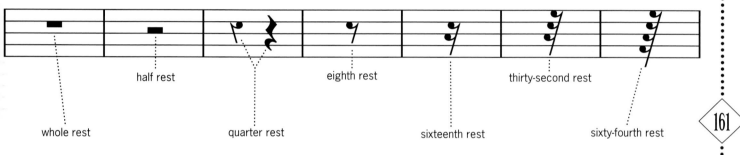

whole rest

half rest

quarter rest

eighth rest

sixteenth rest

thirty-second rest

sixty-fourth rest

accidentals

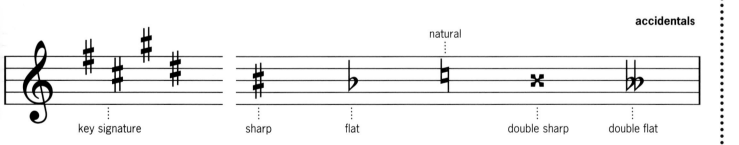

natural

key signature

sharp

flat

double sharp

double flat

ornaments

appoggiatura

trill

turn

mordent

STRINGED INSTRUMENTS

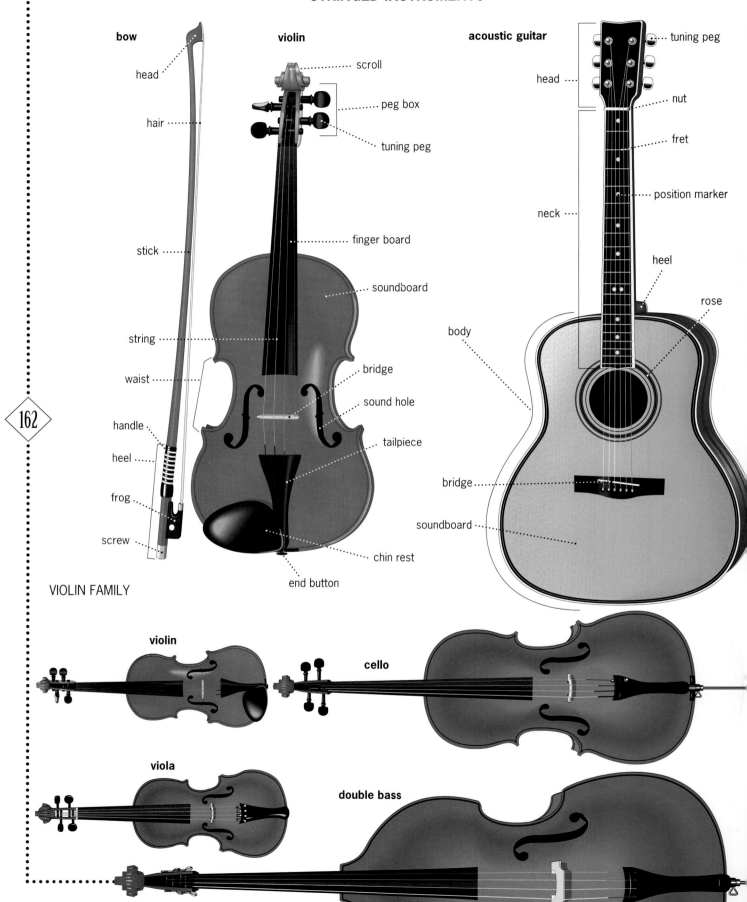

bow

head

hair

stick

string

waist

handle

heel

frog

screw

violin

scroll

peg box

tuning peg

finger board

soundboard

bridge

sound hole

tailpiece

chin rest

end button

acoustic guitar

tuning peg

head

nut

fret

position marker

neck

heel

rose

body

bridge

soundboard

162

VIOLIN FAMILY

violin

cello

viola

double bass

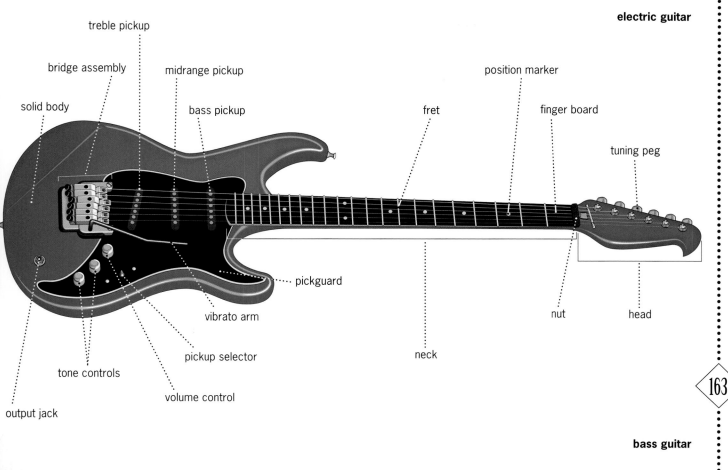

electric guitar

treble pickup

bridge assembly

midrange pickup

position marker

solid body

bass pickup

fret

finger board

tuning peg

pickguard

vibrato arm

nut

head

pickup selector

neck

tone controls

volume control

output jack

163

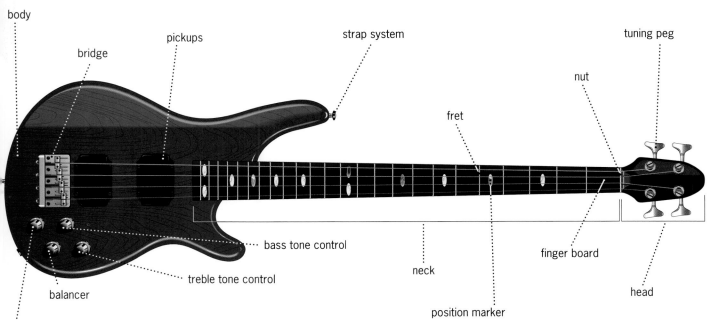

bass guitar

body

pickups

strap system

tuning peg

bridge

nut

fret

neck

finger board

bass tone control

treble tone control

balancer

position marker

head

volume control

WIND INSTRUMENTS

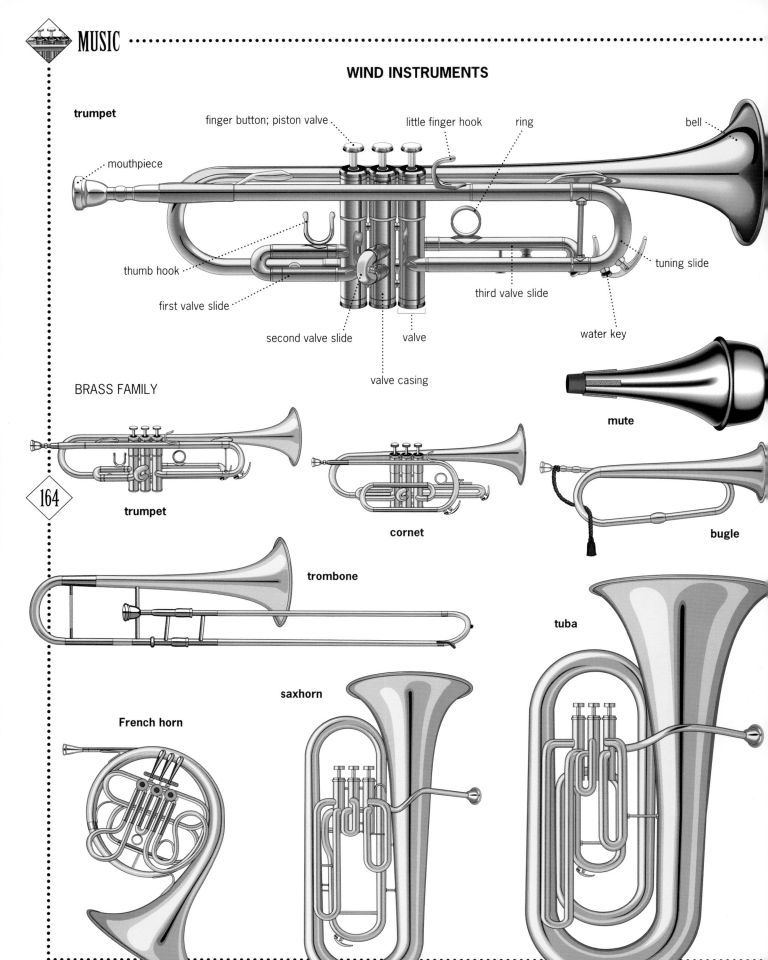

trumpet

finger button; piston valve

little finger hook

ring

bell

mouthpiece

thumb hook

first valve slide

second valve slide

valve

valve casing

third valve slide

water key

tuning slide

BRASS FAMILY

trumpet

cornet

mute

bugle

trombone

tuba

saxhorn

French horn

crook

ligature

reed

mouthpiece

octave mechanism

REEDS

single reed

double reed

saxophone

WOODWIND FAMILY

saxophone

piccolo

bell

bell brace

body

thumb rest

key

flute

recorder

oboe

clarinet

English horn

bassoon

PERCUSSION INSTRUMENTS

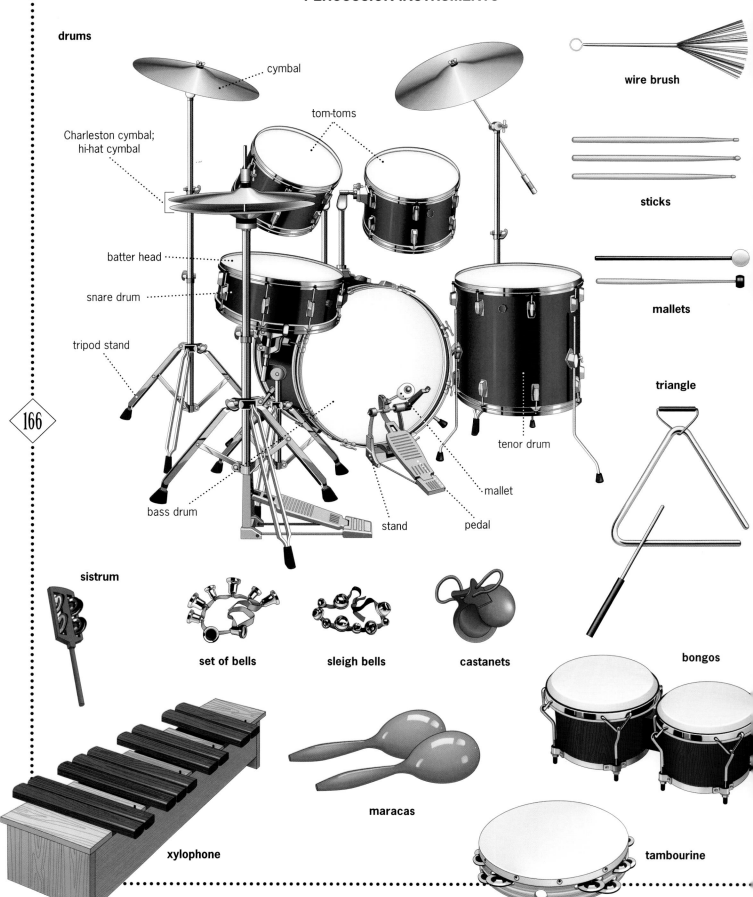

drums

cymbal

tom-toms

Charleston cymbal;
hi-hat cymbal

batter head

snare drum

tripod stand

166

bass drum

stand

mallet

pedal

tenor drum

wire brush

sticks

mallets

triangle

sistrum

set of bells

sleigh bells

castanets

bongos

xylophone

maracas

tambourine

SYMPHONY ORCHESTRA

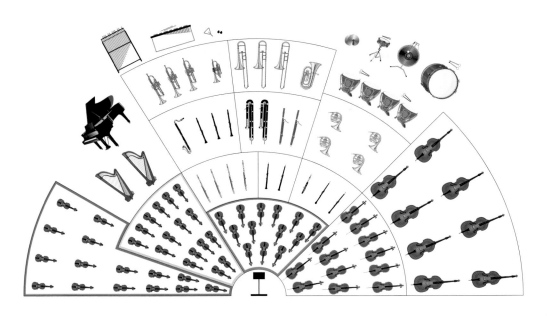

conductor's podium

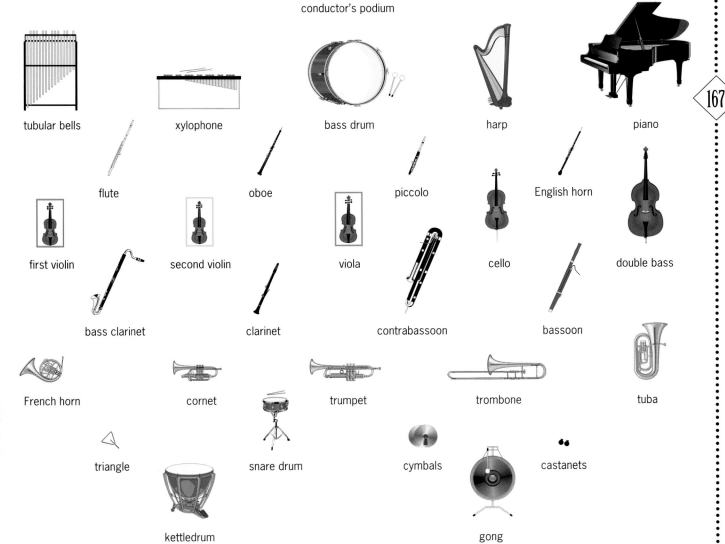

tubular bells

xylophone

bass drum

harp

piano

flute

oboe

piccolo

English horn

first violin

second violin

viola

cello

double bass

bass clarinet

clarinet

contrabassoon

bassoon

French horn

cornet

trumpet

trombone

tuba

triangle

snare drum

cymbals

castanets

kettledrum

gong

BASEBALL

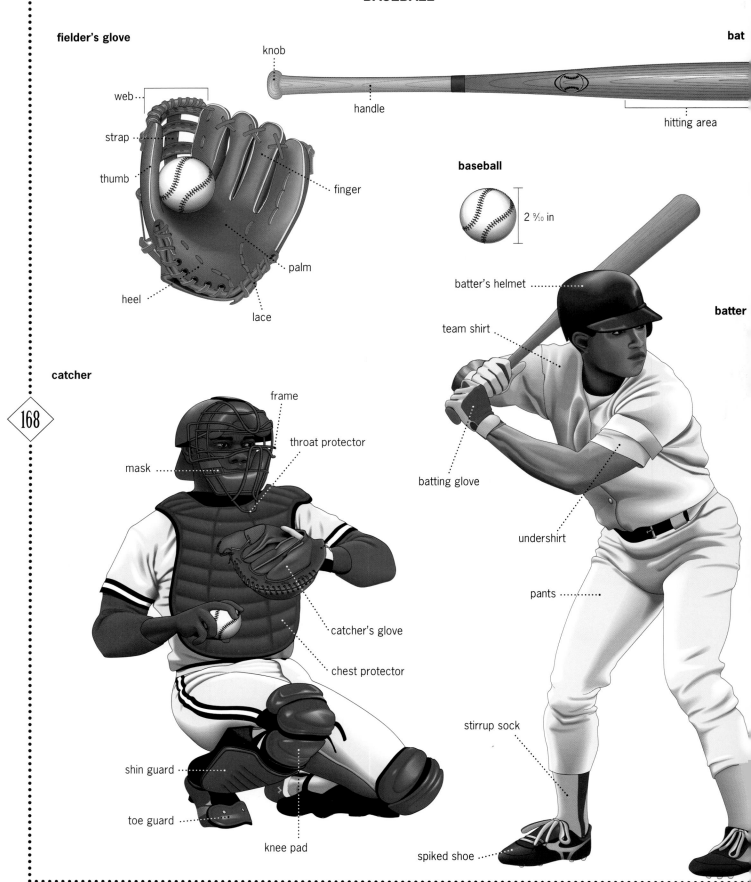

fielder's glove

web

strap

thumb

heel

lace

palm

finger

knob

handle

bat

hitting area

baseball

2 ⁹⁄₁₀ in

batter

batter's helmet

team shirt

batting glove

undershirt

pants

stirrup sock

spiked shoe

catcher

frame

throat protector

mask

catcher's glove

chest protector

shin guard

toe guard

knee pad

168

field

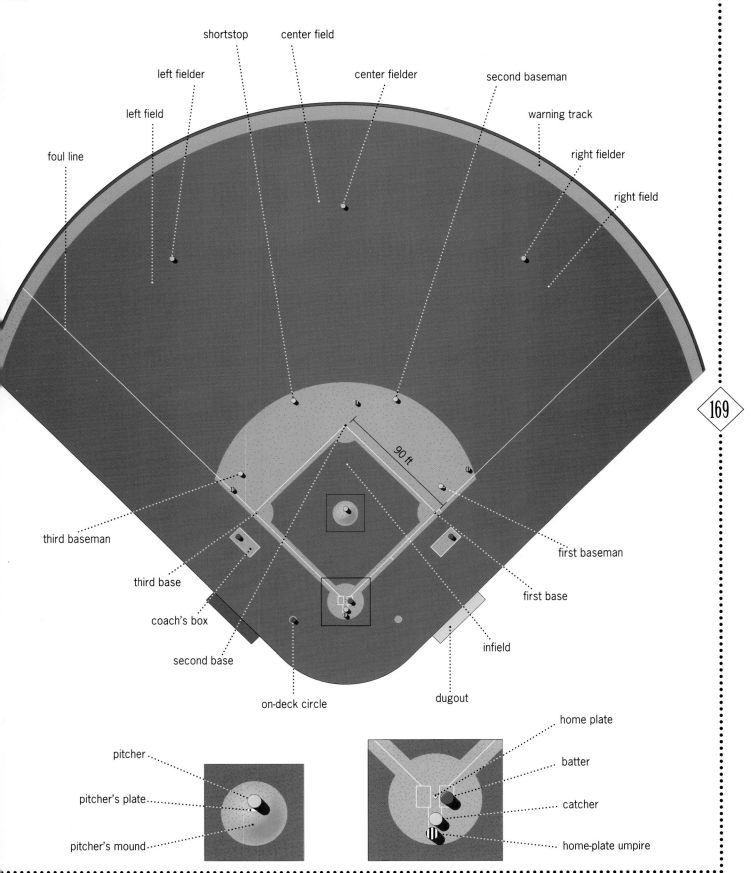

shortstop

center field

left fielder

center fielder

second baseman

left field

warning track

right fielder

foul line

right field

third baseman

90 ft

first baseman

third base

first base

coach's box

second base

infield

on-deck circle

dugout

home plate

pitcher

batter

pitcher's plate

catcher

pitcher's mound

home-plate umpire

FOOTBALL

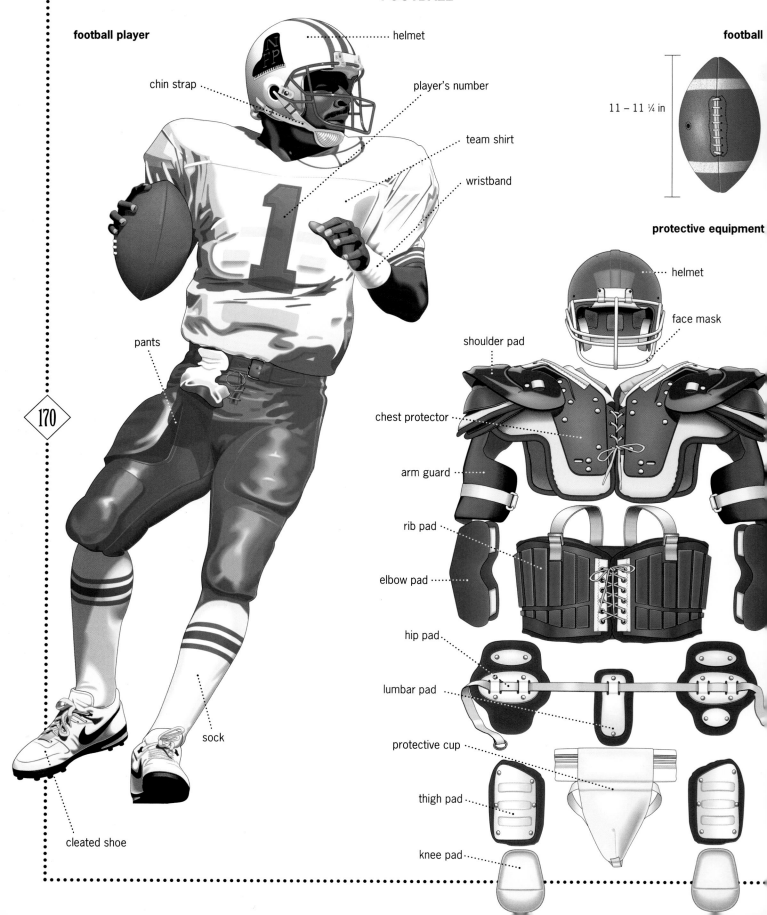

football player

chin strap

helmet

player's number

team shirt

wristband

pants

sock

cleated shoe

football

11 – 11 ¼ in

protective equipment

helmet

face mask

shoulder pad

chest protector

arm guard

rib pad

elbow pad

hip pad

lumbar pad

protective cup

thigh pad

knee pad

170

scrimmage

OFFENSE

DEFENSE

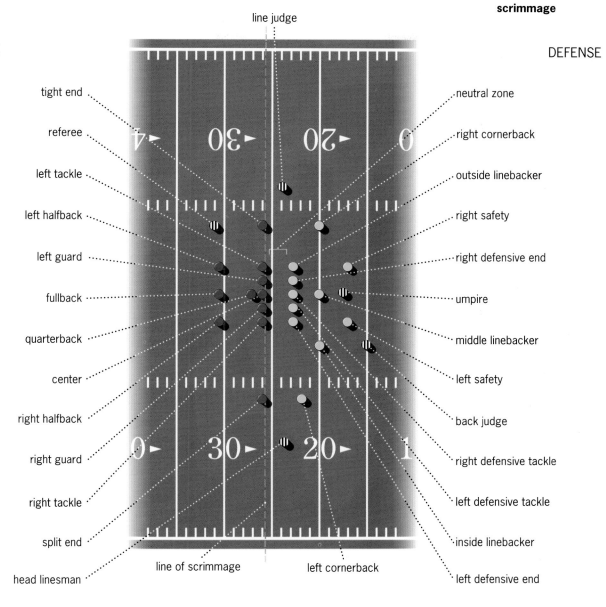

line judge

tight end

referee

left tackle

left halfback

left guard

fullback

quarterback

center

right halfback

right guard

right tackle

split end

head linesman

line of scrimmage

left cornerback

neutral zone

right cornerback

outside linebacker

right safety

right defensive end

umpire

middle linebacker

left safety

back judge

right defensive tackle

left defensive tackle

inside linebacker

left defensive end

playing field for football

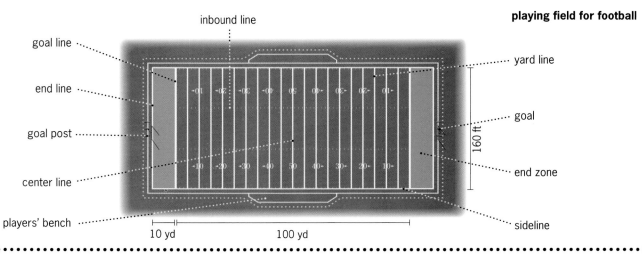

inbound line

goal line

end line

goal post

center line

players' bench

yard line

goal

end zone

sideline

160 ft

10 yd

100 yd

SOCCER

soccer player

soccer ball

team shirt

8 ⅗ - 8 ⁹⁄₁₀ in

shorts

shin guard

soccer shoe

interchangeable studs

playing field

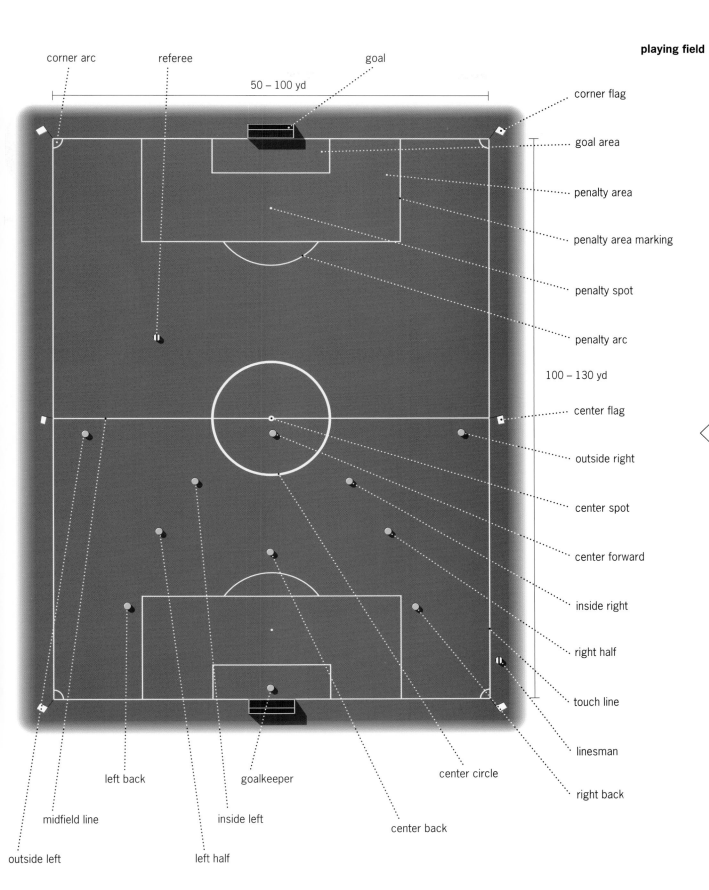

corner arc

referee

goal

50 – 100 yd

corner flag

goal area

penalty area

penalty area marking

penalty spot

penalty arc

100 – 130 yd

center flag

outside right

center spot

center forward

inside right

right half

touch line

linesman

right back

center circle

goalkeeper

inside left

center back

midfield line

left back

left half

outside left

173

court

VOLLEYBALL

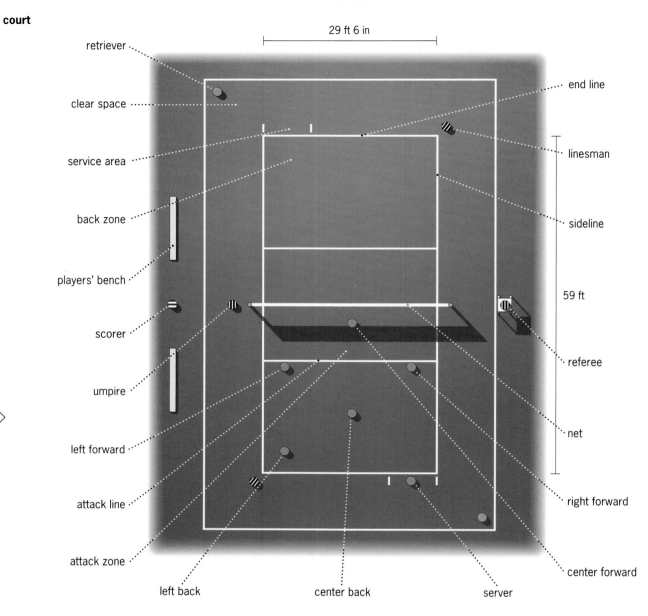

retriever

clear space

service area

back zone

players' bench

scorer

umpire

left forward

attack line

attack zone

29 ft 6 in

end line

linesman

sideline

59 ft

referee

net

right forward

center forward

left back

center back

server

174

net

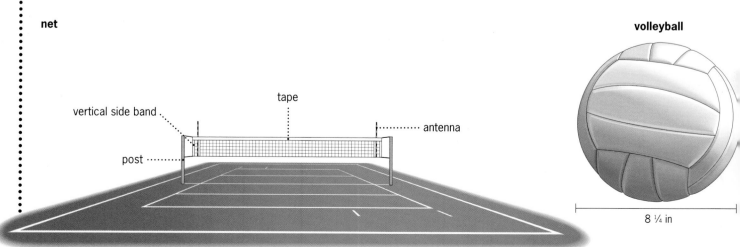

tape

vertical side band

antenna

post

volleyball

8 ¼ in

FIELD HOCKEY

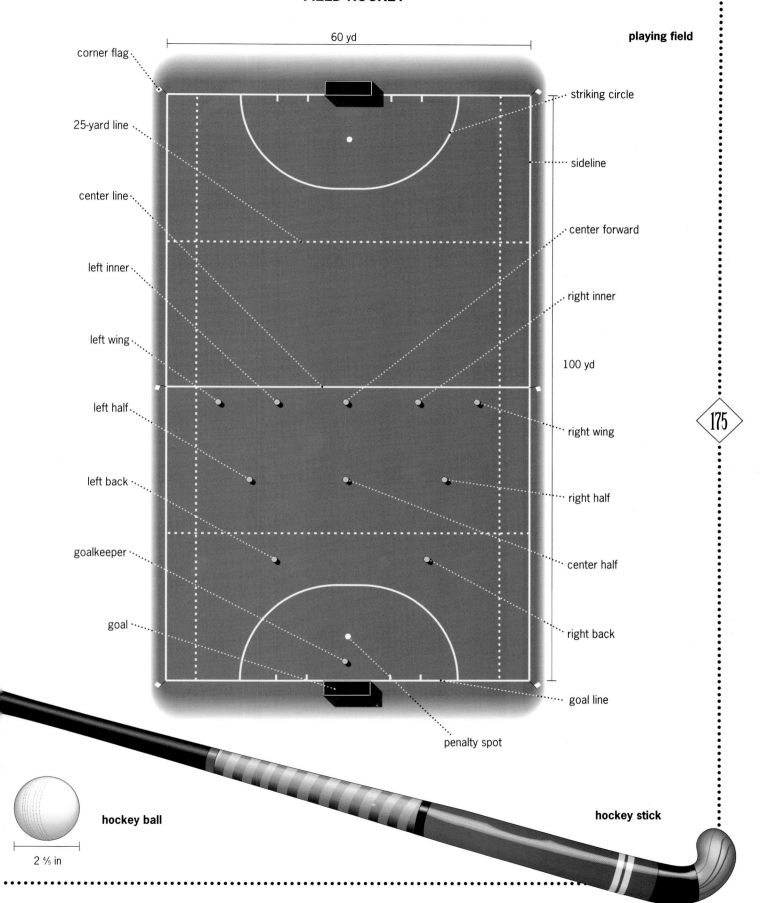

playing field

corner flag

25-yard line

center line

left inner

left wing

left half

left back

goalkeeper

goal

60 yd

100 yd

striking circle

sideline

center forward

right inner

right wing

right half

center half

right back

goal line

penalty spot

hockey ball

2 ⅘ in

hockey stick

ICE HOCKEY

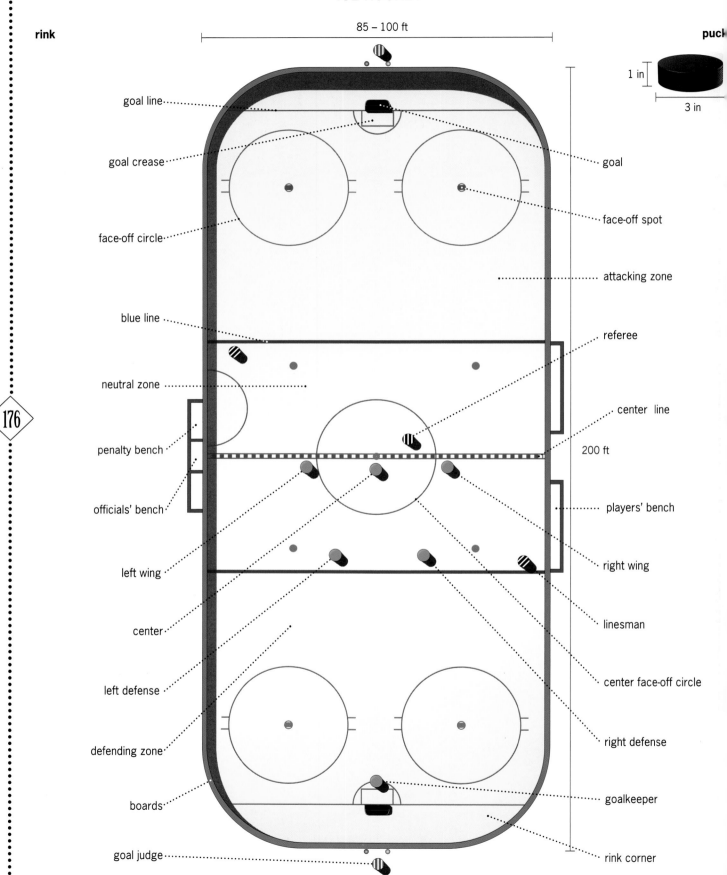

85 – 100 ft

rink

puck

1 in

3 in

goal line

goal crease

goal

face-off spot

face-off circle

attacking zone

blue line

referee

neutral zone

center line

200 ft

penalty bench

officials' bench

players' bench

left wing

right wing

center

linesman

left defense

center face-off circle

defending zone

right defense

boards

goalkeeper

goal judge

rink corner

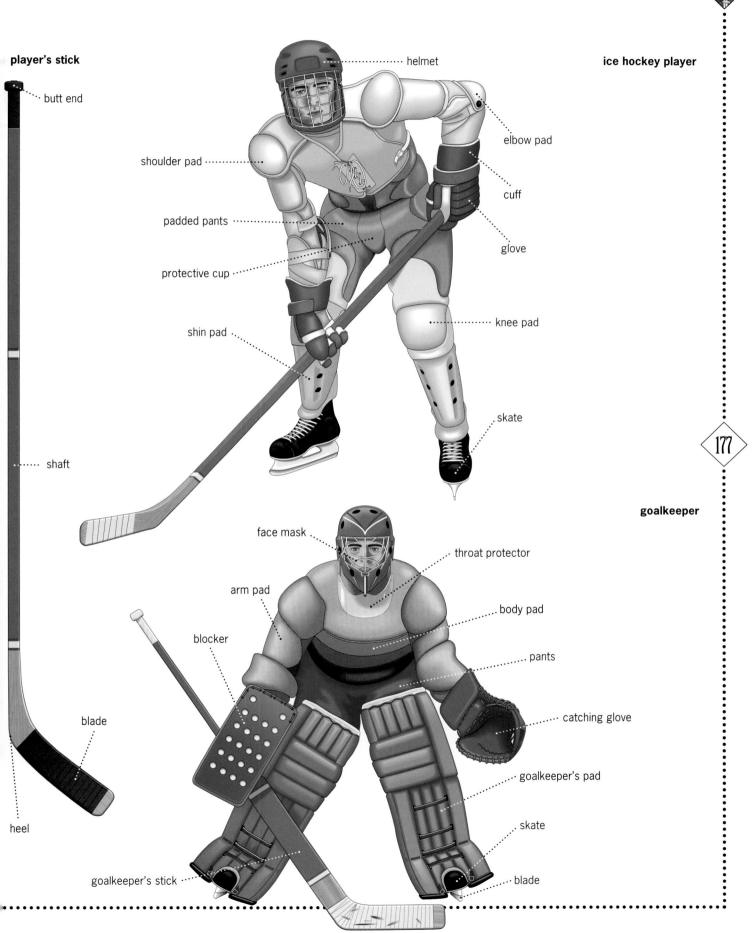

player's stick

butt end

shoulder pad

padded pants

protective cup

shin pad

shaft

blade

heel

helmet

elbow pad

cuff

glove

knee pad

skate

goalkeeper

face mask

throat protector

arm pad

body pad

blocker

pants

catching glove

goalkeeper's pad

skate

goalkeeper's stick

blade

BASKETBALL

court

50 ft

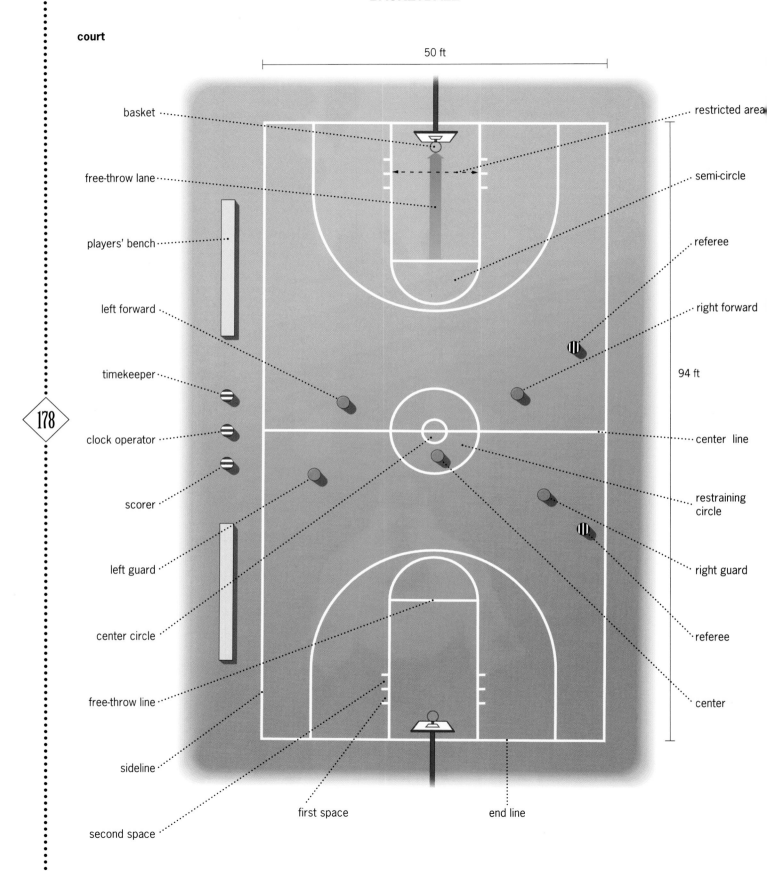

basket

restricted area

free-throw lane

semi-circle

players' bench

referee

left forward

right forward

timekeeper

94 ft

clock operator

center line

scorer

restraining circle

left guard

right guard

center circle

referee

free-throw line

center

sideline

first space

end line

second space

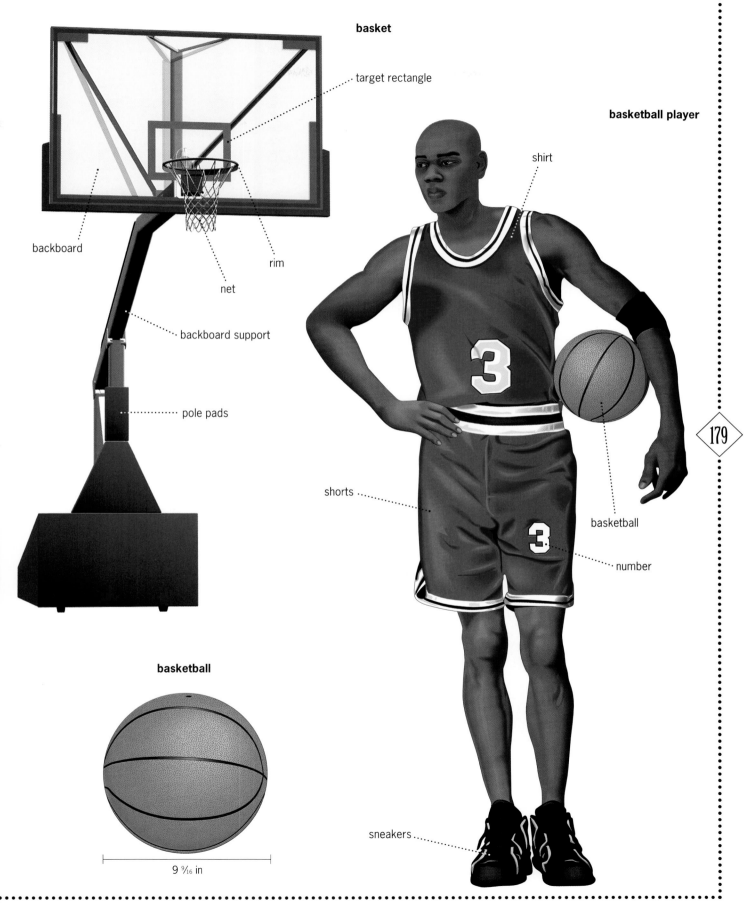

basket

target rectangle

basketball player

shirt

backboard

rim

net

backboard support

pole pads

shorts

basketball

number

basketball

9 ⁹⁄₁₆ in

sneakers

TENNIS

court

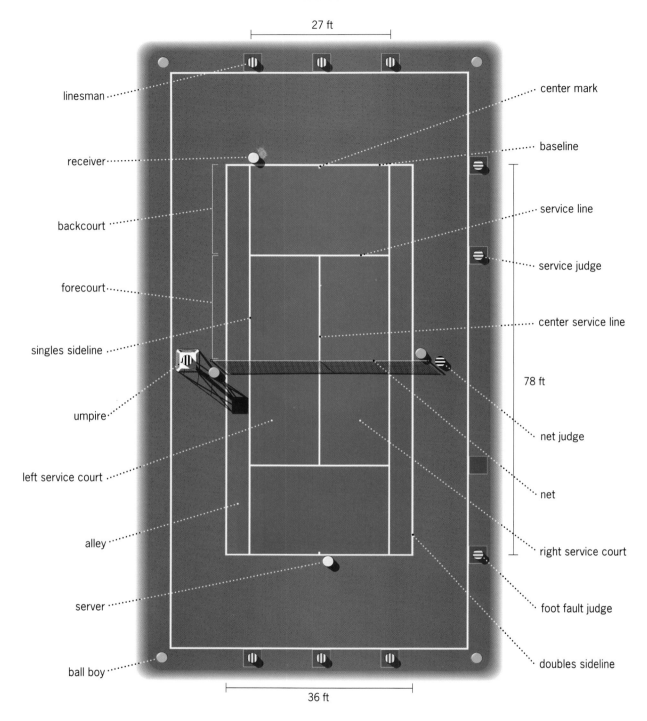

27 ft

linesman

center mark

receiver

baseline

backcourt

service line

forecourt

service judge

singles sideline

center service line

umpire

78 ft

left service court

net judge

alley

net

server

right service court

ball boy

foot fault judge

doubles sideline

36 ft

net

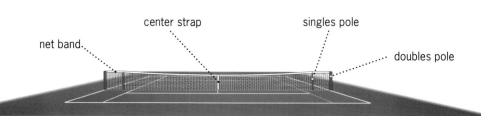

center strap

singles pole

net band

doubles pole

tennis ball

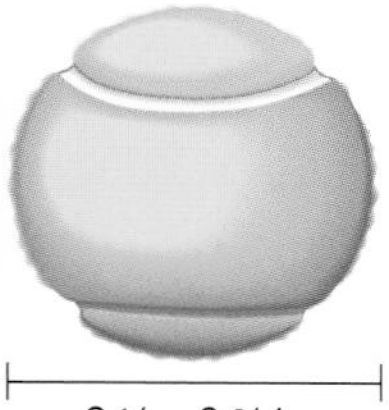

2 ½ – 2 ⅝ in

tennis player

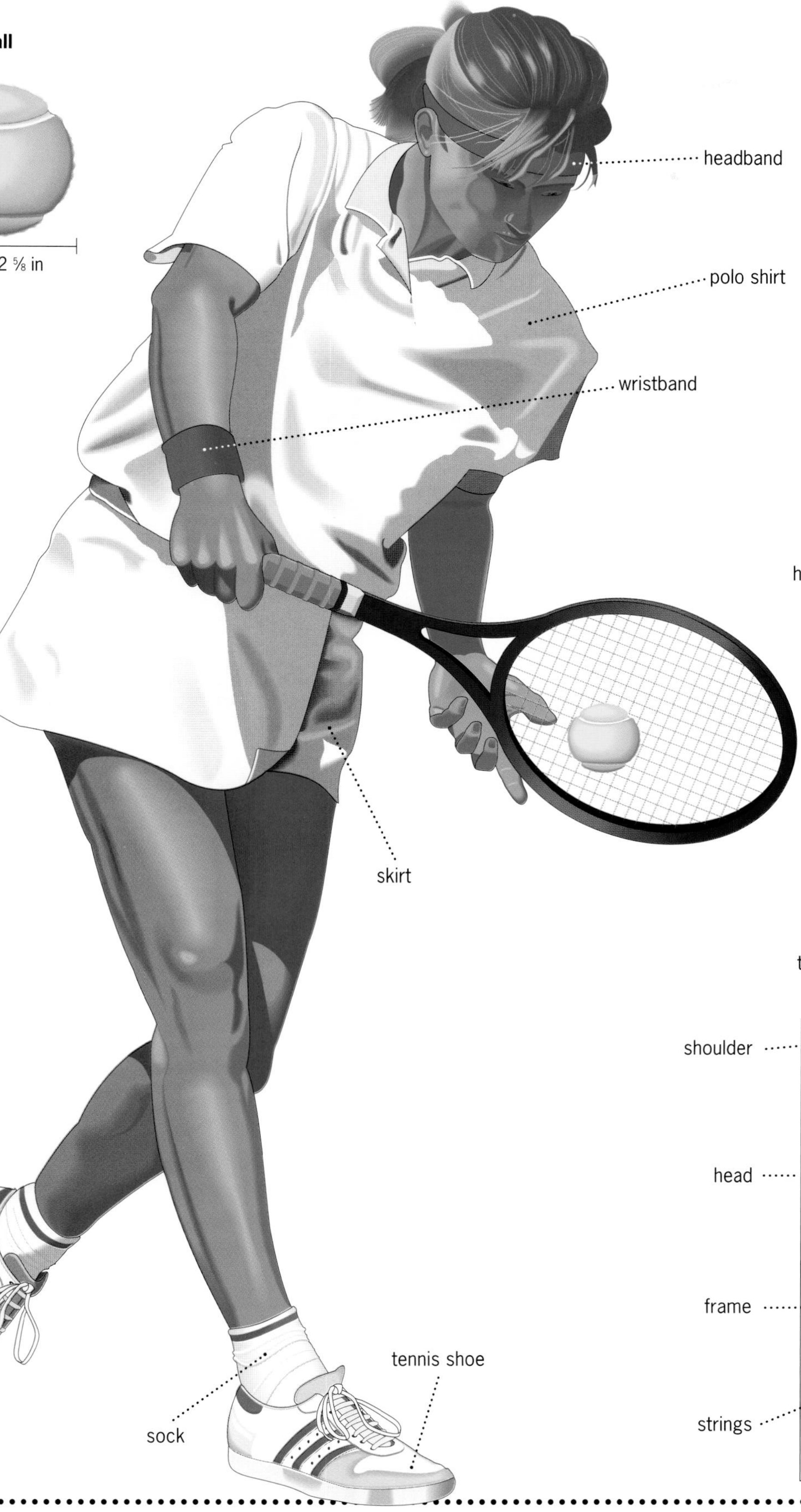

headband

polo shirt

wristband

skirt

sock

tennis shoe

tennis racket

butt

handle

shaft

throat

shoulder

head

frame

strings

181

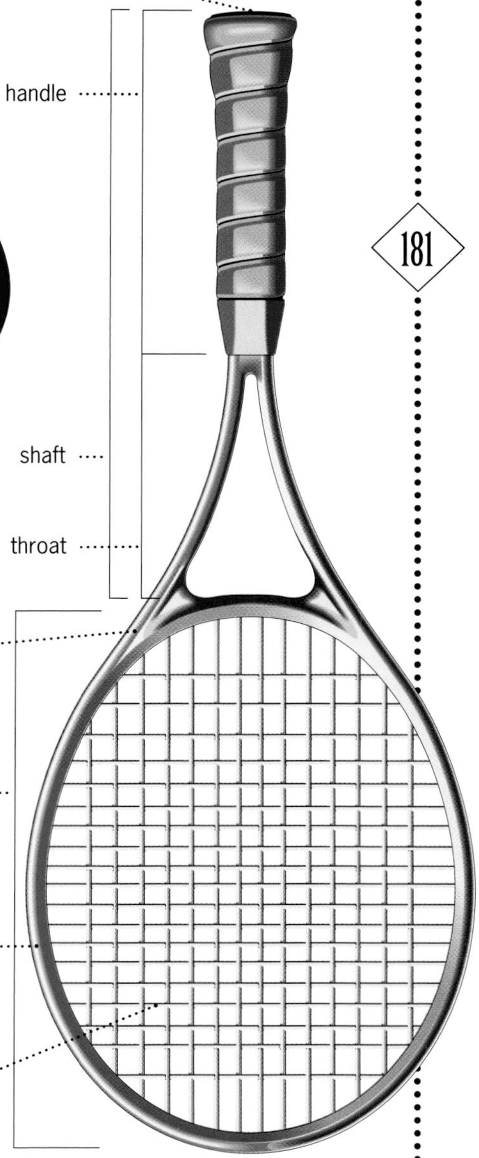

SWIMMING

competitive course

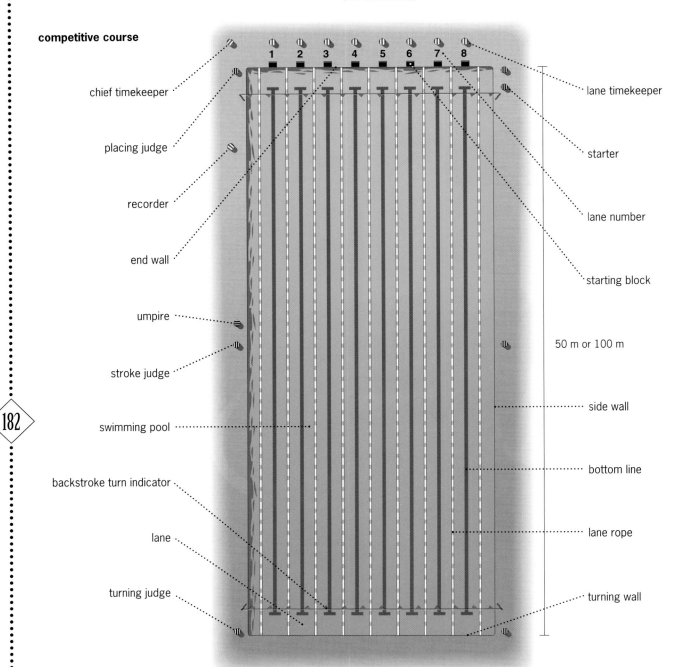

chief timekeeper

placing judge

recorder

end wall

umpire

stroke judge

swimming pool

backstroke turn indicator

lane

turning judge

lane timekeeper

starter

lane number

starting block

50 m or 100 m

side wall

bottom line

lane rope

turning wall

starting block

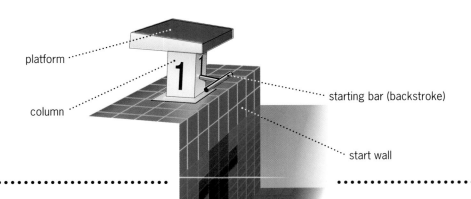

platform

column

starting bar (backstroke)

start wall

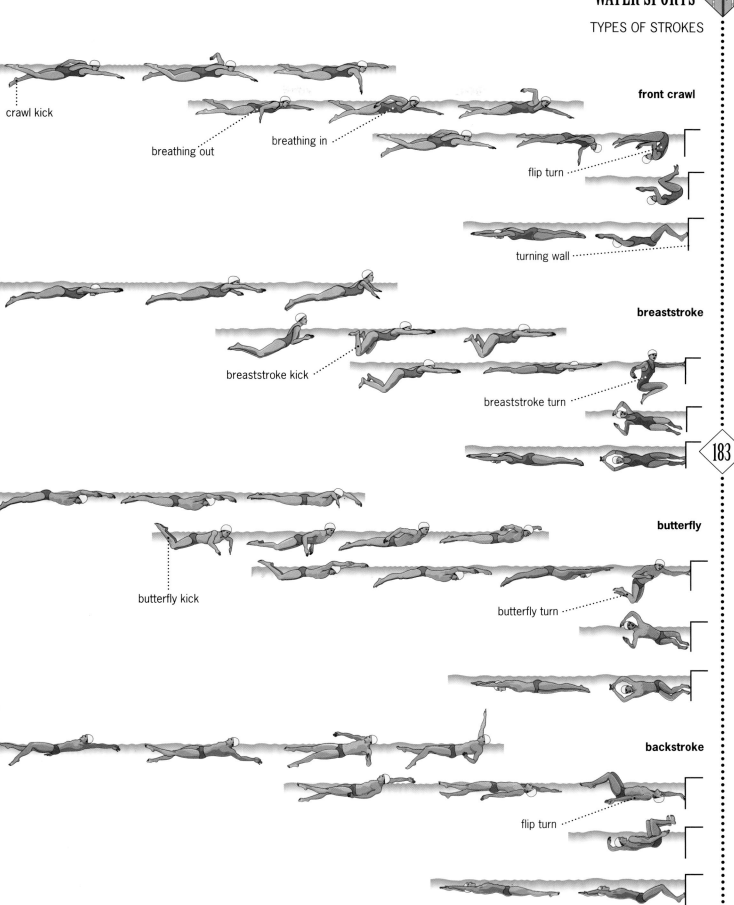

crawl kick

breathing out

breathing in

front crawl

flip turn

turning wall

breaststroke kick

breaststroke

breaststroke turn

183

butterfly kick

butterfly

butterfly turn

backstroke

flip turn

SAILBOARD

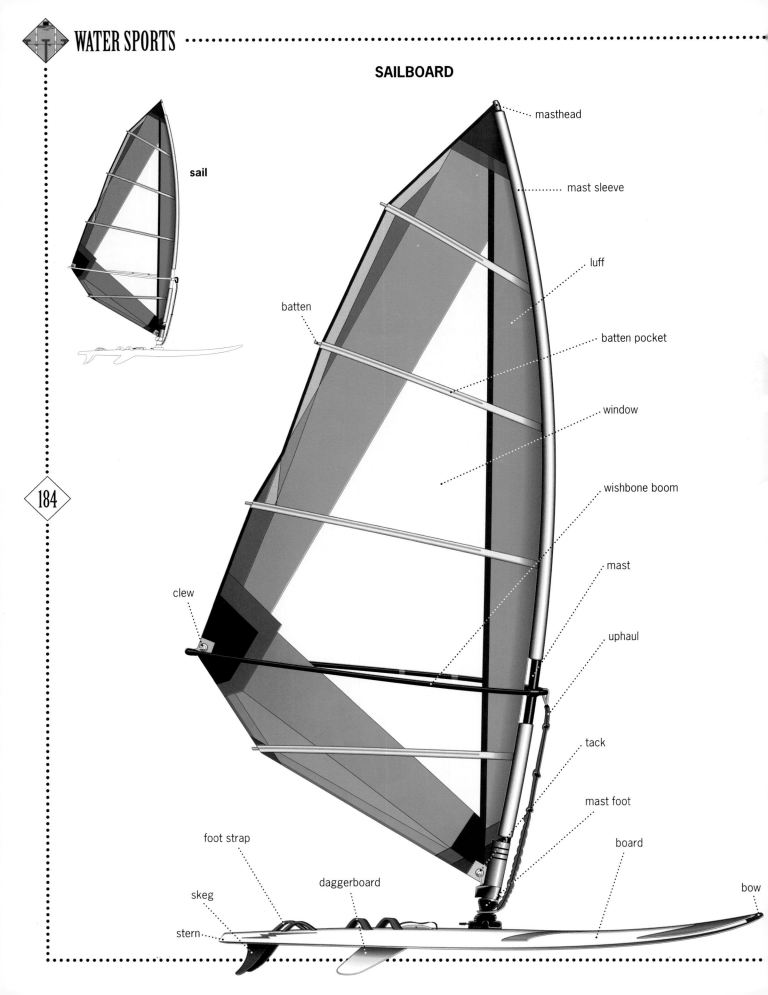

sail

masthead

mast sleeve

luff

batten pocket

batten

window

wishbone boom

mast

uphaul

clew

tack

mast foot

board

foot strap

daggerboard

bow

skeg

stern

SKATING

in-line skate

inner boot

upper shell

adjusting buckle

boot

axle

wheel

truck

heel stop

speed skate

hockey skate

tendon guard

boot

toe box

point

blade

figure skate

hook

backstay

eyelet

boot

stanchion

edge

blade

tongue

lace

sole

toe pick

skate guard

185

SKIING

alpine skier

ski boot

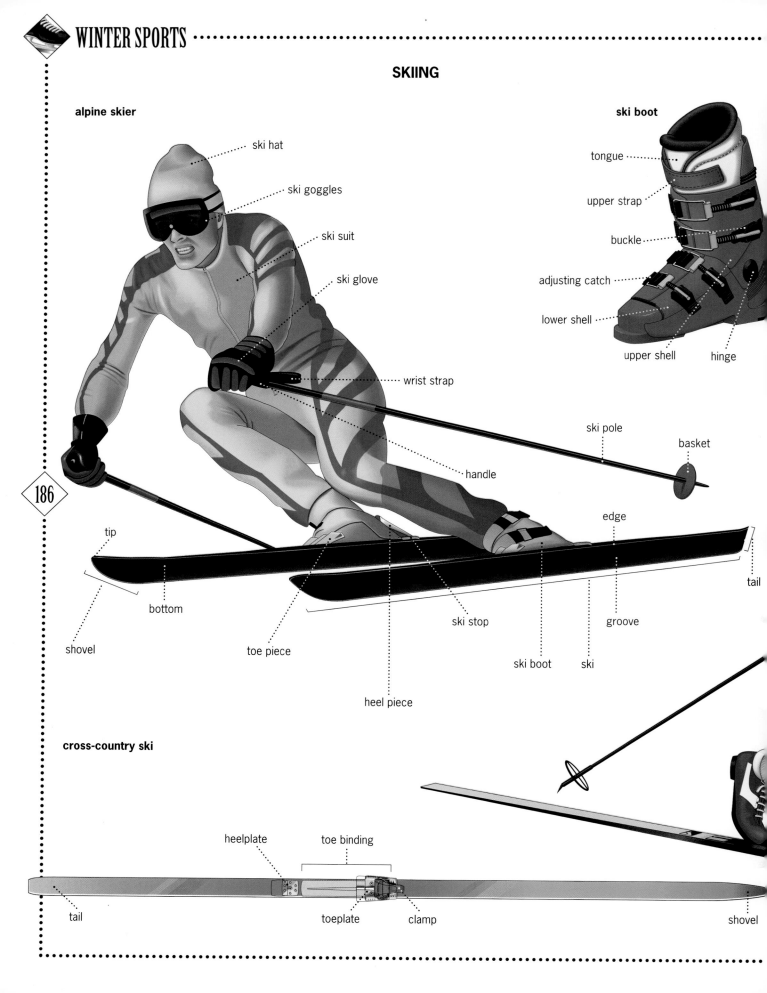

ski hat

ski goggles

ski suit

ski glove

tongue

upper strap

buckle

adjusting catch

lower shell

upper shell   hinge

wrist strap

ski pole

basket

handle

edge

tip

tail

bottom

ski stop

groove

shovel

toe piece

ski boot   ski

heel piece

cross-country ski

heelplate   toe binding

tail

toeplate   clamp

shovel

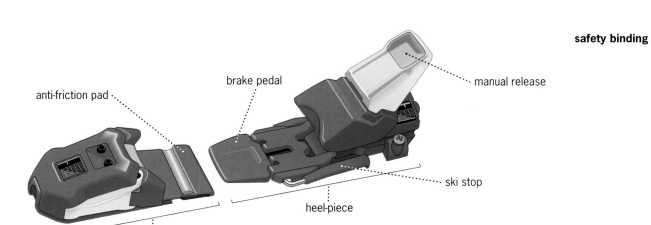

safety binding

manual release

brake pedal

anti-friction pad

ski stop

heel-piece

toe-piece

cross-country skier

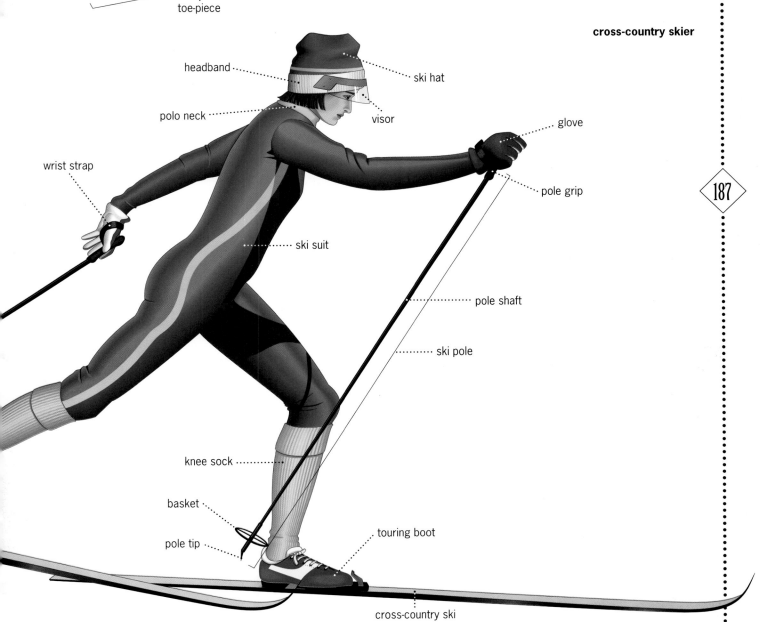

headband

ski hat

polo neck

visor

glove

wrist strap

pole grip

ski suit

pole shaft

ski pole

knee sock

basket

touring boot

pole tip

cross-country ski

GYMNASTICS

pommel horse

horse

base

neck

saddle

croup

pommel

fastening system

vault

balance beam

springboard

trampoline

safety pad

bed

leg

spring

frame

uneven bars

horizontal bar; high bar

steel bar

upright

rings

frame

cable

parallel bars

ring

fastening system

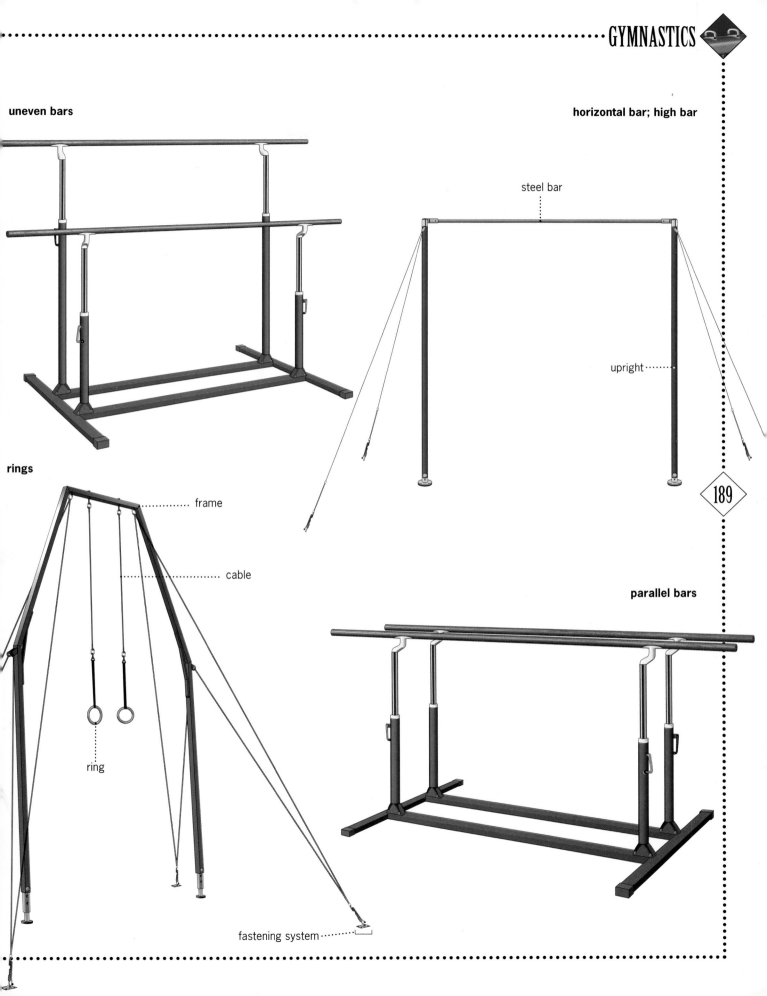

TENTS

two-person tent

rainfly

door

awning

guy line

strainer

zipper

inner tent

stake

190 MAJOR TYPES OF TENTS

wagon tent

wall tent

pup tent

dome tent

pop-up tent

family tent

one-person tent

SLEEPING EQUIPMENT

foam pad

self-inflating mattress

BEDS AND MATTRESSES

inflator

inflator-deflator

folding cot

air mattress

mummy

semi-mummy

SLEEPING BAGS

rectangular

CAMPING EQUIPMENT

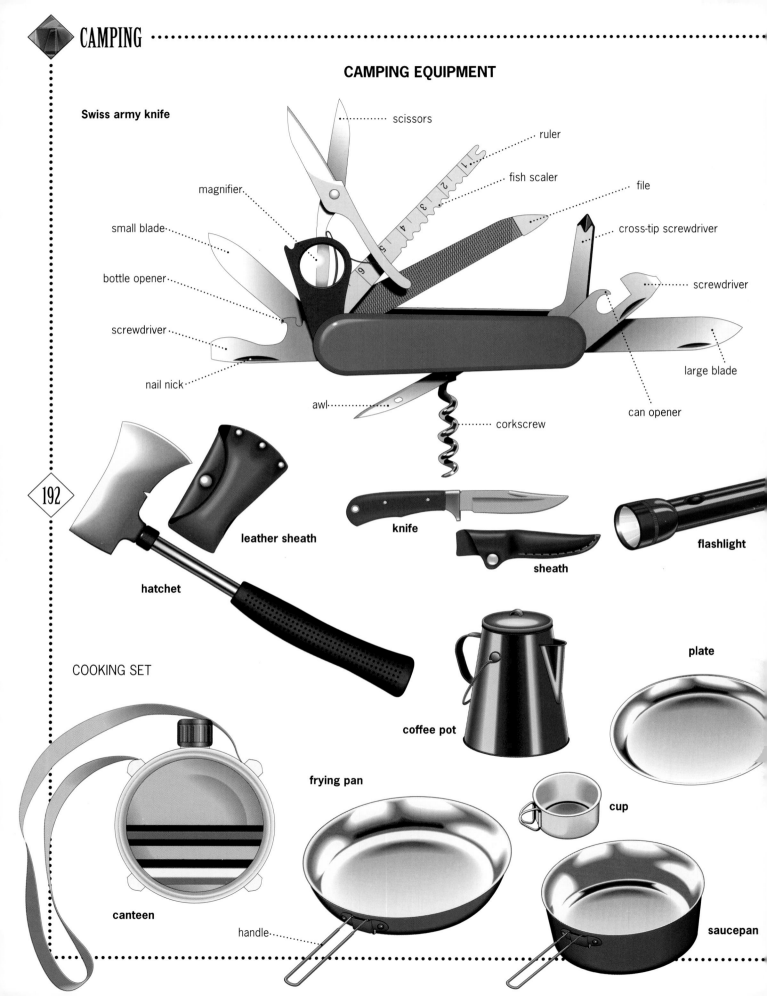

Swiss army knife

scissors

ruler

magnifier

fish scaler

file

small blade

cross-tip screwdriver

bottle opener

screwdriver

screwdriver

nail nick

large blade

awl

can opener

corkscrew

leather sheath

knife

flashlight

hatchet

sheath

plate

COOKING SET

coffee pot

frying pan

cup

canteen

handle

saucepan

backpack

top flap

shoulder strap

side compression strap

internal frame

waist belt

tightening buckle

strap loop

front compression strap

first aid kit

magnetic compass

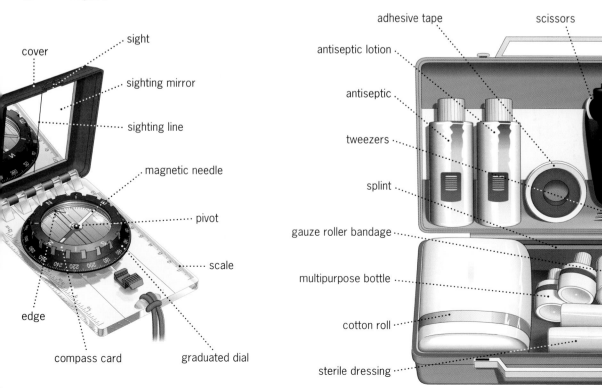

cover

sight

sighting mirror

sighting line

magnetic needle

pivot

scale

edge

compass card

graduated dial

adhesive tape

antiseptic lotion

antiseptic

tweezers

splint

gauze roller bandage

multipurpose bottle

cotton roll

sterile dressing

scissors

small bandage

CARD GAMES

heart

diamond

club

spade

Ace

King

Queen

Jack

Joker

DICE

DOMINOES

poker die

ordinary die

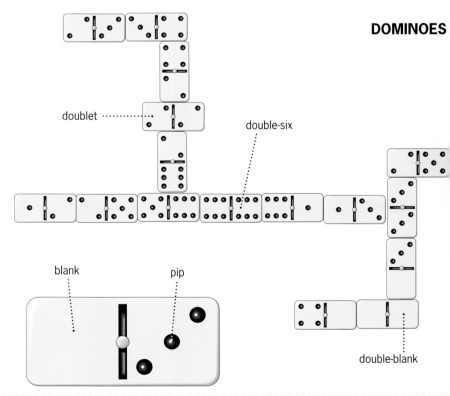

doublet

double-six

blank

pip

double-blank

CHESS

chessboard

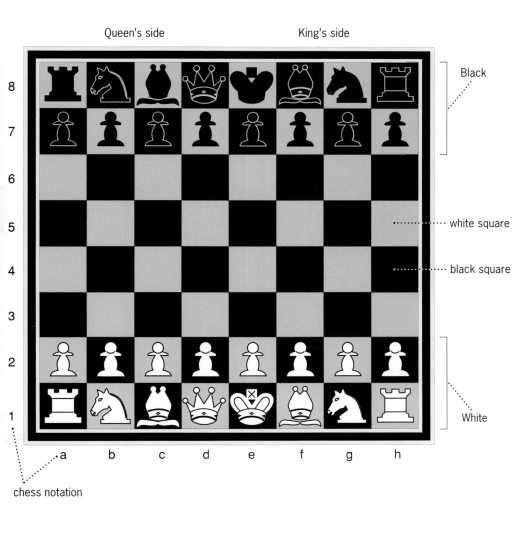

Queen's side   King's side

Black

white square

black square

White

a   b   c   d   e   f   g   h

chess notation

Pawn   **Knight**

Bishop   **Rook**

types of movements

vertical movement

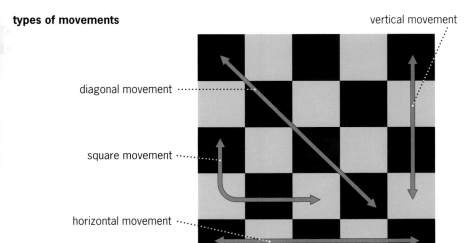

diagonal movement

square movement

horizontal movement

Queen   **King**

BACKGAMMON

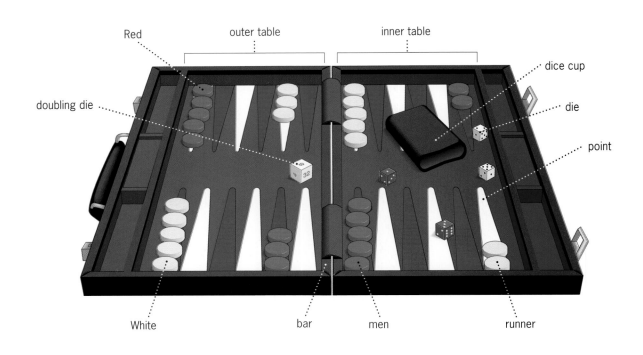

Red

outer table

inner table

dice cup

doubling die

die

point

White

bar

men

runner

CHECKERS

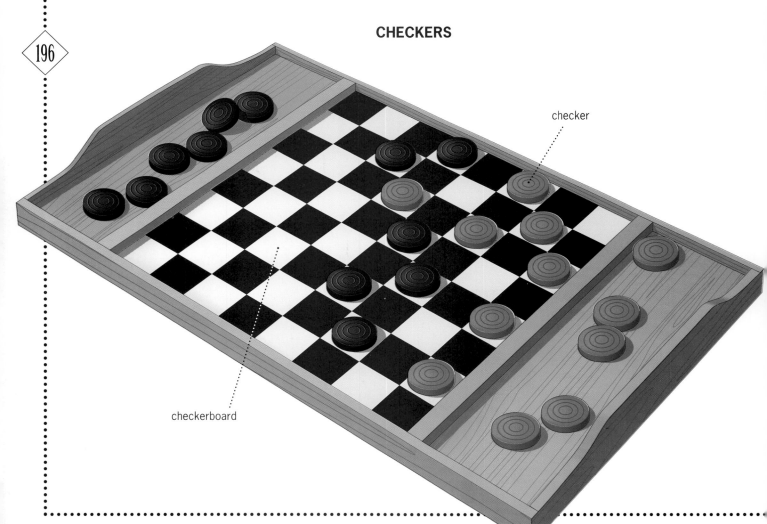

checker

checkerboard

VIDEO ENTERTAINMENT SYSTEM

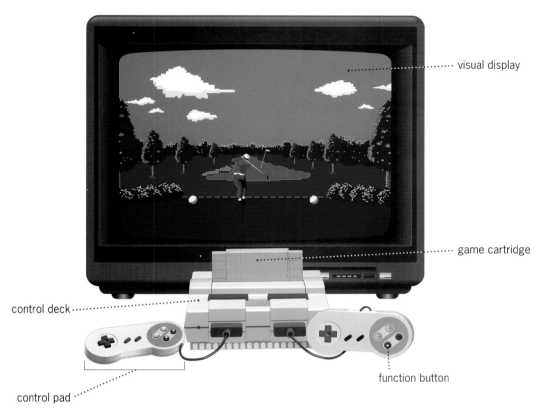

visual display

game cartridge

control deck

function button

control pad

GAME OF DARTS

dart

dartboard

flight

segment score number

shaft

double ring

triple ring

barrel

bull's-eye

25 ring

point

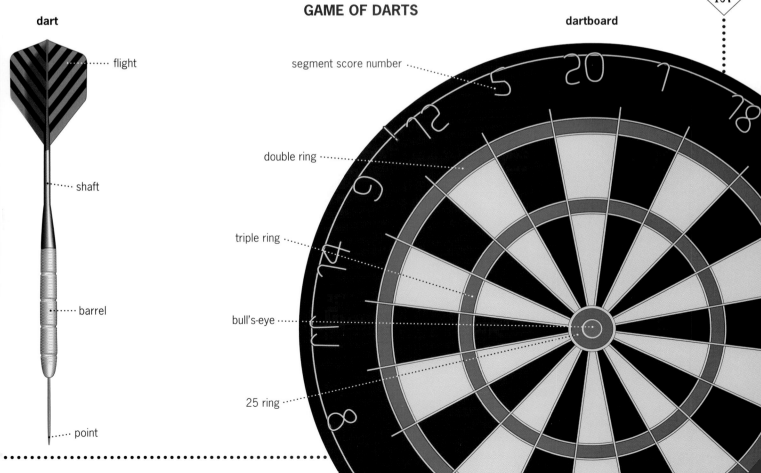

MEASURE OF TIME

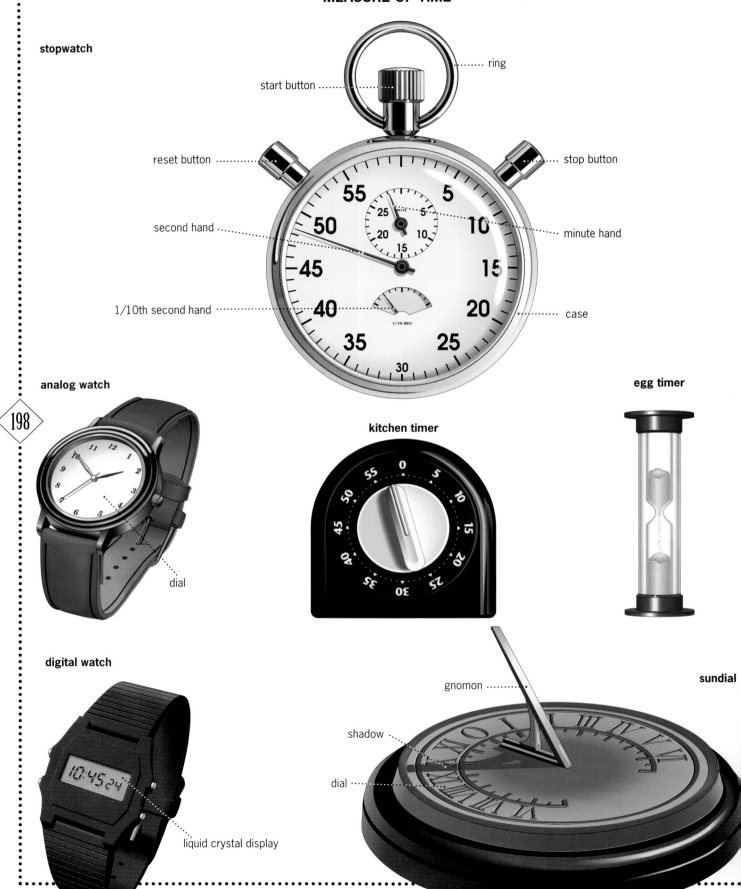

stopwatch

ring

start button

reset button

stop button

second hand

minute hand

1/10th second hand

case

1/10 SEC

analog watch

dial

kitchen timer

egg timer

digital watch

10:45 24

liquid crystal display

gnomon

shadow

dial

sundial

MEASURE OF TEMPERATURE

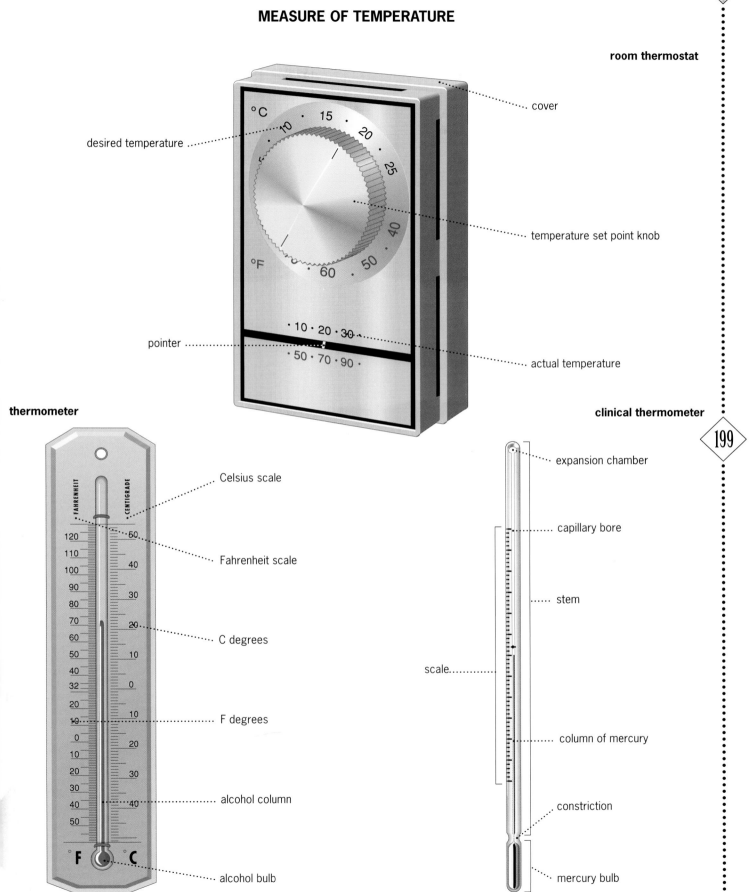

room thermostat

cover

desired temperature

°C

15

10

20

5

25

40

°F

50

60

temperature set point knob

pointer

· 10 · 20 · 30 ·

· 50 · 70 · 90 ·

actual temperature

thermometer

clinical thermometer

FAHRENHEIT

CENTIGRADE

Celsius scale

Fahrenheit scale

expansion chamber

capillary bore

120 · 50

110 · 40

100

90 · 30

80

70 · 20

60

50 · 10

40

32 · 0

20

10 · 10

0

10 · 20

20

30 · 30

40 · 40

50

C degrees

F degrees

alcohol column

stem

scale

column of mercury

constriction

F °C

alcohol bulb

mercury bulb

 **MEASURING DEVICES**

MEASURE OF WEIGHT

balance

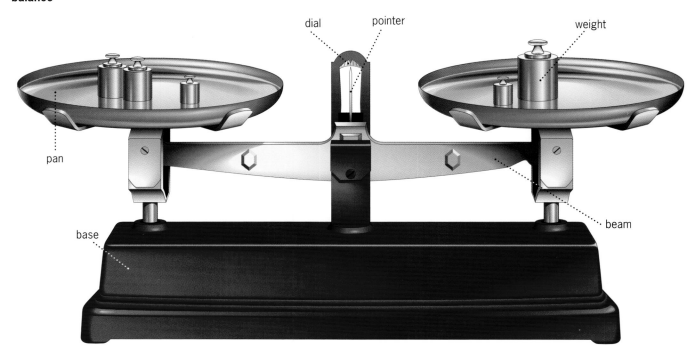

dial

pointer

weight

pan

base

beam

steelyard

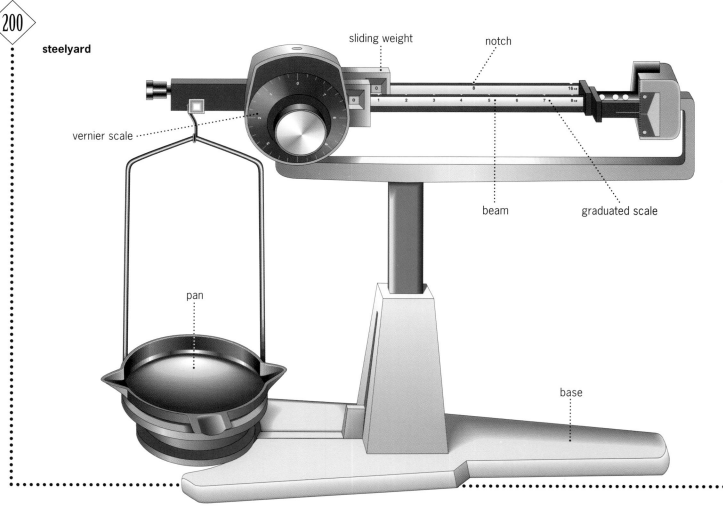

sliding weight

notch

vernier scale

pan

beam

graduated scale

base

MEASURING DEVICES

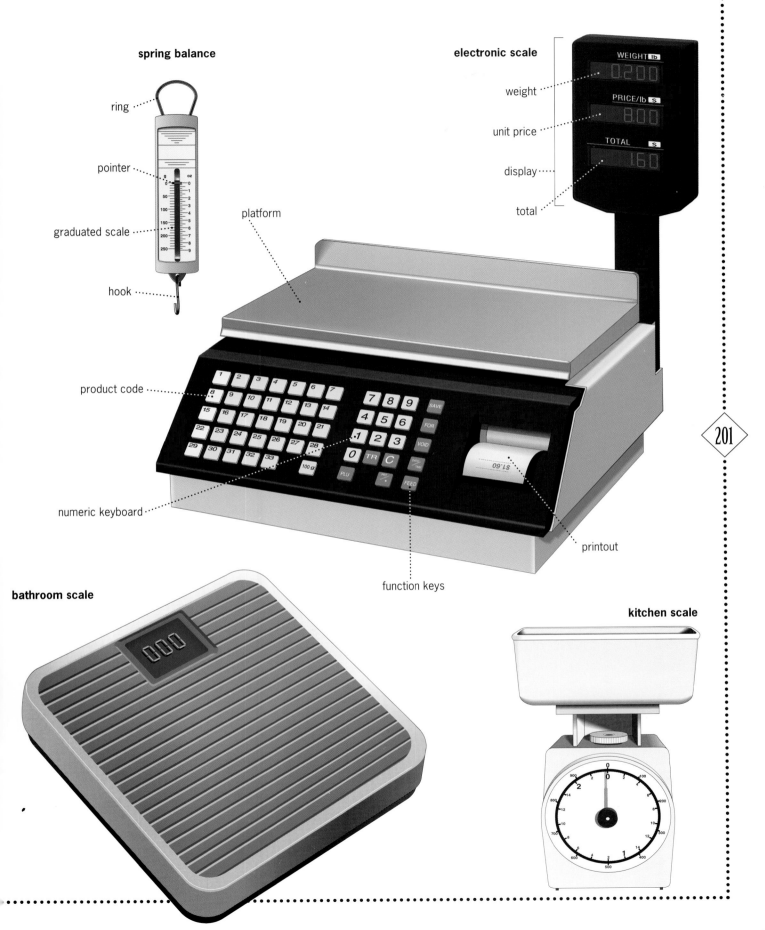

spring balance

ring

pointer

graduated scale

hook

electronic scale

weight

unit price

display

total

platform

product code

numeric keyboard

function keys

printout

bathroom scale

kitchen scale

OIL

GROUND TRANSPORT

PROSPECTING

surface prospecting

DRILLING

drilling rig

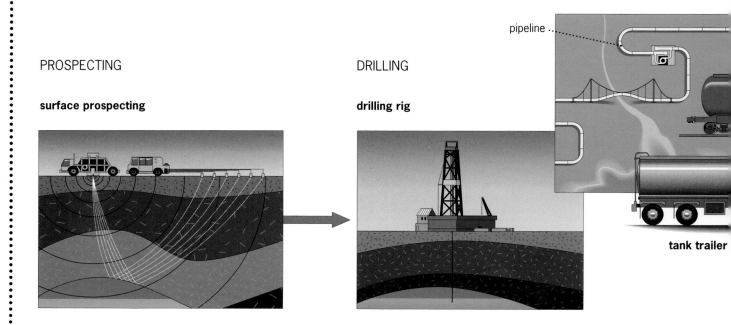

pipeline

tank trailer

offshore prospecting

production platform

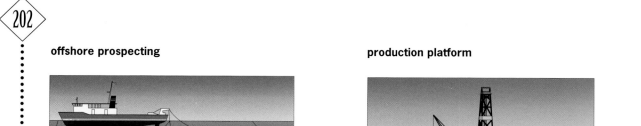

shock wave

seismographic recording

petroleum trap   blasting charge

MARITIME TRANSPORT

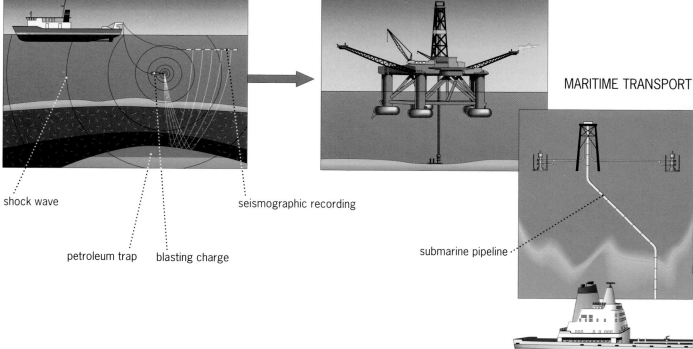

submarine pipeline

REFINERY PRODUCTS

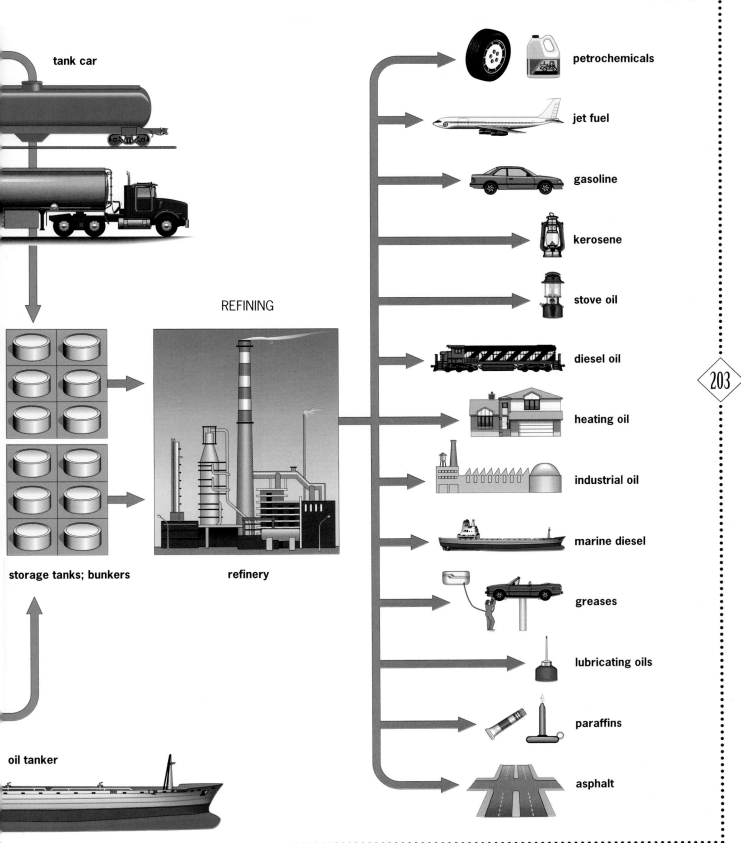

tank car

REFINING

storage tanks; bunkers

refinery

oil tanker

petrochemicals

jet fuel

gasoline

kerosene

stove oil

diesel oil

heating oil

industrial oil

marine diesel

greases

lubricating oils

paraffins

asphalt

HYDROELECTRIC ENERGY

hydroelectric complex

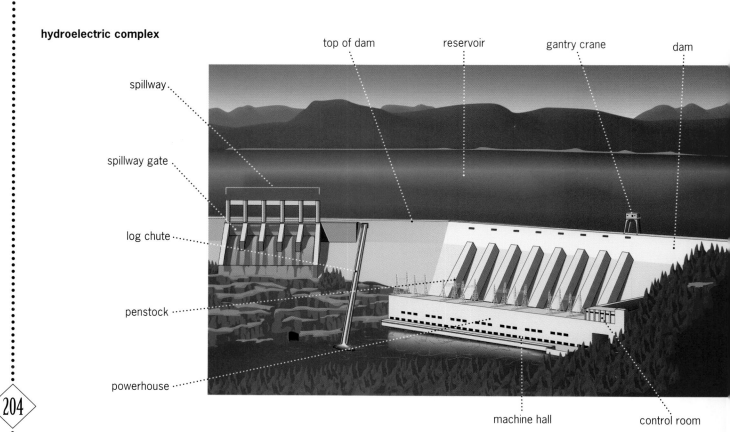

top of dam

reservoir

gantry crane

dam

spillway

spillway gate

log chute

penstock

powerhouse

machine hall

control room

cross section of hydroelectric power station

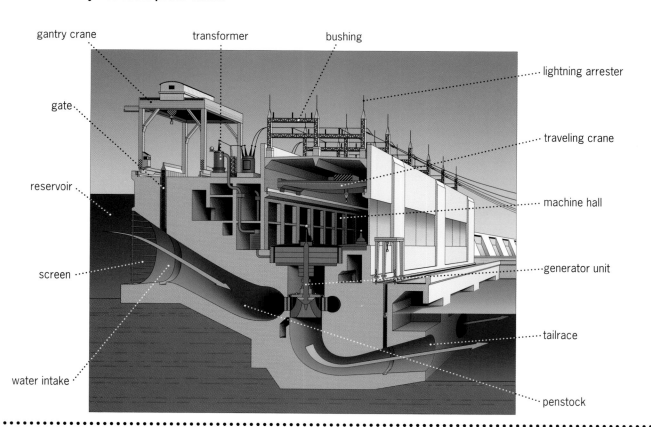

gantry crane

transformer

bushing

lightning arrester

gate

traveling crane

reservoir

machine hall

screen

generator unit

water intake

tailrace

penstock

electric circuit

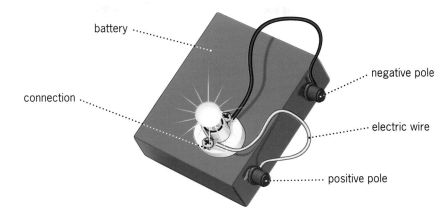

battery ....

connection ....

negative pole

electric wire

positive pole

steps in production of electricity

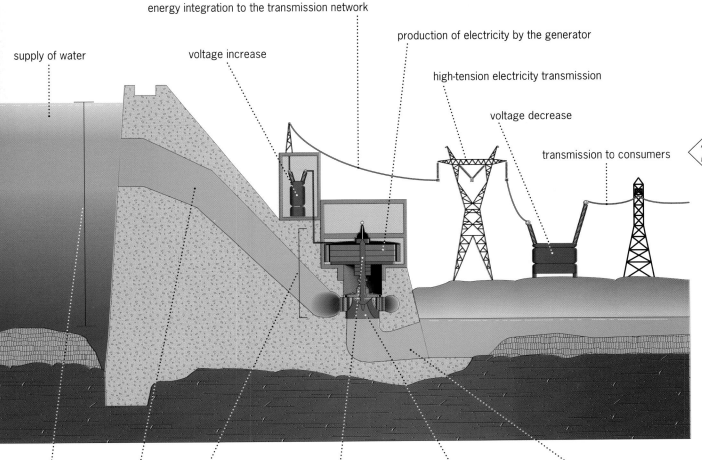

energy integration to the transmission network

production of electricity by the generator

supply of water

voltage increase

high-tension electricity transmission

voltage decrease

transmission to consumers

head of water

turbined water draining

water under pressure

transmission of the rotative movement to the rotor

transformation of mechanical work into electricity

rotation of the turbine

NUCLEAR ENERGY

nuclear power station

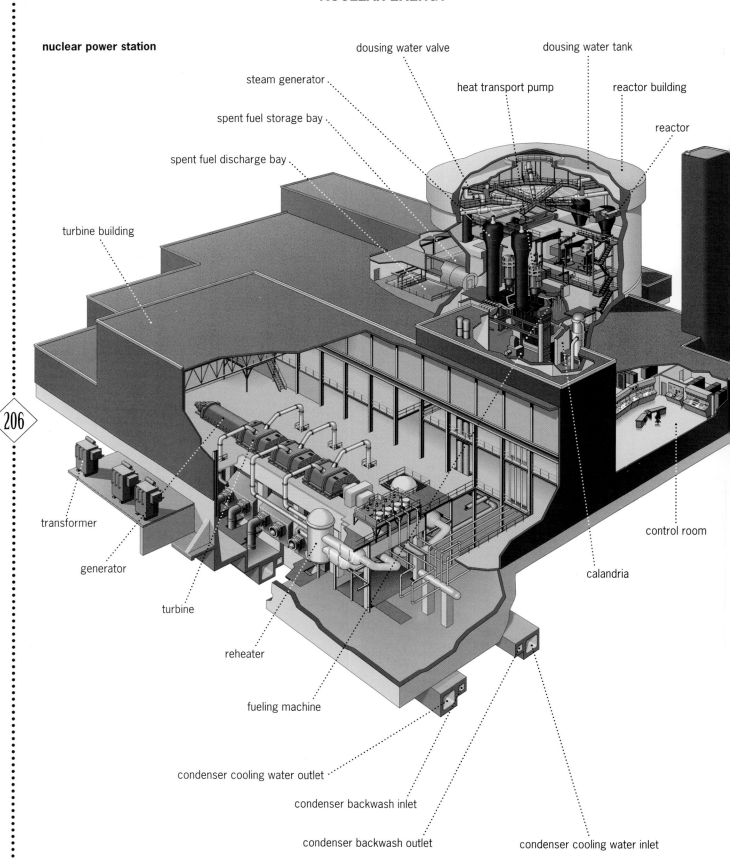

dousing water valve

dousing water tank

steam generator

heat transport pump

reactor building

spent fuel storage bay

reactor

spent fuel discharge bay

turbine building

transformer

generator

turbine

reheater

fueling machine

control room

calandria

condenser cooling water outlet

condenser backwash inlet

condenser backwash outlet

condenser cooling water inlet

production of electricity from nuclear energy

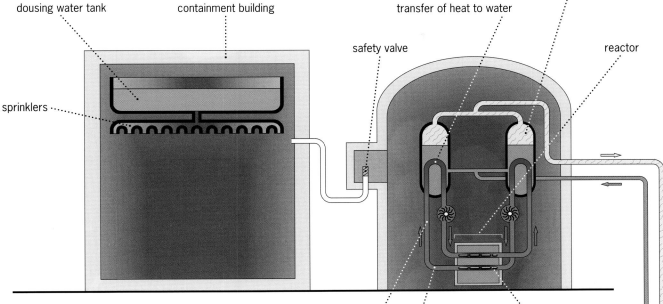

water turns into steam

dousing water tank

containment building

transfer of heat to water

safety valve

reactor

sprinklers

coolant transfers the heat to the steam generator

fission of uranium fuel

heat production

207

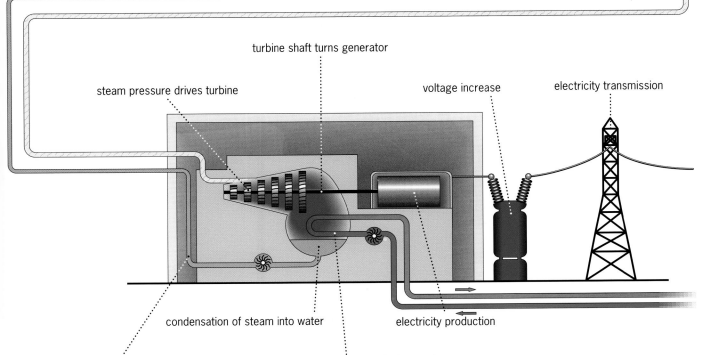

turbine shaft turns generator

steam pressure drives turbine

voltage increase

electricity transmission

condensation of steam into water

electricity production

water is pumped back into the steam generator

water cools the used steam

SOLAR ENERGY

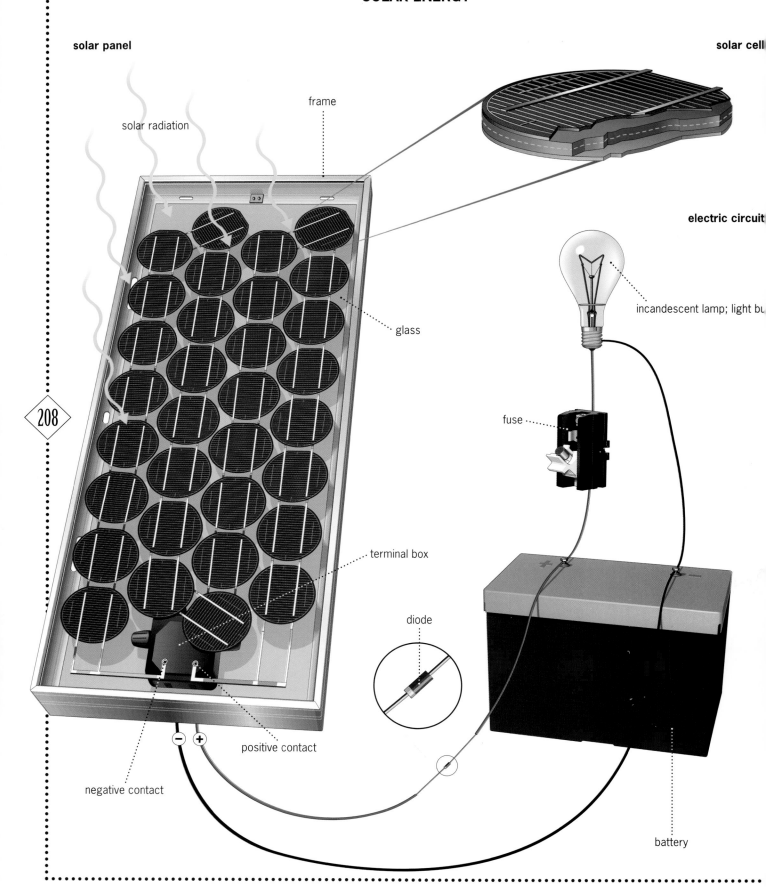

solar panel

solar cell

frame

solar radiation

electric circuit

incandescent lamp; light bu

glass

fuse

terminal box

diode

positive contact

negative contact

battery

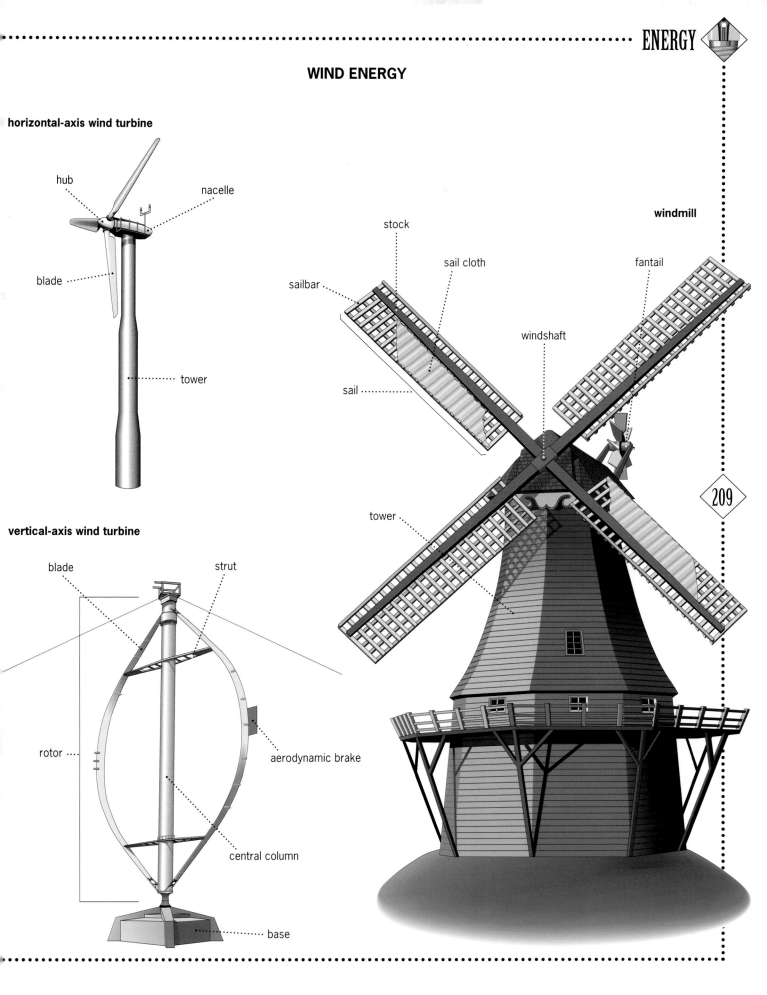

WIND ENERGY

horizontal-axis wind turbine

hub

nacelle

blade

tower

windmill

stock

sail cloth

fantail

sailbar

windshaft

sail

tower

vertical-axis wind turbine

blade

strut

rotor

aerodynamic brake

central column

base

209

FIRE PREVENTION

fire hose

portable fire extinguisher

fire hydrant

operating nut

water supply point

cap

upright pipe

fire engine

elevating cylinder

turntable mounting

telescopic boom

spotlight

storage compartment

outrigger

hydrant intake

control panel

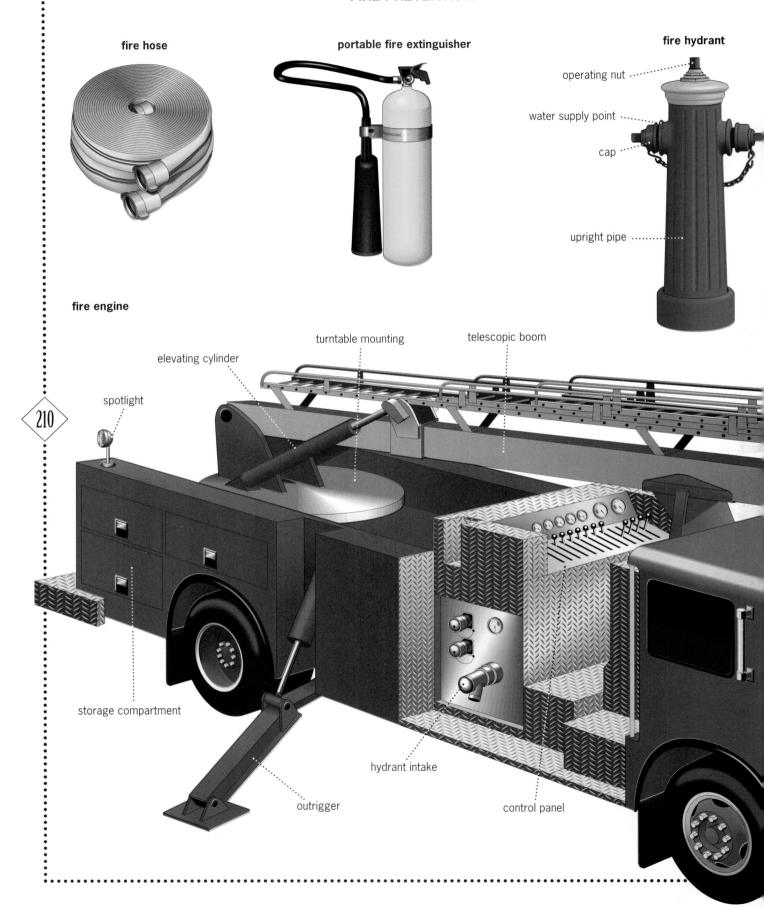

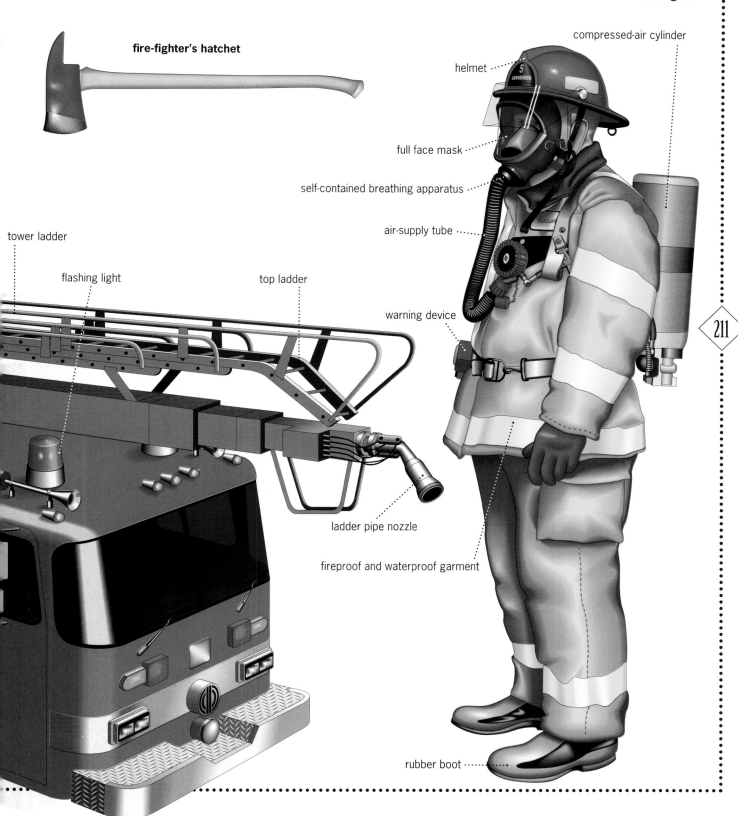

pike pole

fire-fighter's hatchet

fire-fighter

compressed-air cylinder

helmet

full face mask

self-contained breathing apparatus

air-supply tube

tower ladder

flashing light

top ladder

warning device

ladder pipe nozzle

fireproof and waterproof garment

rubber boot

211

HEAVY VEHICLES

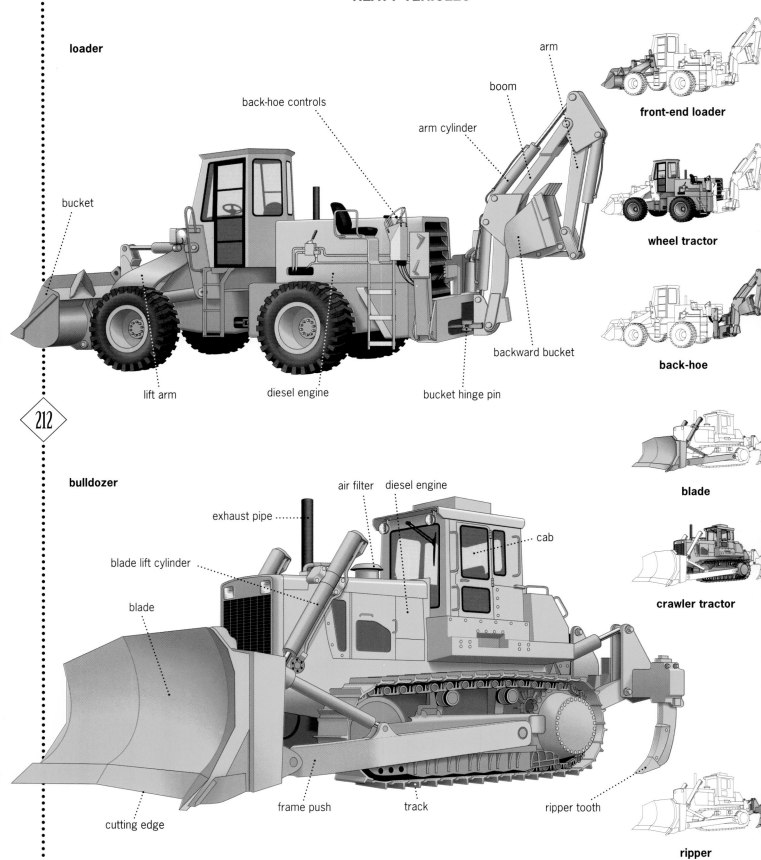

loader

back-hoe controls

arm

boom

arm cylinder

bucket

backward bucket

lift arm

diesel engine

bucket hinge pin

front-end loader

wheel tractor

back-hoe

blade

crawler tractor

ripper

bulldozer

air filter

diesel engine

exhaust pipe

cab

blade lift cylinder

blade

cutting edge

frame push

track

ripper tooth

212

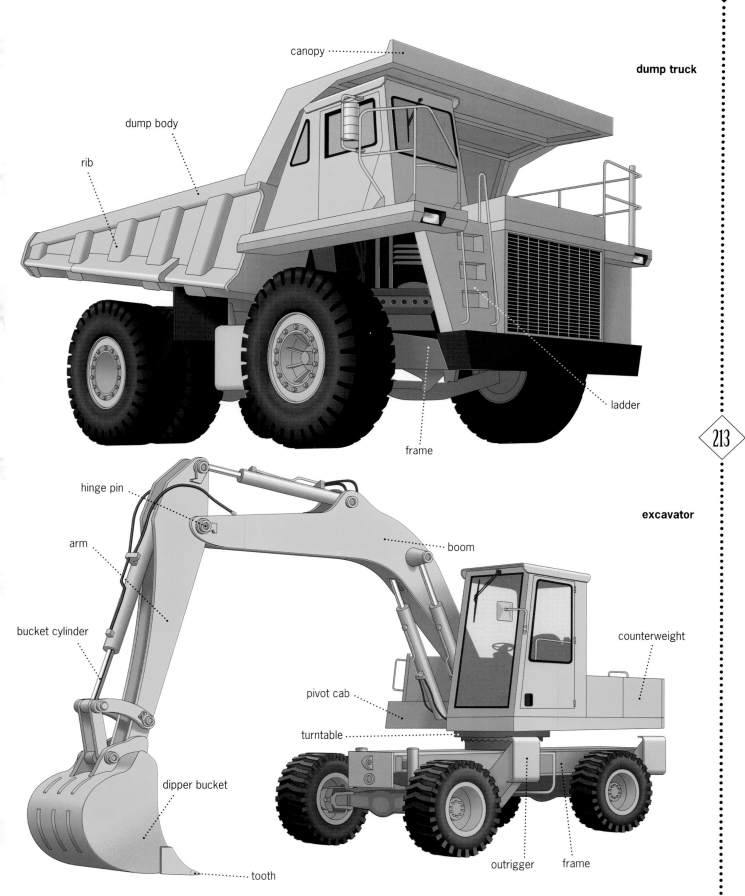

canopy

dump truck

dump body

rib

ladder

frame

213

hinge pin

excavator

arm

boom

bucket cylinder

counterweight

pivot cab

turntable

dipper bucket

tooth

outrigger

frame

HEAVY MACHINERY

tower crane

jib

trolley

trolley pulley

crane runway

operator's cab

hoisting rope

hoisting block

hook

street sweeper

collection body

central brush

watering tube

lateral brush

snowblower

projection device

worm

tower mast

counterweight

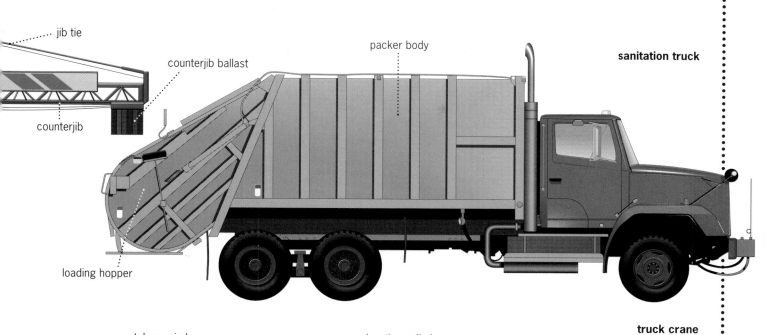

jib tie

counterjib ballast

packer body

sanitation truck

counterjib

loading hopper

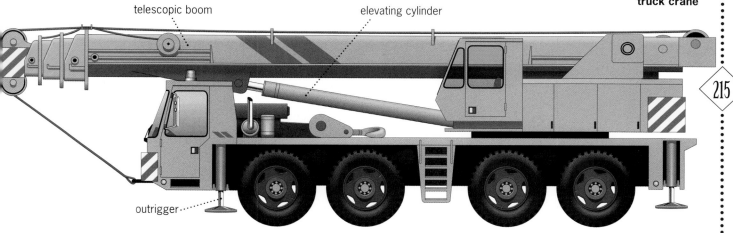

truck crane

telescopic boom

elevating cylinder

215

outrigger

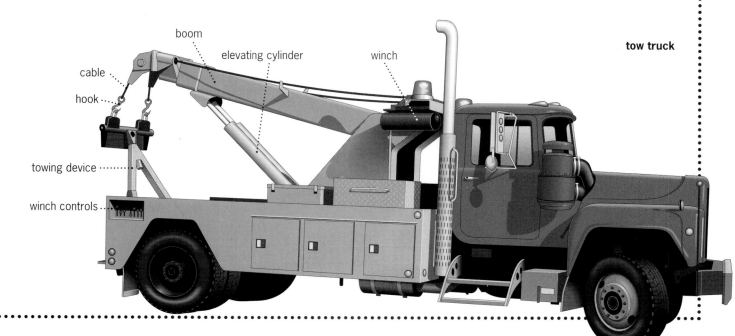

boom

tow truck

elevating cylinder

winch

cable

hook

towing device

winch controls

COMMON SYMBOLS

women's rest room

men's rest room

wheelchair access

hospital

telephone

no smoking

camping (tent)

camping prohibited

stop at intersection

SAFETY SYMBOLS

corrosive

electrical hazard

explosive

flammable

radioactive

poisonous

PROTECTION

eye protection

ear protection

head protection

hand protection

foot protection

respiratory system protection

1/10th second hand 198.
25 ring, dartboard 197.
25-yard line, field hockey 175.
35 mm still camera 149.

A

a 160.
abdomen 61.
abdomen 57, 59, 74.
ablutions fountain 87.
absorbed heat 28.
accelerator pedal 132.
access road 146.
accessory shoe 125, 127.
accidentals, musical notation 161.
accordion 158.
Ace 194.
achene 44.
acid precipitation 31.
acid rain 32, 33.
acoustic guitar 162.
action of wind 31.
actual temperature 199.
Adam's apple 78.
add in memory 154.
add key 154.
adhesive tape 193.
adjustable channel 109.
adjustable wrench 109.
adjusting band 128.
adjusting buckle 185.
adjusting catch 186.
adjusting screw 109.
adjustment slide 112.
aerodynamic brake 209.
aerosol 29.
Africa 19.
aftermast 141.
aileron 144.
air compressor 139.
air concentrator 122.
air conditioner 29.
air filter 139, 212.
air horn 134.
air inlet 145.
air mattress 191.
air pressure, measure 23.
air pump 134.
air space 75.
air unit 121.
air vent 132.
air-outlet grille 122.
air-supply tube 211.
AIRPORT 146.
airport 27.
airport ground equipment 146.
ala 84.
albumen 75.
alcohol bulb 199.
alcohol column 199.
alighting board 59.
alley 180.
almond 45.
alpine skier 186.
alternator 138.
altitude clamp 11.
altitude fine adjustment 11.
AM antenna 128.
ambulatory 89.
AMPHIBIANS 60.
amphibians 60.
amplifier 128.
anal fin 63.
analog watch 198.
anchor-windlass room 142.
anemometer 23.
ankle 78.
ankle boot 119.
annual ring 40.
annular eclipse 10.
ant 56.
Antarctic Circle 12.
Antarctica 18.
antenna 57, 58, 61, 129, 131, 145, 174.
antennule 61.
anther 38.
anti-friction pad 187.
anti-slip shoe 111.
anti-torque tail rotor 145.
antiseptic 193.
antiseptic lotion 193.
aortic arch 81.
appendix 81.

apple 46.
appoggiatura, musical notation 161.
apricot 45.
apron 97, 146.
aquatic bird 74.
Arabian camel 73.
archipelago 26.
Arctic 18.
Arctic Circle 12, 24.
Arctic Ocean 19.
arm 67, 79, 97, 155, 212, 213.
arm guard 170.
arm pad 177.
armchair 96, 97.
armpit 78.
arterial blood 81.
artery, anterior tibial 81.
artery, common carotid 81.
artery, femoral 81.
artichoke 49.
artichoke, Jerusalem 51.
ash layer 15.
Asia 19.
asparagus 52.
asphalt 203.
asteroid belt 6.
Atlantic Ocean 18.
atmosphere 12, 20.
atmospheric pollution 30.
attack line 174.
attack on human beings 31.
attack on nature 31.
attack zone 174.
attacking zone 176.
audio system 129.
auditory canal 83.
auditory nerve 83.
auditory ossicles 83.
auger bit 110.
auricle 83.
Australia 19.
auto reverse 129.
autofocus on/off switch 153.
automatic dialer 124.
automatic drip coffee maker 105.
automobile car 138.
autumn 20.
autumn squash 49.
autumnal equinox 20.
auxiliary handle 110.
avocado 48.
awl 192.
awning 190.
axillary bud 36.
axis of rotation 152.
axle 138, 185.
azimuth clamp 11.
azimuth fine adjustment 11.

B

b 160.
back 66, 67, 75, 79, 97, 101.
back judge 171.
back zone 174.
back, left 175.
back, right 175.
back-hoe 212.
back-hoe controls 212.
backboard 179.
backboard support 179.
backcourt 180.
BACKGAMMON 196.
backguard 107.
backpack 193.
backstay 185.
backstroke 183.
backstroke turn indicator 182.
backup light 133.
backward bucket 212.
bag, drawstring 123.
baggage compartment 145.
baggage conveyor 146.
baggage trailer 147.
bagpipes 158.
bailey 88.
balaclava 114.
balalaika 158.
balance 200.
balance beam 188.
balancer 185.
ball boy 180.
ballast 140.
ballerina 119.

ballpoint pen 150.
banana 48.
band 129.
banjo 158.
bar 123, 196.
bar line 160.
bar stool 96.
BARK, FOUR-MASTED 141.
bark, inner 40.
bark, outer 40.
barograph 23.
barrel 122, 197.
base 99, 140, 152, 155, 188, 200, 209.
base plate 110.
BASEBALL 168.
baseball 168.
baseball, field 169.
baseline 180.
baseman, first 169.
baseman, second 169.
baseman, third 169.
basement 93.
basement window 93.
basic source of food 28.
basket 179.
basket 105, 178, 186, 187.
BASKETBALL 178.
basketball 179.
basketball 179.
basketball player 179.
basketball, court 178.
bass bridge 159.
bass clarinet 167.
bass drum 166, 167.
bass guitar 163.
bass keyboard 158.
bass pickup 163.
bass register 158.
bass tone control 163.
bassoon 165.
bassoon 167.
bat 168.
bat 168.
bathrobe 116.
bathroom scales 201.
batten 184.
batten pocket 184.
batter 168.
batter 169.
batter head 166.
batter's helmet 168.
battery 127, 138, 205, 208.
battery eject switch 127.
batting glove 168.
bayonet base 99.
beach 14.
beam 200.
bean sprouts 52.
beater 105.
beater ejector 105.
beaver 70.
BED 95.
bed 188, 191.
bedrock 34.
beer mug 100.
beet 51.
begonia 38.
belfry 89.
bell 164, 165.
bell brace 165.
bell tower 89.
bellows 158.
belly 67.
belt 112.
belt carrier 112.
belt highway 27.
bench 96.
beret 114.
Bering Sea 19.
Bermuda shorts 115.
berries, major types 44.
BERRY FRUITS 44.
berry, section 44.
BICYCLE 136.
bicycle bag 136.
bile duct 81.
bill 74.
bills, principal types 74.
birch 42.
BIRD 74.
bird feeder 75.
bird of prey 74.
bird's nest 75.
bird, morphology 74.
birdhouse 75.

BIRDS, EXAMPLES 76.
Bishop 195.
bitter taste 84.
Black 195.
black bass 63.
black currant 44.
Black Sea 19.
black square 195.
blackboard 152.
bladder 81.
blade 212.
blade 36, 101, 109, 110, 111, 177, 185, 209, 212.
blade guard 110.
blade tilting mechanism 110.
blank 194.
blanket 95.
blasting charge 202.
blastodisc 75.
blender 105.
blocker 177.
blouse 114.
blow pipe 158.
blue 157.
blue line 176.
blue-green 157.
blueberry 44.
board 184.
boarding step 145.
boarding walkway 147.
boards 176.
bodies, types 133.
body 130.
body 162, 163, 165.
body flap 148.
body pad 177.
bolster 95.
bolt 109.
bongos 166.
book bag 151.
boom 212, 213, 215.
booster parachute 148.
boot 119.
boot 185.
bottle opener 102.
bottle opener 192.
bottom 186.
bottom line 182.
boulevard 90.
bow 162.
bow 142, 184.
bow thruster 142.
bow window 92.
bowl 101.
bowsprit 141.
box car 138.
box spring 95.
boxer shorts 112.
bra 116.
brake cable 137.
brake caliper 135.
brake lever 137.
brake light 133.
brake pedal 132, 187.
branch 43.
branch 40.
branches 40.
brass family 164.
brassiere cup 116.
brattice 88.
bread and butter plate 100.
breast 74.
breast pocket 112.
breast welt pocket 113.
breaststroke 183.
breaststroke kick 183.
breaststroke turn 183.
breathing in 183.
breathing out 183.
bridge 123, 162, 163.
bridge assembly 163.
briefcase 151.
briefs 116.
bristles 111, 122.
broad beans 52.
broccoli 49.
brush 111.
Brussels sprouts 53.
bubble 135.
bucket 212.
bucket hinge pin 212.
buckle 186.
bud 50.
bud, flower 36.
bud, terminal 34, 36.
bugle 164.
built-in microphone 127.

bulb 99.
bulb 99.
bulb vegetables 50.
bulb, energy saving 97.
bulbil 50.
bulk terminal 142.
bulkhead flat car 139.
bull's-eye 197.
bulldozer 212.
bumper 130.
bunkers 203.
burner 104, 107.
bushing 204.
butt 181.
butt end 177.
butter compartment 106.
butter dish 100.
butter knife 101.
BUTTERFLY 57.
butterfly kick 183.
butterfly stroke 183.
butterfly turn 183.
butterfly, hind leg 57, 59.
button 112, 117.
button loop 112.
by-pass runway 146.

C

c 160.
C clef 160.
C-clamp 108.
cab 212.
cabbage lettuce 53.
cabin 143.
cabinet 126.
cable 110, 129, 189, 215.
caboose 139.
calandria 206.
calculator, pocket 154.
calf 68.
calf 79.
Callisto 6.
calyx 38.
cambium 40.
camera body 125.
camera, 35 mm still 149.
camera, pocket 125.
camera, single lens reflex 125.
camera, video 127.
camping (tent) 216.
CAMPING EQUIPMENT 192.
camping prohibited 216.
can opener 102.
can opener 192.
canal lock 142.
canine 70, 85.
cannon 67.
canopy 123, 213.
cantaloupe 49.
canteen 192.
cap 113.
cap 35, 210.
cape 26.
capillary bore 199.
capital 26.
CAR 130, 132.
car lights 133.
car wash 134.
carafe 100.
carafe 105.
carapace 61, 64.
carbon dioxide 33.
CARD GAMES 194.
card reader 124.
cardigan 117.
cardoon 52.
cargo bay door 148.
Caribbean Sea 18.
carnassial 70.
carnation 39.
carnivore's jaw 70.
carnivores 29, 33.
CARPENTRY TOOLS 108.
carpus 80.
carrier 136.
carrot 51.
CARTOGRAPHY 24, 26.
cartridge film 125.
case 108, 154, 159, 198.
casement window 94.
casement window (inward opening) 94.
casing 54.

217

Caspian Sea 19.
casserole 104.
cassette 129.
cassette 129.
cassette compartment 127.
cassette eject switch 127.
cassette film 125.
cassette player 129.
cassette player controls 124, 129.
cassette tape deck 128.
castanets 166.
castanets 167.
CASTLE 88.
castle 88.
CAT 66.
catcher 168.
catcher 169.
catcher's glove 168.
catching glove 177.
catenary 140.
catering vehicle 147.
caterpillar 57.
cathedral 90.
CATHEDRAL, GOTHIC 89.
caudal fin 63.
cauliflower 49.
CAVE 13.
cave 14.
ceiling fixture 98.
celeriac 51.
celery 52.
cell 57, 59.
cello 162.
cello 167.
Celsius scale 199.
center 171, 176, 178.
center back 173, 174.
center circle 173, 178.
center console 132.
center face-off circle 176.
center field 169.
center fielder 169.
center flag 173.
center forward 173, 174, 175.
center half 175.
center hole 129.
center line 171, 175, 176, 178.
center mark 180.
center post 131.
center service line 180.
center spot 173.
center strap 174.
Central America 18.
central brush 214.
central column 209.
central incisor 85.
central nave 87.
central processing unit 154.
cephalothorax 61.
cereal bowl 100.
chain guide 136.
chain wheel 136.
CHAIRS 97.
chaise longue 96.
chameleon 65.
champagne flute 100.
champagne glass 100.
change sign key 154.
channel scan buttons 126.
channel selector controls 126.
chanter 158.
chapel 88.
chapel, Lady 89.
chapel, side 89.
Charleston cymbal 166.
Charon 7.
checker 196.
checkerboard 196.
CHECKERS 196.
cheek 66, 78.
cheese knife 101.
cherimoya 48.
cherry 45.
CHESS 195.
chess notation 195.
chessboard 195.
chest 67, 78.
chest protector 168, 170.
chestnut 67.
chevet 89.
chick 68.
chick peas 52.
chicory 53.
chief timekeeper 182.
chilli 49.
chimney 93.
chin 74, 78.

chin protector 135.
chin rest 162.
chin strap 170.
China Sea 19.
Chinese cabbage 53.
chives 50.
choir 89.
chrysalis 57.
chrysalis 59.
chuck 110.
chuck key 110.
church 91.
ciliate 37.
circle 156.
circular body 158.
circular saw 110.
circular saw blade 110.
cirque 9.
cirque, glacial 16.
citrus fruit, section 47.
CITRUS FRUITS 47.
citrus fruits, major types 47.
city 26.
clamp 186.
clarinet 165.
clarinet 167.
clavicle 80.
claw 57, 61, 64, 66, 75, 108.
clear key 154.
clear space 174.
clear-entry key 154.
clefs 160.
clew 184.
cliff 9, 14, 17.
CLIMATES OF THE WORLD 21.
clinical thermometer 199.
clip 150.
clock 132.
clock operator 178.
clock timer 107.
cloud 22.
cloud of volcanic ash 15.
club 194.
clutch lever 135.
clutch pedal 132.
coach's box 169.
coarse adjustment knob 155.
COASTAL FEATURES 14.
cob 52.
cobra 64.
coccyx 80.
cochlea 83.
cock 68.
cockpit 145.
cod 63.
coffee cup 100.
coffee plunger 100.
coffee pot 192.
coffee spoon 101.
coin return tray 124.
coin slot 124.
colander 103.
cold shed 143.
collar 36, 112, 113, 121.
collar point 112.
collecting funnel 23.
collecting vessel 23.
collection body 214.
color circle 157.
color television camera 149.
colored pencils 157.
column 13, 182.
column of mercury 199.
coma 10.
COMET 10.
comforter 95.
commercial premises 91.
commissure of lips 84.
COMMON SYMBOLS 216.
COMMUNICATION BY TELEPHONE 124.
compact camera 125.
compact disk 129.
compact disk 129.
compact disk player 128.
compact disk player 129.
COMPASS CARD 27.
compass card 193.
compass, magnetic 193.
compound eye 57, 58.
compound leaves 36.
compost bin 55.
compressed air reservoir 139.
compressed-air cylinder 211.
computer, personal 154.

concealed pocket 113.
concentration of gases 29.
condensation 31.
condensation of steam into water 207.
condenser 155.
condenser backwash inlet 206.
condenser backwash outlet 206.
condenser cooling water inlet 206.
condenser cooling water outlet 206.
conductor's podium 167.
cone 14, 43, 156.
cone 128.
CONFIGURATION OF THE
    CONTINENTS 18.
conical projection 25.
CONIFER 43.
coniferous forest 20.
connection 205.
constriction 199.
contact 99.
container 23, 105.
container car 138.
container ship 142.
container terminal 143.
container-loading bridge 142.
container/pallet loader 146.
containment building 207.
continental climates 21.
contrabassoon 167.
control deck 141, 197.
control dial 125.
control knob 107.
control pad 197.
control panel 107, 125, 210.
control room 204, 206.
control stand 138.
control stick 145.
control tower 146.
control tower cab 146.
controls 127.
convection zone 8.
convention center 90.
conventional door 92.
convertible 133.
COOKING APPLIANCES 107.
cooking set 192.
COOKING UTENSILS 104.
cooktop 107.
coolant transfers the heat to the steam
    generator 207.
cordless telephone 124.
core 8, 46.
corkscrew 192.
corkscrew, lever 102.
corn salad 53.
corner arc 173.
corner flag 173, 175.
corner tower 88.
cornerback, left 171.
cornerback, right 171.
cornet 164.
cornet 167.
cornice 92, 93.
corolla 38.
corona 8.
coronet 67.
corrosive 216.
cotton roll 193.
cotyledons 34.
counter 121.
counterjib 215.
counterjib ballast 215.
counterweight 11, 140, 213, 214.
country 26.
coupler head 139.
courtyard 87.
cover 99, 123, 193, 199.
covered parapet walk 88.
cow 68.
crab 61.
cradle 11.
cranberry 44.
crane runway 214.
crane, floating 142.
crane, gantry 204.
crane, quayside 143.
crane, tower 214.
crank 136.
crater 9, 15.
crawl kick 183.
crawler tractor 212.
crayfish 61.
crayons 157.
creamer 100.
crease 112.
crenate 37.

crenel 88.
crest 17.
crevasse 16.
crew neck sweater 117.
crisper 106.
crocodile 64.
crocus 39.
crook 165.
cross-country ski 186.
cross-country ski 187.
cross-country skier 187.
cross-tip screwdriver 192.
crossbuck sign 140.
crossing 89.
crossing gate mechanism 140.
crosspiece 97.
crotch 112.
croup 67, 188.
crow 76.
crown 40, 74, 85, 113.
CRUISE LINER 142.
CRUSTACEANS 61.
cube 156.
cucumber 49.
cuff 112, 177.
culottes 115.
cultivated mushroom 35.
cup 100, 192.
curly endive 53.
curly kale 53.
curtain wall 88.
customs house 143.
cutting blade 105.
cutting edge 101, 212.
cylinder 156.
cylinder 75, 212, 213, 215.
cylindrical projection 25.
cymbal 166.
cymbals 167.
cypress scalelike leaves 43.

D

d 160.
daffodil 39.
daggerboard 184.
dairy compartment 106.
dairy products 33.
dam 204.
dandelion 53.
damper pedal 159.
dart 197.
dartboard 197.
dashboard 132.
dashboard 135.
data display 127.
date 45.
daddy forepaw
dead bolt 93.
deadly mushroom 35.
decanter 100.
deciduous forest 20.
decimal key 154.
declination setting scale 11.
decomposers 29.
deer, white-tailed 73.
defending zone 176.
defense 171.
deflector 54.
deforestation 29.
degrees, C 199.
degrees, F 199.
Deimos 6.
delivery ramp 90.
delta wing 144.
DENTAL CARE 122.
dental floss 122.
dentate 37.
dentin 85.
depressed center flat car 139.
depth of focus 13.
desert 21.
desired temperature 199.
destroying angel 35.
dew 22.
dew shield 11.
dewclaw 66.
diagonal movement 195.
dial 198, 200.
diamond 194.
diaphragm 81, 128.
diastema 70.
dice cup 196.
die 196.

diesel engine 139, 212.
diesel engine ventilator 138.
diesel oil 203.
diesel, marine 203.
DIESEL-ELECTRIC LOCOMOTIVE 138.
digit 60.
digital pad 66.
digital watch 198.
dining room 142.
dinner fork 101.
dinner knife 101.
dinner plate 100.
DINNERWARE 100.
diode 208.
dipper bucket 213.
direct-reading rain gauge 23.
direction of Mecca 87.
disk 154.
disk brake 135.
disk drive 154.
disk player controls 129.
dispersed heat 29.
display 124, 154, 201.
divide key 154.
dock 143.
DOG 66.
dog's forepaw 66.
dog, morphology 66.
dolphin 72.
dome tent 190.
DOMINOES 194.
door 93.
door 87, 107, 131, 145, 190.
door handle 93, 131.
door lock 131.
doors, types 92.
dormant volcano 14.
dorsum of nose 84.
double bass 162.
double bass 167.
double boiler 104.
double flat, musical notation 161.
double reed 165.
double ring 197.
double sharp, musical notation 161.
double-blank 194.
double-breasted jacket 113, 114.
doubles pole 180.
doubles sideline 180.
doublet 194.
double-six 194.
doubling die 196.
dousing water tank 206, 207.
dousing water valve 206.
DOWNTOWN 90.
dragonfly 56.
drainpipe 92.
draw tube 155.
drawbridge 88.
drawer 97, 107.
DRAWING 157.
drawstring 113, 123.
drawstring bag 123.
dress 114.
drilling 202.
drilling rig 202.
drip molding 131.
drive chain 136.
driver's cab 138, 140.
driveway 92.
driving glove 118.
dromedary 73.
drone pipe 158.
drone, honey-bee 58.
drop-leaf 97.
drums 166.
drupelet 44.
dry continental - arid 21.
dry continental - semiarid 21.
dry dock 143.
dry gallery 13.
dry subtropical 21.
dual seat 135.
duck 68.
duffle coat 113.
dugout 169.
dump body 213.
dump truck 213.
dune 14.
duodenum 81.
dust 30, 31.
dust tail 10.
dynamic brake 138.
dynamics propeller 141.

218

The terms in **bold type** correspond to an illustration; those in CAPITALS indicate a title.

E

e 160.
EAR 83.
ear 78, 97.
ear cushion 128.
ear drum 83.
ear flap 113.
ear protection 216.
ear, parts 83.
eardrum 60, 64.
earphone 128.
earpiece 124.
Earth 6, 10.
EARTH COORDINATE SYSTEM 12.
Earth's crust 12, 13.
EARTHQUAKE 13.
East 27.
East-northeast 27.
East-southeast 27.
Eastern hemisphere 24.
Eastern meridian 24.
eclipse, annular 10.
eclipse, partial 10.
ECLIPSE, SOLAR 10.
eclipse, total 10.
ECOLOGY 28, 30, 32.
edge 185, 186, 193.
edible crustaceans 61.
edible mushroom 35.
edit/search buttons 127.
eel 63.
egg 75.
egg 59.
egg beater 102.
egg timer 198.
egg tray 106.
eggplant 49.
eggs 60.
eighth note 161.
eighth rest 161.
elastic 95.
elastic waistband 113.
elbow 66, 67, 79.
elbow pad 170, 177.
electric circuit 205, 208.
electric drill 110.
electric guitar 163.
electric range 107.
ELECTRIC TOOLS 110.
electric wire 205.
electrical hazard 216.
electricity production 207.
electricity transmission 207.
electronic flash 125.
electronic scale 201.
electronic viewfinder 127.
elephant 73.
elevating cylinder 210, 215.
ELEVATION ZONES AND VEGETATION
    20.
elevator 144.
elevon 148.
enamel 85.
end button 162.
end line 171, 174.
end wall 182.
end zone 171.
endive, broad-leaved 53.
endocarp 45, 46.
energy integration to the transmission
    network 205.
ENERGY, HYDROELECTRIC 204.
ENERGY, NUCLEAR 206.
ENERGY, SOLAR 208.
energy, solar 28.
ENERGY, WIND 209.
engine 135.
engine room 143.
engines 149.
English horn 165.
English horn 167.
entire 37.
entrance 59.
entrance slide 59.
epicenter 13.
equal key 154.
Equator 12, 24.
equinox, autumnal 20.
eraser 150.
eraser holder 150.
escutcheon 93.
espadrille 119.
Eurasia 19.
Europa 6.

Europe 19.
Eustachian tube 83.
evaporation 30, 31.
excavator 213.
exercise wear 120, 121.
exhaust pipe 135, 145, 212.
exhaust stack 134.
exit cone 59.
exocarp 44, 45, 46.
expansion chamber 199.
explosive 216.
exposure button 125.
extension ladder 111.
exterior of a house 92.
external ear 83.
external gills 60.
external tank 148.
EYE 82.
eye 61, 64, 74, 78.
eye protection 216.
eye, compound 57, 58.
eye, simple 57.
eyeball 60.
eyebrow 82.
eyelash 82.
eyelashes 66.
eyelet 121, 185.
eyelid 64.
eyepiece 11, 127, 155.
eyepiece holder 11.

F

f 160.
f clef 160.
facade 89.
face 78, 108.
face mask 170, 177.
face-off circle 176.
face-off spot 176.
Fahrenheit scale 199.
fallout 31.
family tent 190.
fan 122.
fang 64.
fantail 209.
FARM ANIMALS 68.
farm animals 29.
farm pollution 32.
fast forward 126.
fast-forward button 129.
fastening system 188, 189.
fauces 84.
fault 13.
feet, principal types 74.
female cone 43.
femur 80.
fender 130.
fennel 52.
ferryboat 143.
fertilizers 29, 32.
fetlock 67.
fetlock joint 67.
fibula 80.
FIELD HOCKEY 175.
fielder's glove 168.
fielder, left 169.
fielder, right 169.
fifth wheel 134.
fifth, musical interval 160.
fig 48.
figure skate 185.
filament 38, 99.
file 192.
film advance button 125.
film leader 125.
film pack 125.
film rewind button 125.
film speed 125.
fin 144, 145.
fin, anal 63.
fin, caudal 63.
fin, pectoral 62.
fin, pelvic 62.
fin, second dorsal 63.
fin-mounted tail unit 145.
finderscope 11.
fine adjustment knob 155.
finger 168.
finger board 162, 163.
finger button 164.
finger, little 82.
finger, middle 82.

finger, third 82.
fingernail 82.
fir needles 43.
fire engine 210.
fire extinguisher 210.
fire fighter 211.
fire fighter's hatchet 211.
fire hose 210.
fire hydrant 210.
FIRE PREVENTION 210.
fireproof and waterproof garment 211.
firn 16.
first aid kit 193.
first base 169.
first baseman 169.
first dorsal fin 62.
first floor 92.
first leaves 34.
first molar 85.
first premolar 85.
first quarter 9.
first space 178.
first valve slide 164.
first violin 167.
FISH 62.
fish scaler 192.
fishes, morphology 62.
fission of uranium fuel 207.
fixed jaw 109.
flamingo 76.
flammable 216.
flank 67, 75.
flanking tower 88.
flap 113.
flare 8.
flashing light 140, 211.
flashlight 192.
flashtube 125.
flat brush 157.
flat car 139.
flat mirror 11.
flat, musical notation 161.
flesh 44, 45, 46.
FLESHY FRUITS 44, 47.
fleshy leaves 50.
FLESHY POME FRUITS 46.
FLESHY STONE FRUITS 45.
flews 66.
flexible skirt 141.
flight 197.
flight deck 145, 149.
flip turn 183.
floating crane 142.
floating rib 80.
floor lamp 98.
flounder 63.
flower 36.
flower bud 36.
FLOWERS 38.
flowers, examples 38.
fluorescent tube 99.
fluorescent tube 99.
flute 165.
flute 167.
fly 56.
fly 112.
fly agaric 35.
flying buttress 89.
flying jib 141.
FM antenna 128.
foam pad 191.
focus 13.
focus setting ring 125.
focusing knob 11.
fog 22.
fog light 133, 134.
folding chair 96.
folding cot 191.
folding door 92.
foliage 40.
fondue fork 101.
fondue pot 104.
fondue set 104.
food chain 28.
food pollution in water 32.
food pollution on ground 32.
foot 75, 78, 79.
foot fault judge 180.
foot protection 216.
foot strap 184.
FOOTBALL 170.
football 170.
football player 170.
football, playing field 171.
footboard 95.
footbridge 88.
footless tights 121.

footrest 135.
footstool 96.
footstrap 115.
fore royal sail 141.
forearm 66, 79.
forecastle 142.
forecourt 180.
forehead 74, 78.
foreleg 57, 58.
forelimb 60.
forelock 67.
foremast 141.
foresail 141.
forest 17.
forest, coniferous 20.
forest, deciduous 20.
forest, tropical 20.
forewing 57.
fork 55, 101.
fork 11, 137.
forked tongue 64.
forks, types 101.
fortified wall 87.
forward slide change 153.
forward, left 178.
forward, right 178.
fossil fuels 28.
foul line 169.
fountain pen 150.
four-door sedan 133.
four-four time 160.
FOUR-MASTED BARK 141.
four-toed hoof 71.
fourth, musical interval 160.
frame 94, 112, 136, 168, 181, 188,
    189, 208, 213.
frame push 212.
framing square 108.
free-throw lane 178.
free-throw line 178.
freeway 90.
freezer compartment 106.
FREIGHT CARS, TYPES 138.
French horn 164.
French horn 167.
fret 162, 163.
frog 60.
frog 113, 162.
frog, life cycle 60.
front 112.
front apron 112.
front brake 137.
front compression strap 193.
front crawl 183.
front derailleur 136.
front fender 135.
front lights 133.
front pocket 123.
front steps 92.
front-end loader 212.
fruit vegetables 49.
frying pan 104, 192.
fuel gauge 132.
fuel tank 134, 135, 139, 145.
fuel tanks 148.
fueling machine 206.
full face mask 211.
full Moon 9.
fullback 171.
fumarole 14.
function button 197.
function keys 201.
function selectors 124.
funnel 103.
funnel 143.
fuse 208.
fuselage 144.
fuselage mounted tail unit 145.

G

g 160.
g clef 160.
gable 93.
gaff sail boom 141.
gaff topsail 141.
gall bladder 81.
gallery 89.
game cartridge 197.
GAME OF DARTS 197.
gantry crane 204.
Ganymede 6.
garage 92.
garden sorrel 53.

GARDENING 54.
garlic 50.
gas 30, 31, 99.
gas tail 10.
gas tank door 131.
gaskin 67.
gasoline 203.
gasoline pump 135.
gate 204.
gate arm 140.
gate arm lamp 140.
gate arm support 140.
gauze roller bandage 193.
gear lever 137.
gearchange pedal 135.
gearshift lever 132.
generator 136, 206.
generator unit 204.
GEOMETRY 156.
germ 34.
GERMINATION 34.
geyser 15.
gill 35.
gills 62.
gills, external 60.
giraffe 72.
glacial cirque 16.
GLACIER 16.
glacier 20.
glacier tongue 16.
glass 100.
glass 208.
glass cover 106.
glass lens 123.
glass slide 155.
GLASSES 123.
GLASSWARE 100.
glazed frost 22.
globe 152.
globe of Earth 152.
glottis 64.
glove 177, 187.
glove compartment 132.
glove finger 118.
GLOVES 118.
gloves 118.
glue stick 150.
gnomon 198.
goal 171, 173, 175, 176.
goal area 173.
goal crease 176.
goal judge 176.
goal line 171, 175, 176.
goal post 171.
goalkeeper 177.
goalkeeper 173, 175, 176.
goalkeeper's pad 177.
goalkeeper's stick 177.
goat 69.
gondola car 139.
gong 167.
goose 68.
gooseberry 44.
gorge 13.
GOTHIC CATHEDRAL 89.
gour 13.
grab handle 134.
graduated dial 193.
graduated scale 200, 201.
grain terminal 142.
granivorous bird 74.
grape 44.
grapefruit 47.
graphic equalizer 128.
grassbox 54.
grasshopper 56.
grater 103.
greases 203.
green 157.
green bean 49.
green cabbage 53.
green peas 52.
green pepper 49.
greenhouse effect 28.
greenhouse gases 29.
Greenland Sea 18.
grid system 24.
grille 130.
groove 186.
ground moraine 16.
ground transport 202.
grounding terminal 99.
guard rail 106.
guard, left 178.
guard, right 178.

The terms in **bold type** correspond to an illustration; those in CAPITALS indicate a title.

guardhouse 88.
guava 48.
guide roller 129.
gulf 26.
gum 84, 85.
gutter 92.
guy line 190.
GYMNASTICS 188-189.

H

hair 79, 162.
hair pick 122.
hair-dryer 122.
hairbrush 122.
HAIRDRESSING 122.
half note 161.
half rest 161.
half, left 175.
half, right 175.
half-slip 116.
halfback, left 171.
halfback, right 171.
hammer 159.
hammer rail 159.
hammer, carpenter's 108.
hammer, claw 108.
HAND 82.
hand 79.
hand blender 105.
hand cultivator 54.
hand fork 54.
hand mixer 105.
hand protection 216.
handbrake 132.
handgrip 135.
handle 54, 95, 101, 108, 109, 110, 111, 122, 123, 129, 162, 168, 181, 186, 192.
handlebars 137.
handsaw 109.
handset 124.
handset cord 124.
hanger loop 117.
hanging glacier 16.
hanging pendant 98.
HARBOR 142.
hard palate 84.
harmonica 158.
harp 167.
hatch 148.
hatchback 133.
hatchet 192.
head 10, 57, 58, 79, 108, 109, 122, 162, 163, 181.
head linesman 171.
head of water 205.
head protection 216.
headband 128, 129, 181, 187.
headboard 95.
header 93.
headlamp 137.
headland 14.
headlight 130, 135, 139, 140.
headlight/turn signal 132.
headphone 129.
headphone jack 129.
headphone plug 129.
headphones 128.
heart 194.
heart 81.
heartwood 40.
heat production 207.
heat selector switch 122.
heat shield 149.
heat transport pump 206.
heater control 132.
heating oil 203.
heavy duty boot 119.
HEAVY MACHINERY 214.
HEAVY VEHICLES 212.
heel 79, 118, 121, 162, 168, 177.
heel piece 186.
heel stop 185.
heel-piece 187.
heelplate 186.
HELICOPTER 145.
helix 83.
helmet 149, 170, 177, 211.
hemispheres 24.
hen 68.
herbivore's jaw 70.

herbivores 29, 33.
hi-hat cymbal 166.
high bar 189.
high beam 133.
high beam indicator light 132.
high-rise apartment 91.
high-speed exit runway 146.
HIGH-SPEED TRAIN 140.
high-tension electricity transmission 205.
highland climates 21.
highland climates 21.
highlighter pen 150.
highway 27.
HIGHWAY CROSSING 140.
highway crossing bell 140.
highway number 27.
hill 17.
hind leg, butterfly 57, 59.
hind limb 60.
hind toe 75.
hind wing 57.
hinge 93, 186.
hinge pin 213.
hip 79.
hip pad 170.
hitting area 168.
hive 59.
hive body 59.
hock 66, 67.
hockey ball 175.
hockey skate 185.
hockey stick 175.
hockey, playing field 175.
hoisting block 214.
hoisting rope 111, 214.
home plate 169.
home-plate umpire 169.
honey cell 59.
HONEYBEE 58.
honeycomb 59.
honeycomb section 59.
hood 113, 130.
hooded sweat shirt 120.
hoof 67.
HOOFS, TYPES 71.
hook 94, 108, 185, 201, 214, 215.
hopper car 138.
horizontal bar 189.
horizontal movement 195.
horizontal pivoting window 94.
horizontal stabilizer 144, 145.
horizontal-axis wind turbine 209.
horn 132, 138.
horns of giraffe 71.
horns of mouflon 71.
horns of rhinoceros 71.
HORNS, MAJOR TYPES 71.
horny beak 64.
HORSE 67.
horse 70.
horse 188.
horseradish 51.
hospital 216.
hot pepper 49.
hot-shoe contact 125.
hotel 91.
HOUSE 92.
house on stilts 86.
house, exterior 92.
HOUSES, TRADITIONAL 86.
housing 99, 110, 129.
HOVERCRAFT 141.
hub 137, 209.
huckleberry 44.
HUMAN ANATOMY 81.
HUMAN BODY 78, 79.
HUMAN DENTURE 85.
humerus 80.
humid - long summer 21.
humid - short summer 21.
humid subtropical 21.
humidity, measure 23.
hummingbird 77.
hunting cap 113.
husk 52.
hut 87.
hydrant 210.
hydrant intake 210.
hydroelectric complex 204.
HYDROELECTRIC ENERGY 204.
hydroelectric power station, cross section 204.
hydrosphere 20.
hygrograph 23.

I

ice 30.
ice cream scoop 103.
ice cube tray 106.
ice dispenser 134.
ICE HOCKEY 176.
ice hockey player 177.
ice hockey, rink 176.
igloo 86.
ignition key 54.
ignition switch 132.
ilium 80.
in-line skate 185.
inbound line 171.
incandescent lamp 99.
incandescent lamp 208.
incisor 70.
incisors 85.
incoming message cassette 124.
index finger 82.
Indian fig 48.
Indian Ocean 19.
indicators 126.
industrial oil 203.
industrial pollution 32, 33.
inert gas 99.
infield 169.
infiltration 30.
inflator 191.
inflator-deflator 191.
inflorescent vegetables 49.
inner bark 40.
inner boot 185.
inner core 12.
inner table 196.
inner tent 190.
inner, left 175.
inner, right 175.
inorganic matter 29.
insectivores 29.
insectivorous bird 74.
INSECTS 56.
inside 101.
inside left 173.
inside linebacker 171.
inside right 173.
instep 118.
instrument panel 132.
instrument panel 132.
instrument shelter 23.
insulation tiles 148.
interchangeable studs 172.
internal boundary 26.
internal ear 83.
internal frame 193.
international boundary 26.
internode 36.
interrupted projection 25.
intervals 160.
Io 6.
iris 82.
island 26.
isthmus 26.

J

Jack 194.
jacket 113.
jacket 114.
jalousie 94.
jamb 93.
Japanese persimmon 48.
Japanese plum 46.
jaw 109, 110.
jaw, carnivore's 70.
jaw, herbivore's 70.
jaw, rodent's 70.
JAWS, TYPES 70.
jay 77.
jeans 115.
Jerusalem artichoke 51.
jet fuel 203.
jib 214.
jib tie 215.
jib, flying 141.
jigger topgallant staysail 141.
jigger topmast staysail 141.
Joker 194.
journal box 138.
Jupiter 6.

K

kangaroo 73.
keep 88.
kernel 52.
kerosene 203.
kettle 105.
kettledrum 167.
key 159, 165.
key case 123.
key signature, musical notation 161.
keybed 159.
keyboard 154, 159.
keyboard cable 154.
KEYBOARD INSTRUMENT 159.
King 194, 195.
King's side 195.
kiosk 135.
KITCHEN APPLIANCES 105.
kitchen scale 201.
kitchen timer 198.
KITCHEN UTENSILS 102.
kiwi 48.
knapsack 123.
knee 67, 78.
knee pad 168, 170, 177.
knee sock 187.
knee-high sock 118.
knife 101, 192.
Knight 195.
knitted hat 114.
knives, types 101.
knob 97, 168.
knob handle 110.
knuckle 82.
kohlrabi 51.

L

label 129.
labial palp 57.
lace 168, 185.
ladder 213.
ladder pipe nozzle 211.
ladle 102.
Lady chapel 89.
ladybug 56.
lagoon 14.
lake 9, 17, 26.
lamb 69.
lanceolate 37.
Land camera, Polaroid® 125.
landing light 145.
landing window 145.
lane 160.
lane number 182.
lane rope 182.
lane timekeeper 182.
larch 43.
large blade 192.
large intestine 81.
last quarter 9.
latch 107.
latch bolt 93.
lateral brush 214.
lateral incisor 85.
lateral moraine 17.
latitude 12.
latitude, lines 24.
lava flow 15.
lava layer 15.
lawn rake 55.
lawnmower 54.
lead-in wire 99.
leading edge 144.
leaf 37.
leaf 34, 36.
leaf axil 37.
leaf margins 37.
leaf node 36.
leaf vegetables 53.
leather end 112.
LEATHER GOODS 123.
leather sheath 192.
leaves, compound 36.
leaves, simple 37.
leaves, types 43.
ledger line 160.
leek 50.
left back 173, 174, 175.

left channel 128.
left cornerback 171.
left defense 176.
left defensive end 171.
left defensive tackle 171.
left field 169.
left fielder 169.
left forward 174, 178.
left guard 171, 178.
left half 173, 175.
left halfback 171.
left inner 175.
left safety 171.
left service court 180.
left tackle 171.
left wing 175, 176.
leg-warmer 121.
leg 64, 79, 95, 97, 118, 188.
lemon 47.
lemon squeezer 103.
lentils 52.
leotard 120.
level 108.
leveling-adjustment foot 153.
lever 105, 109.
license plate light 133.
life raft 141.
lifeboat 141, 143.
lift arm 212.
ligature 165.
light 11.
light bulb 208.
LIGHTING 99.
lightning 22.
lightning arrester 204.
lightning rod 93.
LIGHTS 98.
lily 39.
lily of the valley 39.
limb 40.
lime 47.
limousine 133.
line 160.
line judge 171.
line of scrimmage 171.
linear 37.
linebacker, inside 171.
linebacker, middle 171.
linebacker, outside 171.
linen 95.
lines of latitude 24.
lines of longitude 24.
linesman 173, 174, 176, 180.
linesman, head 171.
lining 113, 121.
lion 70, 72.
lip 66, 67.
liquid crystal display 198.
listen button 124.
litchi 48.
lithosphere 20.
little finger hook 164.
liver 81.
livestock car 138.
lizard 65.
loader 212.
loading hopper 215.
loafer 119.
lobate 37.
lobate toe 74.
lobe 74, 83.
lobster 61.
lock 93, 136.
lock 93.
lock ring 153.
locking device 111.
locking pliers 109.
LOCOMOTIVE, DIESEL-ELECTRIC 138.
log cabin 86.
log chute 204.
loin 67.
long-nose pliers 109.
long-range jet 144.
longitude 12.
longitude, lines 24.
loop 112.
loophole 88.
loose-leaf paper 151.
loudspeakers 128.
louver-board 89.
louvred window 94.
loveseat 96.
low beam 133.
lower eyelid 60, 66, 82.
lower fore topgallant sail 141.

220

The terms in **bold type** correspond to an illustration; those in CAPITALS indicate a title.

lower fore topsail 141.
lower lip 84.
lower mantle 12.
lower shell 186.
lubricating oils 203.
lubricating system 139.
luff 184.
lumbar pad 170.
LUNAR ECLIPSE 10.
lunar eclipses, types 10.
lunar features 9.
lung, left 81.
lung, right 81.
lunula 82.
lyre 158.

M

machicolation 88.
machine hall 204.
magma 15.
magma chamber 15.
magnetic compass 193.
magnetic needle 193.
magnifier 192.
magnifying glass 155.
main engines 148.
main landing gear 144.
main mirror 11.
main tube 11.
main vent 15.
mainmast 141.
mainsail 141.
maintenance 134.
maintenance hangar 147.
male cone 43.
mallet 108.
mallet 166.
mallets 166.
mandarin 47.
mandible 57, 58, 62, 80.
mandolin 158.
mane 67.
maneuvering engine 148.
mango 45.
manned maneuvering unit 149.
manual focusing knob 153.
manual release 187.
map projections 25.
maple 41.
maracas 166.
margin 36.
marine 21.
marine diesel 203.
maritime transport 202.
marker 150.
marker light 134.
Mars 6.
mask 168.
mast 140, 145, 184.
mast foot 184.
mast sleeve 184.
masthead 184.
mattress 95, 191.
mattress cover 95.
maxilla 62, 80.
maxillary bone 85.
maxillipeds 61.
maximum thermometer 23.
measure of air pressure 23.
measure of humidity 23.
measure of rainfall 23.
measure of temperature 23.
MEASURE OF WEIGHT 200.
measure of wind direction 23.
measure of wind strength 23.
measuring spoons 102.
measuring tube 23.
meat 33.
meat tray 106.
mechanical pencil 150.
mechanics 134.
medial moraine 16.
median strip 90.
Mediterranean Sea 19.
Mediterranean subtropical 21.
melody strings 158.
meltwater 17.
memory cancel 154.
memory recall 154.
men 195, 196.
MEN'S CLOTHING 112.

men's rest room 216.
Mercury 6.
mercury barometer 23.
mercury bulb 199.
meridian band 152.
merlon 88.
mesocarp 44, 45, 46, 47.
metacarpus 80.
metal frame 159.
metals 33.
metatarsus 80.
METEOROLOGICAL MEASURING
 INSTRUMENTS 23.
metronome 159.
microscope 155.
microwave oven 107.
middle ear 83.
middle leg 57, 58.
middle linebacker 171.
middle panel 93.
middle toe 74.
midfield line 173.
midrange 128.
midrange pickup 163.
midrib 37.
midsole 121.
Mihrab dome 87.
minaret 87.
minimum thermometer 23.
minivan 133.
minute hand 198.
mirror 134, 135, 152, 155.
mist 22.
mitten 118.
mixed forest 20.
mizzenmast 141.
moat 88.
moccasin 119.
mode selectors 129.
moisture in the air 30.
molar 70.
molar, cross section 85.
molars 85.
monkey 72.
MOON 9.
Moon 6, 10.
Moon's orbit 10.
moons 6.
moraine, ground 16.
moraine, lateral 17.
moraine, medial 16.
moraine, terminal 17.
mordent, musical notation 161.
MOSQUE 87.
motor 54, 110.
MOTORCYCLE 135.
MOUNTAIN 17.
mountain bike 137.
mountain range 9, 26.
mountain slope 17.
mountain torrent 17.
mounting foot 125.
mouse 154.
MOUTH 84.
mouth 60, 78.
mouthpiece 124, 164, 165.
mouthpipe 158.
movable jaw 109.
movable maxillary 64.
movements, chess 195.
mud flap 131, 134.
mud hut 86.
mudguard 136.
muffler felt 159.
muffler pedal 159.
mug 100.
multiply key 154.
multipurpose bottle 193.
multipurpose vehicle 133.
mummy 191.
muntin 94.
museum 91.
MUSHROOM 35.
mushroom, structure 35.
music stand 159.
musical accessories 159.
MUSICAL INSTRUMENTS,
 TRADITIONAL 158.
MUSICAL NOTATION 160.
musical scale 160.
muskmelon 49.
mute 164.
muzzle 66, 67.
mycelium 35.

N

nail 108.
nail nick 192.
nape 75, 79.
nasal septum 84.
national park 27.
natural arch 14.
natural, musical notation 161.
nave 89.
navel 78.
navigation light 144.
neck 64, 67, 78, 79, 85, 162, 163, 188.
neck end 112.
nectarine 45.
negative contact 208.
negative pole 205.
Neptune 7.
net 174, 180.
net 174, 179, 180.
net band 180.
net judge 180.
neutral zone 171, 176.
new crescent 9.
new Moon 9.
nictitating membrane 66.
nightingale 77.
no smoking 216.
North 27.
North America 18.
North Pole 12.
North Sea 19.
North-northeast 27.
North-northwest 27.
Northeast 27.
Northern hemisphere 12, 24.
Northwest 27.
NOSE 84.
nose 67, 78, 145.
nose landing gear 145.
nose leather 66.
nose of the quarter 121.
nose pad 123.
nostril 60, 62, 67, 84.
notch 200.
note symbols, musical notation 161.
notebook 151.
notepad 151.
nozzle 148.
NUCLEAR ENERGY 206.
nuclear power station 206.
nucleus 10.
number 179.
number key 154.
number of tracks sign 140.
numeric keyboard 201.
nut 109, 162, 163.
nutcracker 102.

O

oak 41.
objective 155.
objective lens 11, 125, 153.
oboe 165.
oboe 167.
observation window 148.
ocean 9, 26, 31.
Oceania 19.
octave 160.
octave mechanism 165.
odometer 132.
offense 171.
office 134.
office building 91, 143.
office tower 90.
officials' bench 176.
offshore prospecting 202.
OIL 202.
oil tanker 143.
oil terminal 143.
oil, diesel 203.
oil, heating 203.
oils, lubricating 203.
okra 49.
olive 45.
old crescent 9.
omnivores 28.
on-deck circle 169.
on-off switch 105, 122.

on/off button 126, 129.
on/off switch 153.
on/off/volume control 129.
one-person tent 190.
one-toe hoof 71.
onion, pickling 50.
onion, yellow 50.
open strings 158.
operating nut 210.
operator's cab 214.
operculum 60.
optical lens 152.
optical stage 152.
orange 47.
orange 157.
orange-red 157.
orange-yellow 157.
orbiculate 37.
orbits of the planets 6.
orchid 38.
ORGAN OF HEARING 83.
ORGAN OF SIGHT 82.
ORGAN OF SMELL 84.
ORGAN OF TASTE 84.
ORGAN OF TOUCH 82.
ornaments, musical notation 161.
ostrich 76.
outer bark 40.
outer core 12.
outer table 196.
outer toe 74.
outgoing announcement cassette 124.
outlet 99.
output jack 163.
outrigger 210, 213, 215.
outside left 173.
outside linebacker 171.
outside mirror 130.
outside right 173.
outsole 121.
outwash plain 17.
ovary 38.
oven 107.
oven control knob 107.
overcoat 114.
overhead projector 152.
ovule 38.
owl 77.
ox 69.
ozone layer 29.

P

Pacific Ocean 18.
packer body 215.
padded pants 177.
paint roller 111.
paintbrush 157.
PAINTING UPKEEP 111.
pajamas 116.
palm 82, 118, 168.
palm tree 42.
palmar pad 66.
palmate 36.
pan 200.
pane 94.
panel 93.
panpipes 158.
pantograph 140.
pants 112, 120.
pants 168, 170, 177.
papaya 48.
paper clips 150.
paraffins 203.
parallel 24.
parallel bars 189.
parallelepiped 156.
parallelogram 156.
park 90.
parking area 147.
parking lot 91.
parrot 76.
parsnip 51.
partial eclipse 10.
parts 95.
pass 17.
passenger cabin 141, 145.
passenger car 140.
passenger terminal 143, 147.
passenger transfer vehicle 147.
pastern 67.
patch pocket 113.
patella 80.

pause 126.
Pawn 195.
pay phone 124.
peach 45.
peacock 77.
peak 17, 113, 114.
pear 46.
pear-shaped body 158.
pectoral fin 62.
pedal 136, 166.
pedal rod 159.
pedicel 38, 44, 45, 46.
peeler 102.
peg box 162.
pelvic fin 62.
pen, ballpoint 150.
pen, fountain 150.
pen, highlighter 150.
penalty arc 173.
penalty area 173.
penalty area marking 173.
penalty bench 176.
penalty spot 173.
pencil 150.
pencil sharpener 150.
pendulum bar 159.
peninsula 26.
penstock 204.
penumbra shadow 10.
pepper shaker 100.
percent key 154.
perch 75.
perching bird 74.
PERCUSSION INSTRUMENTS 166.
perforation 125.
pericarp 47.
perpetual snows 17.
personal AM-FM cassette player 129.
personal computer 154.
pesticides 32.
petal 38.
petiole 37.
petrochemicals 203.
petroleum trap 202.
phalanges 80.
phases of the Moon 9.
philtrum 84.
Phobos 6.
phosphorescent coating 99.
photoelectric cell 125.
PHOTOGRAPHY 125.
physical map 26.
piano 167.
piccolo 165.
piccolo 167.
pickguard 163.
pickling onion 50.
pickup selector 163.
pickup truck 133.
pickups 163.
pig 69.
piggyback car 139.
pike 63.
pike pole 211.
pillar 89.
pillow 95.
pillow protector 95.
pillowcase 95.
pilot 139, 140.
pin 99.
pin base 99.
pin block 159.
pine needles 43.
pine seeds 43.
pineapple 48.
pinnatifid 36.
pip 44, 46, 47, 194.
pipeline 202.
pistil 38.
pistol grip handle 110.
pitcher 169.
pitcher's mound 169.
pitcher's plate 169.
pith 40.
pivot 193.
pivot cab 213.
placing judge 182.
placket 112.
plain 26.
PLANE 144.
plane projection 25.
plane surfaces 156.
planetarium 90.
planets 6.
planets, orbits 6.
PLANT AND SOIL 34.

221

The terms in **bold type** correspond to an illustration; those in CAPITALS indicate a title.

plant litter 34.
plastron 64.
plate 192.
plateau 17, 26.
platform 182, 201.
platform ladder 111.
play 126.
play button 129.
player's number 170.
player's stick 177.
players' bench 171, 176, 174, 178.
playing area 143.
playing window 129.
pleated skirt 115.
plexus of blood vessels 85.
plexus of nerves 85.
plug 110.
plug, American 99.
plug, European 99.
plum 45.
Pluto 7.
pocket 112, 117.
pocket calculator 154.
pocket camera 125.
point 101, 185, 196, 197.
point of interest 27.
pointer 199, 200, 201.
poisonous 216.
poisonous mushroom 35.
poker die 194.
polar bear 72.
polar climates 21.
polar ice cap 21.
polar tundra 21.
Polaroid® Land camera 125.
pole grip 187.
pole pads 179.
pole shaft 187.
pole tip 187.
political map 26.
pollen basket 58.
pollen cell 59.
pollution, atmospheric 30.
pollution, food 32.
pollution, industrial 33.
polo neck 187.
polo shirt 117.
polo shirt 181.
pome fruit, section 46.
pome fruits, major types 46.
pomegranate 48.
pommel 188.
pommel horse 188.
poncho 114.
poop 141.
pop-up tent 190.
poplar 41.
poppy 38.
port hand 142.
portable CD AM/FM cassette recorder 129.
portable cellular telephone 124.
portable fire extinguisher 210.
portable life support system 149.
PORTABLE SOUND SYSTEMS 129.
portal 89.
porthole 143.
position light 140, 145.
position marker 162, 163.
positive contact 208.
positive pole 205.
post 174.
potato 51.
potato masher 102.
power button 127.
power car 140.
power zoom button 127.
powerhouse 204.
prairie 26.
prayer hall 87.
precipitation 30, 31.
premolar 70.
premolars 85.
preset buttons 126, 127.
pressed area 129.
pressure bar 159.
pressure cooker 104.
pressure regulator 104.
primary colors 157.
primary root 34, 36.
prime meridian 24.
printed document 154.
printer 154.
printout 154, 201.
prism 156.
proboscis 57.
procedure checklist 149.

product code 201.
production of electricity by the
  generator 205.
**production of electricity from nuclear
  energy 207.**
production of electricity, steps 205.
production platform 202.
projection device 214.
projection head 152.
projection screen 153.
projector, overhead 152.
proleg 57.
promenade deck 143.
prominence 8.
propellant level gauge 149.
propeller 143.
propeller duct 141.
prospecting 202.
PROTECTION 216.
protection layer 149.
protective cup 170, 177.
protective equipment 170.
protective helmet 135, 137.
protractor 151.
province 26.
pruning shears 54.
puck 165.
pulley 111.
pulp 47, 85.
pump 119.
pump island 135.
pumpkin 49.
punch hole 112.
pup tent 190.
pupil 66, 82.
purse 123.
push button 105.
push buttons 124.
push-button telephone 124.
pushpins 150.
pyramid 156.

Q

Qibla wall 87.
quarter 121.
quarter note 161.
quarter rest 161.
quarter-deck 143.
quarterback 171.
quay 142.
quayside crane 143.
Queen 194, 195.
queen cell 59.
Queen's side 195.
queen, honey-bee 58.
quince 46.

R

rack 107.
radar 142.
radial passenger loading area 147.
radiation zone 8.
radiator 139.
radiator grille 134.
radiator panel 148.
radicle 34, 36, 40.
radio antenna 142.
radioactive 216.
radish 51.
radius 80.
rail 93, 97, 140.
railroad 90.
railroad station 90.
rain 22.
rain forest, tropical 21.
rain gauge recorder 23.
rain gauge, direct-reading 23.
rainbow 22.
raindrop 22.
rainfall, measure 23.
rainfly 190.
rake 55.
rake comb 122.
rampart 88.
rangefinder 125.
raspberry, section 44.
rattlesnake 65.
reactor 206, 207.

reactor building 206.
reading start 129.
rear apron 112.
rear brake 136.
rear derailleur 136.
rear light 136.
rear lights 133.
rear shock absorber 135.
rearview mirror 132.
receiver 180.
receptacle 38, 44.
record 129.
record 126.
record announcement button 124.
recorder 165.
recorder 182.
recording tape 129.
recording unit 23.
rectangle 156.
rectangular 191.
red 157.
Red 196.
red currant 44.
Red Sea 15.
red wine glass 100.
red- violet 157.
reed 165.
reeds 165.
referee 171, 173, 176, 174, 178.
refinery 203.
refinery products 203.
refining 203.
reflected heat 28.
reflected ultraviolet rays 28.
REFLECTING TELESCOPE 11.
reflecting telescope, cross section 11.
reflector 136.
REFRACTING TELESCOPE 11.
**refracting telescope, cross section
  11.**
REFRIGERATOR 106.
refrigerator 29.
refrigerator car 139.
refrigerator compartment 106.
reheater 206.
release lever 109.
remote control 126.
remote control 153.
remote control sensor 126.
remote control terminal 125.
remote-control arm 149.
repeat mark 160.
REPTILES 64.
reservoir 105, 204.
reset button 198.
respiratory system protection 216.
rest area 27.
rest symbols, musical notation 161.
restaurant 91.
restraining circle 178.
restricted area 178.
retriever 174.
rev(olution) counter 132.
reverse slide change 153.
revolving nosepiece 155.
rewind 126.
rewind button 129.
rhinoceros 73.
rhombus 156.
rhubarb 52.
rib 123, 213.
rib joint pliers 109.
rib pad 170.
ribbed top 118.
ribbing 117.
ribs 80.
ridge 17.
right ascension setting scale 11.
right back 173, 175.
right channel 128.
right cornerback 171.
right defense 176.
right defensive end 171.
right defensive tackle 171.
right field 169.
right fielder 169.
right forward 174, 178.
right guard 171, 178.
right half 173, 175.
right halfback 171.
right inner 175.
right safety 171.
right service court 180.
right tackle 171.
right wing 175, 176.
rim 123, 135, 137, 179.

rind 47.
ring 35, 123, 164, 189, 198, 201.
ring binder 151.
rings 189.
rink 176.
rink corner 176.
ripper 212.
ripper tooth 212.
river 26.
river estuary 14, 26.
road 27.
road map 27.
road number 27.
roasting pans 104.
robin 77.
rocking chair 96.
rodent's jaw 70.
roller cover 111.
roller frame 111.
rolling pin 102.
romaine lettuce 53.
roof 59, 92, 131.
Rook 195.
room thermostat 199.
rooster 68.
root 50, 85.
root canal 85.
root cap 36.
root hairs 34, 36.
root of nose 84.
root system 36.
root vegetables 51.
root, primary 34, 36.
root, secondary 34, 36.
root-hair zone 40.
rose 38.
rose 162.
rose window 89.
rotation of the turbine 205.
rotor 209.
rotor blade 145.
rotor head 145.
rotor hub 145.
rubber boot 211.
rudder 141, 143, 144, 148.
ruler 151.
ruler 192.
rump 75.
rung 111.
runner 196.
running shoe 121.
runway 146.
runway line 147.
rutabaga 51.

S

sacrum 80.
saddle 188.
safety binding 187.
safety handle 54.
safety pad 188.
safety rail 138.
SAFETY SYMBOLS 216.
safety tether 149.
safety valve 104, 207.
sail 184.
sail 209.
sail cloth 209.
sail, fore royal 141.
sail, lower fore topgallant 141.
sail, upper fore topgallant 141.
sailbar 209.
SAILBOARD 184.
salad bowl 100.
salad dish 100.
salad plate 100.
salad spinner 103.
salsify 51.
salt marsh 14.
salt shaker 100.
salty taste 84.
salamander 60.
sand island 14.
sandbox 139.
sanitation truck 215.
sapwood 40.
sash window 94.
Saturn 7.
saucepan 104, 192.
sauté pan 104.

saxhorn 164.
saxophone 165.
scale 63, 64, 74, 108, 193, 199.
scale leaf 50.
scale, musical 160.
scales, bathroom 201.
scales, electronic 201.
scales, kitchen 201.
scallion 50.
scampi 61.
scapula 80.
scenic route 27.
SCHOOL EQUIPMENT 152, 154.
SCHOOL SUPPLIES 150.
scientific instruments 148.
scissors 192, 193.
sclera 82.
scorer 174, 178.
scraper 111.
screen 126, 204.
screw 108.
screw 162.
screw base 99.
screwdriver 108.
screwdriver, cross-tip 192.
scrimmage 171.
scroll 162.
sea 9, 26.
sea horse 62.
sealed cell 59.
SEASONS OF THE YEAR 20.
seat 97, 136.
seat post 136.
SEATS 96.
second base 169.
second baseman 169.
second dorsal fin 63.
second floor 92.
second hand 198.
second molar 85.
second premolar 85.
second space 178.
second value slide 164.
second violin 167.
second, musical interval 160.
secondary colors 157.
secondary road 27.
secondary root 34, 36.
section of a bulb 50.
seed 34, 44, 45, 46, 47.
seed leaf 36.
seed vegetables 52.
seeds 75.
segment 47.
segment score number 197.
seismic wave 13.
seismographic recording 202.
self-contained breathing apparatus
  211.
self-inflating mattress 191.
semi-circle 178.
semi-mummy 191.
semicircular canals 83.
sensor probe 107.
sepal 38, 44.
serac 16.
server 174, 180.
service area 27, 147, 174.
service court, left 180.
service court, right 180.
service judge 180.
service line 180.
service road 146.
service station 134.
set of bells 166.
set square 151.
seventh, musical interval 160.
shade 98.
shadow 198.
shadow, penumbra 10.
shadow, umbra 10.
shady arcades 87.
shaft 177, 181, 197.
shallot 50.
shallow root 40.
sham 95.
shank 108, 123.
shark 63.
sharp, musical notation 161.
sheath 192.
sheath 37, 66, 67.
sheep 69.
sheet 141.
sheet, fitted 95.
sheet, flat 95.

The terms in **bold type** correspond to an illustration; those in CAPITALS indicate a title.

shelf 106.
shell 64.
shell 75.
shield 65.
shin guard 168, 172.
shin pad 177.
shirt 112.
shirt 179.
shirttail 112.
shock wave 202.
shoelace 121.
SHOES 119.
shoot 36, 40.
shooting adjustment keys 127.
short sock 118.
shorts 115, 121.
shorts 172, 179.
shortstop 169.
shoulder 66, 67, 78, 181.
shoulder blade 79.
shoulder pad 170, 177.
shoulder strap 116, 123, 193.
shovel 55.
shovel 186.
shrimp 61.
shroud 141.
shutter 94.
shutter release button 125.
shuttle 148.
side 141.
side chair 97.
side chapel 89.
side compression strap 193.
side footboard 139.
side light 133.
side molding 131.
side plate 100.
side rail 111.
side vent 15.
side wall 182.
sideline 171, 175, 174, 178.
sight 193.
sighting line 193.
sighting mirror 193.
signal background plate 140.
signal lamp 107.
silk 52.
silos 142.
SILVERWARE 101.
simple eye 57, 58.
simple leaves 37.
single lens reflex (slr) camera 125.
single reed 165.
singles pole 180.
singles sideline 180.
sink-hole 13.
siphon 13.
sistrum 166.
sixteenth note 161.
sixteenth rest 161.
sixth, musical interval 160.
sixty-fourth note 161.
sixty-fourth rest 161.
skate 177.
skate guard 185.
SKATING 185.
skeg 184.
SKELETON 80.
ski 186.
ski boot 186.
ski boot 186.
ski glove 186.
ski goggles 186.
ski hat 186, 187.
ski pants 115.
ski pole 186, 187.
ski stop 186, 187.
ski suit 186, 187.
skid 145.
SKIING 186.
skin 44, 45, 46, 60.
skirt 114, 181.
skull 78, 80.
skylight 92.
skyscraper 91.
sleeping bags 191.
sleeping cab 134.
SLEEPING EQUIPMENT 191.
sleeve 113, 117.
sleigh bells 166.
slide 153.
slide mount 153.
slide projector 153.
slide tray 153.
slide-select bar 153.
sliding door 93.
sliding folding door 92.
sliding folding window 94.

sliding weight 159, 200.
sliding window 94.
slingback 119.
slip joint 109.
slip joint pliers 109.
slot 105.
slow-motion 126.
small bandage 193.
small blade 192.
small intestine 81.
snap fastener 113, 118.
snare drum 166, 167.
sneakers 179.
snout 60.
snow 30.
snowblower 214.
SOCCER 172.
soccer ball 172.
soccer player 172.
soccer shoe 172.
soccer, playing field 173.
sock 118.
sock 170, 181.
sofa 96.
soft palate 84.
soft pedal 159.
soft-drink dispenser 134.
SOIL PROFILE 34.
solar cell 208.
solar cell 154.
SOLAR ECLIPSE 10.
solar eclipses, types 10.
SOLAR ENERGY 208.
solar energy 28.
solar panel 208.
solar radiation 208.
solar shield 149.
SOLAR SYSTEM 6.
sole 118, 185.
solid body 163.
solid rocket booster 148.
solids 156.
sound hole 162.
sound reproducing system, components 128.
soundboard 158, 159, 162.
soup bowl 100.
soup spoon 101.
soup tureen 100.
sour taste 84.
sources of gases 29.
sources of pollution 30.
South 27.
South America 18.
South Pole 12.
South-southeast 27.
South-southwest 27.
Southeast 27.
Southern hemisphere 12, 24.
Southwest 27.
sow 69.
soybeans 52.
space 160.
SPACE SHUTTLE 148.
space shuttle at takeoff 148.
space shuttle in orbit 148.
spacelab 148.
SPACESUIT 149.
spade 55, 194.
spaghetti tongs 103.
spanker 141.
spatula 102.
speaker 124, 129.
speaker cover 128.
speed control 54, 105.
speed selector switch 122.
speed skate 185.
speedometer 132.
spent fuel discharge bay 206.
spent fuel storage bay 206.
sphere 156.
SPIDER 56.
spider 56.
spiked shoe 168.
spillway 204.
spillway gate 204.
spinach 53.
spindle 97.
spiny lobster 61.
spiral 129.
spiral bound notebook 151.
spiral-in groove 129.
spire 89.
spit 14.
spleen 81.
splint 193.

split end 171.
spoiler 144.
spoke 137.
spoon 101.
spoons, types 101.
spores 35.
sports car 133.
SPORTSWEAR 120.
spotlight 210.
spreader 123.
spring 20, 109, 188.
spring balance 201.
spring equinox 20.
springboard 188.
sprinklers 207.
spur 17.
square 156.
square 90.
square movement 195.
square root key 154.
stabilizer fin 143.
stack 14.
stacking chairs 96.
stadium 91.
staff 160.
stage 155.
stage clip 155.
stake 190.
stalactite 13.
stalagmite 13.
stalk 44, 45, 46.
stalk vegetables 52.
stamen 38.
stanchion 185.
stand 98, 135, 166.
staple remover 150.
stapler 150.
staples 150.
star diagonal 11.
starboard hand 142.
start button 198.
start wall 182.
starter 54, 182.
starting bar (backstroke) 182.
starting block 182.
starting block 182.
state 26.
station wagon 133.
staysail, jigger topgallant 141.
staysail, jigger topmast 141.
steak knife 101.
steam generator 206.
steam pressure drives turbine 207.
steel bar 189.
steelyard 200.
steering wheel 132.
stem 35, 36, 137, 141, 199.
stem bulb 142.
step 134.
stepladder 111.
steppe 21.
stereo control 129.
STEREO SYSTEM 128.
sterile dressing 193.
stern 143, 184.
sternum 80.
stick 162.
stick eraser 150.
sticks 166.
stigma 38.
stile 93, 97.
stimulator tip 122.
stinger 59.
stipule 37.
stock 209.
stock pot 104.
stockade 88.
stocking 118.
stocking cap 113.
STOCKINGS 118.
stomach 81.
stone 45.
stone fruit, section 45.
stone fruits, major types 45.
stool 96.
stop 66, 126.
stop at intersection 216.
stop button 198.
stopwatch 198.
storage compartment 134, 153, 210.
storage door 106.
storage tanks 203.
stork 76.
stormy sky 22.

stove oil 203.
straight skirt 115.
straight wing 144.
strainer 103.
strainer 190.
strait 26.
strap 168.
strap loop 193.
strap system 163.
stratosphere 28.
strawberry, section 44.
street 90.
street lamp 91.
street sweeper 214.
striking circle 175.
string 162.
STRINGED INSTRUMENTS 162.
strings 159, 181.
stroke judge 182.
strokes, types 183.
structure of a flower 38.
STRUCTURE OF A PLANT 36.
STRUCTURE OF THE BIOSPHERE 20.
STRUCTURE OF THE EARTH 12.
strut 209.
stud 121.
stump 40.
stump 40.
style 38.
subarctic climates 21.
subarctic climates 21.
sublimation 30.
submarine pipeline 202.
subsoil 34.
subterranean stream 13.
subtract from memory 154.
subtract key 154.
subtropical climates 21.
sugar bowl 100.
suit 114.
summer 20.
summer solstice 20.
summer squash 49.
summit 17.
SUN 8.
Sun 6, 10, 28.
sun visor 132.
Sun's surface 8.
Sun, structure 8.
sundeck 142.
sundial 198.
sunflower 39.
sunlight 28.
sunroof 131.
sunspot 8.
super 59.
supply of water 205.
support 11, 23, 97.
surface insulation 149.
surface prospecting 202.
surface runoff 30, 32.
suspender clip 112.
suspenders 112.
suspension spring 138.
swallow 76.
swallow hole 13.
sweater vest 117.
SWEATERS 117.
sweatpants 120.
sweatshirt 120.
sweet corn 52.
sweet peas 52.
sweet pepper 49.
sweet potato 51.
sweet taste 84.
swept-back wing 144.
swimmerets 61.
SWIMMING 182.
swimming pool 143, 182.
swimming trunks 121.
swimming, competitive course 182.
swimsuit 120.
Swiss army knife 192.
Swiss chard 52.
switch 99.
switch 110.
switch lock 110.
swordfish 62.
SYMBOLS, COMMON 216.
SYMBOLS, SAFETY 216.
SYMPHONY ORCHESTRA 167.

T

T-tail unit 145.
tab 123.
TABLE 97.
table 97.
table lamp 98.
tack 184.
tadpole 60.
tag 121.
tail 61.
tail 65, 66, 67, 75, 144, 186.
tail assembly 144.
tail boom 145.
tail comb 122.
tail light 133.
tail shapes, types 145.
tail skid 145.
tail-out groove 129.
taillight 135.
tailpiece 162.
tailrace 204.
take-up reel 129.
talon 74.
tambourine 166.
tank car 139, 203.
tank top 120.
tank trailer 202.
tape 108, 174.
tape dispenser 151.
tape guide 129.
tape lock 108.
tape measure 108.
tapered wing 144.
taproot 40.
target rectangle 179.
tarsus 80.
taste sensations 84.
team shirt 168, 170, 172.
teapot 100.
teaspoon 101.
technical identification band 129.
technical terms 44, 45, 46, 47.
telecommunication antenna 142.
telephone 216.
telephone answering machine 124.
telephone index 124.
telephone set 124.
telephone, cordless 124.
telephone, portable cellular 124.
TELESCOPE, REFLECTING 11.
TELESCOPE, REFRACTING 11.
telescopic boom 210, 215.
telescopic corridor 147.
telescopic front fork 135.
telescopic umbrella 123.
TELEVISION 126.
television set 126.
temperate climates 21.
temperature control 105.
temperature gauge 132.
temperature set point knob 199.
TEMPERATURE, MEASURE 199.
temperature, measure 23.
temple 78, 123.
tempo scale 159.
tendon guard 185.
TENNIS 180.
tennis ball 181.
tennis player 181.
tennis racket 181.
tennis shoe 119.
tennis shoe 181.
tennis, court 180.
tenor drum 166.
TENTS 190.
tents, major types 190.
tepee 86.
terminal box 208.
terminal bud 34, 36.
terminal moraine 17.
tertiary colors 157.
test tube 155.
thermometer 199.
thermometer, clinical 199.
thermostat control 106.
thigh 66, 67, 79.
thigh pad 170.
thigh-boot 119.
third base 169.
third baseman 169.
third valve slide 164.
third, musical interval 160.
thirty-second note 161.
thirty-second rest 161.

223

The terms in **bold type** correspond to an illustration; those in CAPITALS indicate a title.

thoracic legs **61.**
thorax 57, 58.
thread 108.
threaded rod 109.
three-four time 160.
three-toed hoof 71.
threshold 93.
throat 74, 181.
throat protector 168, 177.
thruster 149.
thumb 82, 118, 168.
thumb hook 164.
thumb rest 165.
thumb tacks 150.
thumbscrew 109.
tibia 80.
tie 112.
tie 123, 140.
tie plate 140.
tight end 171.
tightening band 23.
tightening buckle 193.
tights 118.
time signatures 160.
TIME, MEASURE 198.
timekeeper 178.
tine 101.
tip 36, 108, 110, 123, 186.
tip of nose 84.
tipod 11.
tire 131, 137.
tire pump 136.
tire valve 137.
Titan 7.
toad 60.
toaster 105.
toe 66, 74, 78, 118.
toe binding 186.
toe box 185.
toe clip 136.
toe guard 168.
toe pick 185.
toe piece 186.
toe-piece 187.
toeplate 186.
toggle fastening 113.
tom-toms 166.
tomato 49.
tone controls 163.
tongue 138, 172.
tongue 74, 112, 121, 185, 186.
tongue sheath 64.
tonsil 84.
tool tether 149.
TOOLS, CARPENTRY 108.
tooth 64, 84, 109, 110, 213.
toothbrush 122.
toothpaste 122.
top 40, 97.
top flap 193.
top ladder 211.
top of dam 204.
top rail 94.
topsail, gaff 141.
topsail, lower fore 141.
topsail, upper fore 141.
topsoil 34.
toque 114.
total 201.
total eclipse 10.
touch line 173.
touring boot 187.
tourist route 27.
tow bar 146.
tow tractor 146, 147.
tow truck 215.
tower 89, 209.
tower crane 214.
tower ladder 211.
tower mast 214.
towing device 215.
track 98, 212.
track lighting 98.
track suit 120.
tractor unit 134.
tractor, crawler 212.
TRADITIONAL MUSICAL
    INSTRUMENTS 158.
traffic island 90.
trailing edge 144.
trailing edge flap 144.
trampoline 188.
transept 89.
transept spire 89.
transfer of heat to water 207.
transformation of mechanical work into
    electricity 205.
transformer 98, 204, 206.

transit shed 143.
transmission of the rotative movement
    to the rotor 205.
transmission to consumers 205.
transparency 153.
transpiration 31.
trapezoid 156.
trapped heat 29.
traveling crane 204.
tray 111.
treble bridge 159.
treble keyboard 158.
treble pickup 163.
treble register 158.
treble tone control 163.
TREE 40.
tree frog 60.
tree, structure 40.
trees, examples 41.
triangle 156, 166.
triangle 167.
triangular body 158.
trifoliolate 36.
trigger switch 110.
trill, musical notation 161.
trip odometer 132.
triple ring 197.
triple tail unit 145.
tripod 11.
tripod accessories shelf 11.
tripod stand 166.
Triton 7.
trolley 214.
trolley pulley 214.
trombone 164.
trombone 167.
tropic of Cancer 12, 24.
tropic of Capricorn 12, 24.
tropical climates 21.
tropical forest 20.
TROPICAL FRUITS 48.
tropical fruits, major types 48.
tropical rain forest 21.
tropical savanna 21.
troposphere 28.
trout 62.
trowel 54.
TRUCK 134.
truck 185, 185.
truck crane 215.
truck frame 138.
trumpet 164.
trumpet 167.
trunk 40, 79, 131.
trunk, cross section 40.
tuba 164.
tuba 167.
tuber vegetables 51.
tubular bells 167.
tulip 38.
tumbler 100.
tuna 62.
tundra 20.
tuner 128.
tuner 129.
tungsten-halogen lamp 99.
tuning control 129.
tuning controls 126.
tuning fork 159.
tuning peg 162, 163.
tuning pin 159.
tuning slide 164.
turbine 206.
turbine building 206.
turbine shaft turns generator 207.
turbined water draining 205.
turbojet engine 144.
turkey 68.
turn signal 133, 135.
turn signal indicator 132.
turn, musical notation 161.
turning judge 182.
turning wall 182, 183.
turnip 51.
turntable 128.
turntable 213.
turntable mounting 210.
turret 88.
turtle 64.
turtleneck 117.
tusks of elephant 71.
tusks of walrus 71.
tusks of wart hog 71.
TUSKS, MAJOR TYPES 71.
TV mode 126.
TV on/off button 126.

TV/video button 126.
tweeter 128.
tweezers 193.
twig 36, 40.
twist drill 110.
two-door sedan 133.
two-person tent 190.
two-toed hoof 71.
two-two time 160.
tympanum 89.

U

ulna 80.
umbra shadow 10.
UMBRELLA 123.
umbrella pine 43.
umbrella, telescopic 123.
umpire 171, 174, 180, 182.
under tail covert 75.
underground flow 31, 32.
underground stem 50.
undershirt 112.
undershirt 168.
uneven bars 189.
unison, musical interval 160.
unit price 201.
universal step 146.
uphaul 184.
upper eyelid 60, 66, 82.
upper fore topgallant sail 141.
upper fore topsail 141.
upper lip 84.
upper mantle 12.
upper shell 185, 186.
upper strap 186.
upper tail covert 75.
upright 189.
upright piano 159.
upright pipe 210.
Uranus 7.
usual terms 44, 45, 46, 47.
UTENSILS, KITCHEN 102.
uvula 84.

V

V-neck 117.
V-neck cardigan 117.
valley 17.
valve 164.
valve casing 164.
vamp 121.
vanity mirror 132.
variable geometry wing 144.
vault 188.
VCR controls 126.
VCR mode 126.
VCR on/off button 126.
vegetable steamer 104.
VEGETABLES 49, 50, 52.
vegetables 33.
vein 37.
vein, femoral 81.
vein, subclavian 81.
venom canal 64.
venom gland 64.
venom-conducting tube 64.
venomous snake's head 64.
venous blood 81.
vent, main 15.
vent, side 15.
ventilating fan 139.
Venus 6.
vernal equinox 20.
vernier scale 200.
vertebral column 80.
vertical movement 195.
vertical pivoting window 94.
vertical side band 174.
vertical-axis wind turbine 209.
vibrato arm 163.
VIDEO 127.
video camera 127.
VIDEO ENTERTAINMENT SYSTEM 197.
video monitor 154.
videocassette recorder 127.
videotape operation controls 127.
viewfinder adjustment keys 127.
vine leaf 53.

viola 162.
viola 167.
violet 38.
violet 157.
violet-blue 157.
violin 162.
violin family 162.
visor 135, 140, 187.
visual display 197.
VOLCANO 15.
volcano 28.
VOLLEYBALL 174.
volleyball 174.
volleyball, court 174.
voltage decrease 205.
voltage increase 205, 207.
volume control 124, 126, 129, 163.
volva 35.

W

wading bird 74.
wagon tent 190.
waist 79, 162.
waist belt 193.
waistband 112, 113.
walking leg 57.
wall 9, 47.
wall fixture 98.
wall tent 190.
wallet 123.
waning gibbous Moon 9.
warming plate 105.
warning device 211.
warning light 140.
warning lights 132.
warning track 169.
washer nozzle 130.
watch, digital 198.
water bottle 136.
water bottle clip 136.
water cools the used steam 207.
water cycle 30.
water intake 204.
water is pumped back into the steam
    generator 207.
water key 164.
water pitcher 100.
water supply point 210.
water table 13.
water tank 139.
water turns into steam 207.
water under pressure 205.
watercolors 157.
watercress 53.
waterfall 17.
watering can 54.
watering tube 214.
watermelon 49.
waxing gibbous Moon 9.
WEATHER 22.
weather radar 145.
web 60, 74, 168.
webbed foot 60.
webbed toe 74.
weeping willow 42.
weight 200, 201.
WEIGHT, MEASURE 200.
West 27.
West-northwest 27.
West-southwest 27.
Western hemisphere 24.
Western meridian 24.
whale 72.
wheel 185.
wheel chock 146.
wheel cover 131.
wheel tractor 212.
wheelbarrow 55.
wheelchair access 216.
whisk 102.
whiskers 66.
White 195, 196.
white cabbage 53.
white of eye 82.
white square 195.
white wine glass 100.
whole note 161.
whole rest 161.
wigwam 86.
WILD ANIMALS 72.

winch 215.
winch controls 215.
wind deflector 134.
wind direction, measure 23.
WIND ENERGY 209.
WIND INSTRUMENTS 164.
wind strength, measure 23.
wind vane 23.
windbag 158.
windbreaker 113, 120.
windmill 209.
WINDOW 94.
window 107, 131, 145, 184.
windows, types 94.
windshaft 209.
windshield 130, 135.
windshield wiper 130.
wing 75, 144, 148.
wing shapes, types 144.
wing slat 144.
wing vein 57.
wing, left 175, 176.
wing, right 175, 176.
winglet 144.
winter 20.
winter solstice 20.
wiper switch 132.
wire brush 166.
wisdom tooth 85.
wishbone boom 184.
withers 66, 67.
wok 104.
WOMEN'S CLOTHING 114, 116.
women's rest room 216.
woodwind family 165.
woofer 128.
worker, honey-bee 58.
worm 214.
wrist 66, 79, 82.
wrist strap 186, 187.
wristband 170, 181.

X

xylophone 166.
xylophone 167.

Y

yard line 171.
yellow 157.
yellow onion 50.
yellow-green 157.
yolk 75.
yurt 87.

Z

zebra 73.
zest 47.
zipper 190.
zither 158.
zoom lens 127.
zucchini 49.

224

The terms in **bold type** correspond to an illustration; those in CAPITALS indicate a title.